Se

The Chronicle of a Young Man in the Dark Years
1938 to 1954

A feel good story of a young man's decline and resurrection

"You remind me of Seth,"
said the young girl laughingly,
"Seth in *Cold Comfort Farm*.
Yes, I think we should call you Seth.
It suits you!"

Keswick

1967-2013

Terry Lansbury

Published in 2014 by FeedARead.com Publishing

First Edition

A CIP catalogue record for this title is available from the British
Library.

Prologue

The Mill Hill Scene, London 1938

Those far off pre-war years of suburban life seem now to have been part of a different universe. Dads went off to work, mums looked after the home and family, usually with domestic help, and a young boy could find his entertainments, exploring the world outside the home, in the company of his friends. Summer seemed one glorious blaze of golden sunshine; the green, green fields, shimmering tarmac roads and wide white pavements were safe places to roam, explore and play.

Unused to newfangled central heating, unknowing of the coming marvels of television or computer games, we were perhaps tougher, and our young imaginations less saturated by the instant fantasy adventure spewed out today in the warm environment of the sitting room at the touch of a button. Then, the world outside the house was full of excitement and discovery to capture uncluttered minds. The vegetation bursting out on waste ground and from cracks in the pavements offered new flowers to be found and named as the seasons unfolded. The young explorer could find wonderful wildlife in the long grass and shrubbery along the new Watford Way. The rasping song of grasshoppers filled the air, electric blue dragonflies hovered and darted like sparks, and colourful butterflies fluttered from flower to flower. We chattered and shouted excitedly with each new find. Learning their names was a new delight and competitive game. This, we discovered, was a Red Admiral, that a Peacock and that other plain one, a Cabbage White.

There was endless excitement as new and different caterpillars, beetles, spiders and ants emerged to be collected and compared. Occasionally the very lucky youngster would find a mole, or chase a field mouse or spot a squirrel dashing round to hide behind some rough-barked tree trunk as if deliberately playing hide and seek... Bird life was abundant. The common starlings, blackbirds, thrushes and sparrows were ignored as the more colourful nuthatches, chaffinches and yellowhammers were recognised. The excitement of finding the first wren's nest was matched by the thrill of seeing those little blue eggs in the carefully guarded robin's nest... As summer progressed, the meadows changed from lush wet grass to dry wiry herbage, shot through with rusty sorrel, yellow ragwort and blue thistles. Those squishy cowpats which had bedevilled our progress became hardened into discs, which, after the bright orange dung flies had been brushed off, could be made to fly like the plastic "Frisbees" of today.

Even the advertising hoardings, which towered up wherever there were undeveloped sites, were sources of wonder, admiration and education; not to mention the cigarette cards which were often to be found in carelessly discarded "fag packets". One could learn all about the Kings of England from these and it was much easier than in the books at school.

There were passing motor cars to be identified. Aeroplanes had their own shapes and names; and if we walked down to the bottom of Mill Hill Broadway, there were all the wonders of steam trains to thrill the eyes and ears.

The most adventurous youngsters could stand on the footbridge as an express roared by below enveloping the watchers in steam, smoke and soot specks which stung the eyes and brought recriminations for grimy collars. The more fastidious amongst us ran backwards and forwards through the tunnel under the lines, shouting and screaming in the resonant tube, much to the annoyance of porters and elderly passengers making their way between platforms. Every now and then an express would thunder overhead, causing the more timorous explorers to cower against the tiled walls.

A trip to the cinema was a privilege and a longed-for treat... The flickering screen took us to different worlds. From Wild West cowboys, who in those days were always the heroes being attacked by the treacherous redskins, we were transported magically to ride huge black motor cars with gangsters in Chicago. We flew in our rows of rather smelly fleapit seats; from desert tents of Arabian sheikhs to the igloos of the fur-clad Eskimos. We travelled in time to accompany Richard the Lionheart as he fought the chivalrous Saladin. How we cheered Robin Hood as he humbled the Sheriff of Nottingham! Felix the Cat gave way to Mickey Mouse and Popeye taught us to eat our spinach, but no one ever stole our hearts and minds as absolutely as Snow White, who made a million boys her willing slaves...

Sometimes there were newsreels showing little Japanese soldiers scampering almost comically through smoke and fire. Healthy Germans were shown seeking strength through joy as they exercised in endless ranks of white-clad perfection. Less interesting to impatient children were the grim-faced Englishmen plodding patiently

4

behind huge banners: the hunger marches. We gaped uncomprehendingly at shots of grimy streets in the industrial north with their clogged and shawled passers-by. Sometimes one glimpsed ragged, shoeless children shivering, hungry and snotty-nosed. But they were not part of our universe; and as we emerged, eyes aching, into the blinding daylight after an afternoon matinee, they were soon forgotten along with the redskins and Friar Tuck...

Wars, famine and, poverty existed in another time zone for most of us. We were privileged, protected, spoilt and ignorant; but we were little explorers absorbing our own immediate surroundings. Busy and innocent, we were as unaware of the threatening real world as the two little princesses who we knew lived somewhere in the looming bulk of Buckingham Palace.

It was a wonderful, safe and comfortable world for a well-fed, middle class boy...

* * * * * * * * * * * * * * * * * * *

I feel that I should tell you a little about our family as we were in 1936, just before my story begins. This is how I saw it as I approached my tenth birthday; and I hope you can stay with me and see the world through the eyes of a child, an adolescent and a young man. The style of the narrative may change as we pass through these phases. These stages of human development took place during a time of great decline in the family and indeed the British Nation's fortunes. I hope you will enjoy a journey through a Britain which includes times and events which we were privileged to be part of.

Our family at Mill Hill may have seemed, superficially, to be a pretty typical middle class North London suburban family. We lived in a biggish five-bedroomed house with a live-in maid, a daily girl and a part-time gardener. We had a large car, a small sports car and a motorcycle, the last two belonging to my older brothers. Bill, my dad, went off to work every day with my older brothers, George and Little Billy. My sisters, Esme and Daphne, also went off to business as secretary typists. I was still at school. Jessie, my mother, was sadly incapacitated much of the time with an inexplicable alcoholism. Nevertheless, when sober, she was a much-loved and respected parent.

Having moved from the tough East End of London, my Dad and his late brother Edgar had been successful business people in the timber trade. "Nouveau riche" would not have been an accurate description as their rise had been a story of hard work, troubles and

5

setbacks. Running through the family were pride in public service and a deep interest in politics and culture inherited from both sides of the family. Grandparents, aunts, uncles and cousins had distinguished themselves in public life, politics, literature and the theatre, without accumulating great wealth or the affectations of class. Granddad George Lansbury, for instance, had risen from the labouring classes to become leader of the Labour Party, a Privy Councillor and confidant of the late King George the Fifth. Perhaps this little sub-family at Mill Hill was the most humdrum of a brilliant, bohemian and sometimes eccentric Lansbury clan.

As socialists they could claim an impeccable working class background; and yet they were now regarded, by dint of their address, as "toffs". This was a situation they found embarrassing and sought to deny at every opportunity. Living in a large new house in the best part of a smart suburb did not make this easy. Indeed at times, the older boys, particularly Little Billy, affected a plebeian uncouthness, which embarrassed the rest of the Mill Hill family. George and Billy worked in father's veneer mill, which provided very high quality oak and walnut veneers to the luxury furniture trade.

It was my father's proud boast that his veneers had been used in the renowned Royal Scot exhibition train and in the cabins and staterooms of the newly launched *Queen Mary*, at that time the largest and most luxurious ship afloat. Sadly, the economic recession had dragged on and many of his Jewish cabinetmaker customers were forced to close down; and the business went into recession. Dad kept as many of the men on as possible; but the golden days for crafted furniture were over and the demand for fine veneers continued to decline.

Both my sisters had successful careers before marriage and family demands clipped their able wings. All in all we were a happy, united family, with one great sadness: Mother's alcohol problem, which turned a wonderful and beautiful character into a mumbling stranger whom, at such times, I could hardly recognise as the lovely warm mum I loved.

I had been born eight years later than the others and was both bane and favourite, in accordance with my most recent activities, which were frequently over the top. In those days it was simply "going too far". Modelling myself upon my hero, Richmal Crompton's "William", I frequently disrupted my elder relatives' tranquillity, courtships and other ambitions. Sometimes I was regarded as a pain in

6

the neck, and less frequently, as a little angel! In any other family I think I would have been regarded, perhaps, as an over-imaginative boy.

My freedom to roam with my gang of followers, my unacceptably imaginative schemes and occasional outrages perpetrated on unsuspecting – but in my eyes, unreasonable – adults, came to an abrupt end in September 1936. Then, with my sisters married or committed to careers and my mother ill, "drying out" in a "nursing home", it was decided to send me to board at Belmont, Mill Hill Junior School. I suppose in a way it was "going into care"; but jolly expensive care, and a cause of great distress to my socialist grandfather.

The first term at Belmont was the usual hell of initiations and bullying. One soon learned to "blend into the woodwork" in order to avoid marauding senior boys in search of likely victims. I was thoroughly enjoying life by the second term and indeed, by dint of the family gift for comedy, I had become something of a school "character" by the end of my first year. By the second year, when I was no longer a "new bug" and had had some good class results, I grew rapidly in self-confidence. It seemed that I was embarked on a successful school career in spite of many hard-fought battles. These encounters arose from my singularity in resisting mass psychology and boasting of being a socialist in a dormitory conservative to the last new boy. I made many political enemies and no converts yet somehow remained a "popular boy".

.... And so the story begins!

Chapter 1

Cumberland Sausage

It had been a fine summer in 1938. I reckoned the Hendon Air Display had been the best ever. There had been a fly-past by two hundred and fifty planes. My brother Billy and his friend Ken had hauled me up into a tree in Mill Hill Park to see Handley Page Hereford bombers blow up a model of an Afghan fort, which I had watched the airmen build in plywood the previous week. An observation balloon was shot down in real flames and the Royal Air Force's first monoplane fighters, the Spitfire and Hurricane, were on display. Bristol Blenheim and Handley Page Harrow bombers were shining silver in the sun and our Gloster Gladiator biplanes were the most manoeuvrable in the world. In spite of this, the grown-ups amongst our family and friends were pessimistic about our chances if Hitler and Mussolini got going.

I must admit that I enjoyed the air display too much to worry about the prospect of an imminent war. Yellow Avro biplanes were giving exhibitions of crazy flying: looping, stalling and spinning before recovering just when it seemed they must hit the ground. It was indeed a great day for an air-minded lad and one that I would long remember, especially as Ken bought me a large Aero chocolate bar and Billy gave me fourpence to buy a Walls choc ice. Ken, who was seventeen, had just joined the Auxiliary Air Force but had not yet got his uniform although he was attending drills each weekend. I was pretty sure that he fancied my sister Daphne; but he was too busy preparing himself for the Air Force to pursue her properly.

The family were all at home though Little Billy would soon be going to sea. It was clear that the veneer mills were not going to be Little Billy's career and he always yearned for the sea and ships. Dad had been a sailor and had inspired us all with tales of his apprenticeship on a four-masted square-rigged sailing ship. Soon after his fourteenth birthday, Dad had sailed from Tilbury for Durban. The grossly undermanned crew of seventeen had survived one hundred and twenty days at sea without sight of land, and experiencing severe gales and the heat of the doldrums. When they eventually reached Durban, Dad had spilt a pot of paint on the deck and been given the rope's end. He made an attempt to defend himself and was logged for mutiny after a child's tantrum against the ship's mate. That night, Dad went over the side and somehow crossed South Africa, on foot and by bullock cart, to Bulawayo in Rhodesia. He survived by catching rats during the bubonic plague outbreak for a *tikki* (1p) a tail... Eventually he had returned to England via Australia and Argentina and many adventures before becoming a commercial traveller and later joining his brother Edgar in the timber business.

My big sister, Esme, was married and had moved, with her husband and son Nigel, to Watford. The summer holidays at Folkestone had followed an Easter break at Torquay and it seemed as if the days of sunshine and comfort would go on forever. I had a wonderful time on the beach playing with my first nephew Nigel, and enjoying swimming with him on my shoulders. Mum and Esme were a bit worried about him but he laughed and giggled with delight in the shallow breakers. It was indeed a greengage summer; and everything in the family garden seemed lovely. It was not to last; and once more Mum "went funny" and had to go away to a "refuge" early in the autumn. I had to go back once more as a boarder to Belmont, Mill Hill Junior School.

Everyone was talking about Adolf Hitler and the possibility of war. Hitler, at this time, was demanding the return of all the territories taken from Germany by the Versailles Treaty, after the defeat of the fatherland in 1918. A steady stream of Jewish new boys from central Europe resulted from Hitler's excesses; they had little to say about their experiences and their parents were well-dressed and drove expensive cars. They were the lucky ones who had anticipated Hitler's intentions and escaped with their wealth to start again in England. There was much talk about rearmament and I started to wonder if my father's constant theme, that the Versailles Treaty had made another war inevitable, was perhaps true after all. My grandfather, George Lansbury, was a prominent Labour politician and pacifist who was desperately unhappy about the way things were going. He had made trips to see Hitler, Mussolini, Roosevelt and other heads of state in a vain quest for peace; and I had heard him telling the elders of his fears. The deep vibrant voice which had swayed the hearts of millions in his earlier career in national politics was now racked by the emotions of a sad and disappointed man.

I worried a lot but not all the time. Like all twelve-year-olds I loved my model planes, my ships and my sports. I loved music in an adult way, which made me unappreciative of the simple stuff dished up at school and enjoyed by my peers. Perhaps my obsession with

9

Wagner's Meistersingers was unusual: it had been acquired from hearing the music played on the old paper-roll organ in the family lounge. This magnificent contraption had twenty or more stops simulating various instruments which controlled pipes with sounds pitched close to the instruments they represented. The woodwinds, the reedy sound of oboes, bassoons and clarinet were excellent, as were the deep organ notes. I particularly loved the high volume achieved by operating two huge paddles with my knees as I pedalled my way to the crashing climaxes, which contrasted so well with the plaintive woodwind themes which Wagner set with such effective tension against the rest of the orchestra. The brass stops were less effective but nonetheless, all the instrumental parts echoed constantly in my mind as I whistled – tunelessly, I am now assured – to the annoyance of my friends and family.

I also loved jazz when most boys of my age were not yet listening to dance music and certainly not the sort of "hot" music which my much older brothers and sisters brought home. Names like Duke Ellington and Louis Armstrong were not normal currency at posh prep schools in 1938 and were definitely frowned upon by the Music master. I enjoyed learning to chant psalms, sing descants and best of all, to have the form of orchestral music explained and the sounds of all the instruments identified. The opening of Grieg's "Morning", from the *Peer Gynt Suite*, with one instrumental solo after another repeating the themes, unlocked the door to a lifelong appreciation of music and musical instruments and is something for which I will always be grateful to the Belmont Music master Doctor Foster, however unappreciative of jazz he may have been.

After our return to school in September, we were surprisingly undisturbed by the sight of huge air raid trenches which unemployed labourers were digging in Mill Hill Park. I was a little shocked to hear one of our teachers commenting that the trenches would be more use for burying the bodies in than as protection from German bombs. The first barrage balloons had appeared. I had seen one being filled with gas in Regent's Park and now I could count dozens gleaming silver in the clear blue sky. One or two ancient anti-aircraft guns had been dug in on Hampstead Heath. One boy's father was a World War One artillery colonel and had identified them as pre-1914 vintage and pretty ineffective. "Make a lot of noise and reassure the civvies," was his verdict. "Might have scared the Boer in Africa, but not much use against the Hun!"

I was looking forward to learning to play rugger now that I was a "twelve plus", the age at which the public school system generally abandoned soccer. (Eton school being one of the rare exceptions.) However, on the first games afternoon back at school, we were formed into a crocodile and walked along Mill Hill Ridgeway to St Vincent's convent. Here, we were fitted with gas masks by efficient ladies attired in what were to become the familiar blue air raid warden's overalls. The boys were delighted with the novelty of the gas masks with their simple one-way rubber valve and celluloid eyepiece, with their smell of rubber and the intriguing farting noises which they made with each exhalation. The noises were not only fun to produce but were essential to show that the masks were working properly. It was not often that authority smiled on the production of vulgar noises and we took full advantage of this freedom. Perhaps the most worrying day came when the school groundsmen fitted wooden blast screens to the changing room and Charlie Cannon, the boilerman, had sawn up a set of rugby posts to reinforce them.

One day two Czechoslovakian new boys arrived. They were much more silent and thoughtful than the German and Austrian Jewish boys had been. It was obvious that they were feeling their exile and were extremely worried... The "crisis" was deepening and war fever gripped the school. I came in for some severe abuse from senior boys because my family were known to have Labour Party connections and certain Labour MPs, along with Winston Churchill, were calling for resistance to Hitler now. "Lousy little Labour warmonger!" they sneered. I found this very unfair since I had previously been ostracised for my family's pacifist connections. I was amused rather than upset. Not for the first or last time in my life, I found my elders and "betters" not only ill-informed, but inconsistent.

Early in the term, I and one or two boys from each dormitory were woken up and assembled in the school dining room. After a short homily concerning our selection as being the more responsible and resourceful boys in the school, the Headmaster expressed his confidence that we would not let the school down in the uncertain days immediately ahead. We had to get dressed and collect what clothes we could pack into a small suitcase. It emerged that we were to be a small pilot group travelling to Cumberland in order to prepare for the school's evacuation to a disused girls' school, St Helens at Cockermouth. There was subdued giggling at this unlikely location but it was quickly suppressed by a single serious glance from the

Headmaster. In the school uniform of brown and white velvet cap and blue mackintosh and each carrying a suitcase and gas mask, the pilot party lined up for the bus outside the new Three Hammers pub. I shivered in spite of the mild evening. I remembered the warm summer days in the garden of the old Three Hammers pub, drinking fizzy grapefruit as I waited for the grown-ups who were putting the world right in the bar. My father always seemed to hold court as he gave forth on politics or his days at sea. Nobody ever appeared bored and he was treated as one who spoke with authority.

I shivered again. The valley, which stretched like a long bowl between Mill Hill Ridgeway and Harrow on the Hill, was lit up by a million multicoloured street and advertising lights. A single searchlight rotated on the top of the Ritz cinema at Edgware, calling the faithful to worship Clark Gable, Joan Crawford, Bette Davis and Greta Garbo on the silver screen. Beneath them the lights thinned out leaving a pool of darkness where Hendon Aerodrome lay. I wondered if I would ever see the scene again. Further into London, the first Territorial searchlight units were practising with their new equipment; fingers of blue light wheeled erratically about the sky.

The single-decker bus from Golders Green appeared round the bend past Mill Hill School. Some of my schoolmates were chattering excitedly about whether the senior boys would also be going north. Several had elder brothers there. I did not. My brothers had grown up in a different world and had been wage-earners long before the average Mill Hill schoolboy left school.

Opposite the bus stop, the moon was reflecting in the little pond next to St Paul's hall. I wondered if I would ever fish for tiddlers there again. The little pond had been a favourite haunt of mine before I joined the posh school, and it was a grand spot for sticklebacks and minnows – not to mention the newts and occasional leeches which caused panic in the jamjars and were always thrown back. It was considered to be letting the school down to be seen mixing with the village kids there now.

In a fairly orderly if noisy fashion, we clambered aboard the little bus led by the Second Master, an awe-inspiring man to the boys but one who held no terrors for the cockney bus conductor who kept up a loud lament about his misfortune in having picked up a regiment of boys at this time of night. I caught a glimpse of the lights in our home as the bus lurched round the roundabout at Mill Hill Broadway and wondered what my family were doing. It was so near and so far from that beloved kitchen, the bright lounge, and dancing shadows from the warm fire. In a few minutes we were boarding an underground train to Euston. The familiar clicks, hisses and shouted warnings to "Stand clear of the doors!" were followed by the rocking and swaying as the red tube train flashed and crackled its way over points and bridges, through tunnels and brilliantly lit, clean, colourful stations. My friends were swapping statistics. The tunnel from Hampstead to Morden was the longest in the world. Hampstead was the deepest station; no, it was Highgate!

At Euston there were plenty of seats on the train. A whole coach had been allocated to the party. There was room, for everyone who wanted to, to lie down; but most were too excited. I was not going to miss a moment if I could help it. I had always loved the adventure of a train journey and I walked up and down the train exploring all its facilities and occasionally taking a malicious delight in waking the odd sleeping boy with false news of imminent arrival followed by demoniacal laughter. Rugby was passed and Crewe approaching before the last gritty eyes were shut and most if not all the boys were sleeping.

By the time the train approached industrial Lancashire, dawn was breaking and we peered out of the steamy windows upon landscapes the like of which many had never seen before. The blackened red brick mills and slag heaps were a different world; one which the paintings of Robert Lowry had not yet made acceptable. The strange accents of the station staff, as the train paused at Runcorn, Warrington, and St Helens, jarred on their suburban ears, and most of the boys regarded the scenery and people with distaste. Manchester Shipping Canal stirred some interest as a large ship was passing. It was flying what one knowledgeable boy pronounced to be "the red duster of the merchant navy". I thought of my brother Billy who had just left on his first voyage to New Zealand as an ordinary seaman on the *SS Tekoa*.

Runcorn, Warrington, Wigan, Preston. Ah! Preston: here was something the boys had heard of. Preston had the longest railway platform in the world. "No," said a boy who had lived with his military parents in India. "There is a longer platform in Calcutta." So Preston was dismissed along with the cotton towns and the industrial north. Soon the sun was shining on the wide sweep of Morecombe Bay. Looking out, I saw a magnificent panorama of the blue Lakeland mountains beyond the silvery waters and yellow sands which seemed to stretch for ever. After Carnforth the train stopped and we were ordered to get down from the windows as we strained to see what sort of an extra engine was going to pull us up Shap. Every boy knew of this ascent and the need for a second engine.   The pull up and over Shap provided the now sleepy boys with their first sight of the fells. Most were too tired to take much notice and few saw the Penrith Beacon or the hump of Blencathra as they sped down to Carlisle.

Carlisle station, a grand structure, was more like a baronial castle than a station and we got off the train quietly, as if in awe. Perhaps it was just hunger, for we had not eaten on the long, slow journey. Led by the Second Master, we trooped into a commercial hotel on Botchergate. One of the restaurant staff was bemoaning the necessity of serving a bunch of brats at that early hour but Bertie, as the Second Master was affectionately known to the boys, won her over with a "sorrow more than anger" account of the little boys' long journey away from home. After considerable negotiation, a super breakfast of bacon and eggs was laid on. Levinson, a lad whose vociferousness was matched by his lack of tact, enthused about the breakfast. "If only we got food like this at school!" The school housekeeper who was travelling with the boys looked grim, her already thin lips compressed into a thin, thin line!

The journey on to Cockermouth took some arranging. Apparently the party should have left the train at Penrith to catch the train through Keswick. In the event we travelled on a vintage Victorian train through Aspatria. "What a remarkable Latin name," someone commented. We explored the quaint wooden carriage with its tiny slide-down windows raised or lowered by tattered leather straps. We tried hard but they would not budge. In any case, we had been warned not to put our heads out of the windows. We also tried the flush in the minute lavatory which bore the sign "Ladies only", but with no success. The carriage was really like a small lounge mounted on train wheels. There were old gas lights with no mantles or gas and we even found a small stove with a chimney out through the roof of the carriage. Fortunately it was not alight or, with so many bored boys on board, we might never have reached Maryport without a fire at the very least; but luck was with our escorting form master and the little train chuffed safely on round the coast to Workington. This town appeared to the boys to be a desperately depressed place after the clean tidy suburbs of North London. We were all grateful we did not have to stay there.

The final leg of the journey lay through the Derwent Valley, with magnificent, sweeping bends of beautiful riverbanks, and views of distant hills. Eventually the train rattled to a standstill and at last the boys were at Cockermouth...

The party disembarked and collected their luggage. Each boy was checked to see that he had his suitcase and gas mask. A loose crocodile formed and the boys, after being warned to keep together, set off to walk the two miles to the school. I trailed behind because I was helping a very small boy, a German Jewish refugee, to carry a suitcase which seemed almost bigger than the boy himself.

The natives of the busy little market town found the strange school uniform a great novelty and the boys, in turn, were intrigued by the women's shawls, the clatter of clogs and the strange dialect of the townspeople. At the end of the main street, my companion and I went astray and lost sight of the main party. I had not noticed the narrow entrance to Castlegate and we set off down St Helen's Street. I had never seen quite such a jumble of old and tumbledown dwellings.

We seemed to have attracted the attention of some local street urchins who started to follow us. One bold-faced lad said, "Hast tha cum all t'way fra Lunon?" "Yes," said I politely and proudly, thinking that he would admire me as a young hero of the Blitz, "we have actually." The lad looked at me for a moment, then after turning to his mates for approval, shouted, "Weel, booger off back theer!" I shrugged and walked on in dignified silence; inside, I was mortified.

We came to the end of the houses and St Helen's Street became a country lane. The ups and downs of the roadside path seemed endless. The handles of the heavy suitcases bit into my soft hands and the weight burned my shoulders. Eventually we turned in at the lodge gates and we struggled up the steep drive to St Helen's, the red-roofed schoolhouse in the trees.

The other boys and I spent the rest of the day exploring the schoolhouse. St Helen's – or Wyndham House, as it had been formerly called – was an ugly building, having been built for Lord Leconfield's agent. For some reason, unlike much post-Victorian architecture in the district, it had been built without eaves, giving it a shorn look. It occupied a striking position on the edge of a bluff above Bitter Beck and had magnificent views over Cook's farm towards Grassmoor and the Buttermere fells.

We were allocated bed places on mattresses laid out on the lino floors and already the school housekeeper had engaged a local woman to cook mountains of scrambled eggs and mash. I found myself next to Alistair Duncan, a big, dreamy, studious boy, who was being prepared for a scholarship to Oundle. Duncan and I had greatly differing views on almost everything and had fought frequently and painfully when new boys in 1936. Our main quarrels had been over the Spanish civil war. I had supported the Republican government against Franco. Almost all the boys' parents supported Franco's fascist rebels then, as most of the press in England saw the civil war as a struggle between the church and communism. Even at ten years of age I had marvelled at the blinkers which class-consciousness put on people. Now in 1938, the fight against fascism looked like being Britain's fight; and Conservatives had become strangely silent about their former views. I never pressed my friend about this change; I valued Duncan's friendship too much to score political points off him.

Next day the Second Master arranged a coach trip round the nearby lakes, which we had not yet seen. It also gave the staff an opportunity to prepare the building for the newcomers' occupancy. On the way to Keswick, the bus rounded the Dubwath bend and the first lakeland landscape came into view. For all but a minority of boys who had been to Scotland, this was their first sight of lake and mountain scenery. Few of us, however young, were not touched by its beauty. Before us, mirror-smooth and silver in the weak September morning sun, shimmered Bassenthwaite Lake. Across the lake, a succession of ridges ran up the flanks of Skiddaw mountain, culminating in a great purple whaleback against the cloud-dappled sky. The huge bulk of the mountain was softened by the light and shade of cloud shadows and undulating slopes which rose from the emerald green fields running down to the lakeshore. Sombre pines and fir trees rose above groves of beech and oak trees amongst which clusters of stone farm buildings and a small church were visible. Dark wooded peninsulas thrust out into the lake, and then receded to open grassy bays with stony shores. On Long Side, the golden bracken rose to meet the rocky screes and gullies descending from the crags of grey above.

I gasped at the scene and already I was planning how I would describe it to my parents in my letter home. The coach swept round the lake through Beck Wythop, Thornthwaite, Braithwaite, Portinscale: what names to conjure with. At each successive viewpoint Skiddaw seemed to change in colour, shape and character: now smooth and dark, now shiny bright and crinkly. Then, as the bus slowed into the little mountain town of Keswick, the great mountain seemed to open up and send warm green spurs down from its stony summit to shelter the grey stone buildings clustered in its arms.

Crawling through the market square, the bus squeezed down Lake Road and then sped into the open countryside. The road along the shores of Derwentwater gave glimpses of a very different scene. Across the lake, the striking hump and narrow ridge of Catbells was almost perfectly reflected in the water except where wildfowl made v-shaped wakes which crossed and crisscrossed, forming gentle ripples which rocked the reflected image of the golden fellside. A commotion on the other side of the bus drew my attention to the crags which beetled above the road. Here, tiny figures could be seen climbing on the rock faces of Falcon Crag. Others were walking along the crest of the hill, looking like matchsticks against the bright sky. I longed to tackle these giants as they were doing.

At Grange Bridge, we took advantage of a halt and at once some boys began the traditional sport of skimming pebbles across the crystal clear pools beneath the arches. An elderly lady, who had been sitting on the parapet of the elegant bridge, spoke to me. She asked where the boys came from. Hearing that we were strangers, she began to tell us about the pools beneath the bridge. How salmon used to breed and lay their eggs in the gravel beds before tourists came and used the pools for cooling off on hot days. (True country folk would never do this!) She told us how the Borrowdale hermit, Millican Dalton, would emerge from his cave and sail down the river on his raft and how, many years ago, the villagers had drowned a suspected witch in this very pool. I gazed at the innocent-looking pool and shivered.

The Second Master, Bertie, knew the lakes well from his undergraduate days at Cambridge where there had always been an Oxbridge school of fell walkers and rock climbers. These were based mainly in Wasdale Head where the young men and older dalesmen would gather for intellectual and alcoholic stimulation when not risking their limbs and occasionally their necks in climbing exploits on Sca Fell and Great Gable. The Alpine Club frowned upon this madcap rock-climbing, considering it unacceptable as a Gentleman's recreation. Bertie was no exception to these early tigers, having broken his leg in both skiing and rock-climbing accidents. His well-known liking for alcohol had never affected his appearances at school although he was once found asleep in a blazing chair, having dozed off smoking his notorious pipe. Occasionally he overslept and on one of these days, I – who worshipped him – lost favour.

The occasion was on my turn to read the lesson in chapel and Bertie, in spite of having encouraged me to excel in both chapel and in class readings, had failed to wake up. Later when Bertie had realised his gaffe, I had laughed to hide my disappointment at his absence. Bertie took this as flippant indifference to his interest and had been equally hurt. Since the incident, it had taken considerable time for our respective wounded prides to heal. Now, in this artist's paradise, we stood together, man and boy, finding an affinity of interest as we drank in the view. Few people could have come from more different backgrounds but there was a common bond in our love of beauty and literature. Duncan joined us and the spell was broken. He and I wandered off, drawn by the excited shouts of our companions who – having succeeded in launching a log – were now bombarding it with rocks as it was carried downstream by the swirling river Derwent.

Bertie puffed at his pipe reflectively. He missed his youth; he had never found time to marry and now his eccentricity made it unlikely that he would. His reverie was rudely disturbed by the strident hooter as the bus driver recalled us all to resume our journey of discovery. Two bedraggled boys had fallen into the river and despite their cold discomfort, they were enjoying the attention and wonder of the other boys. Bertie said they had let the side down, but he smiled.

Wending its way back over the narrow road, high above the west side of Derwentwater, the bus passed a small grey stone house with a bright blue garage door. Spotting an elderly man leaning on a stick and looking down the lake towards Skiddaw, Bertie gave an excited start but said nothing. When the bus stopped for the boys to enjoy the view above Abbot's Bay and to hear from the driver about the old mineral mines at Brandlehow, Bertie explained his interest in the old man in the garden. "It was Walpole, the author. I believe he has written some good books about the district. We must read them someday." Duncan and I knew all about Walpole, the prime minister of historical fame, but neither of us had heard of Hugh Walpole, the author whose books were later to play a big part in kindling my own and millions of other readers' love of Cumbria and the Borrowdale valley in years to come through the "Herries Chronicles".

The bus completed a figure of eight, going back to Cockermouth round the east side of Bassenthwaite, past historic Mirehouse, Bassenthwaite village and the Castle Inn. The driver paused on Ouse Bridge to let the boys see the white-breasted dippers.

These smart little birds were swimming underwater, emerging to shake the water off their wings. From a reed bed further up the river, the dippers were watched by a solitary solemn heron, which seemed to frown at the noisy boys before it took off and flapped lazily away towards the heronry at Overwater. Bertie organised a hot bath and dry clothes for the two miserable wretches who had managed to fall into the river, coupled with a little lecture on the need to pull together and not let the school down. After tea, there were few boys who were not ready to snuggle down in their makeshift beds and think of all they had seen and done. There was no time to feel homesick.

Next day, Bertie was tied up with organisation and the boys were put on their honour to behave and were given the freedom of the surrounding countryside. A particularly enterprising boy had found bicycles for hire in one of those small hidden courtyards in which Cockermouth abounded, just behind the old market square. For sixpence a day, two machines were wheeled out for Duncan and me. Duncan's steed was of the "sit up and beg" variety, with oil bath and carbide lamps. Somehow it suited his serious nature; whereas my mount was an early attempt at a sports bicycle with white celluloid mudguards and orange tyres. We agreed to change bicycles periodically if either proved a handicap. We both wanted to go back to the nearest lake and we set off for Bassenthwaite.

Just after the Pheasant Inn, we found a tunnel under the railway which led down to the water. A small wooden jetty beckoned us and we sat looking down the lake. I spotted some bottles lying on the lake floor, tied to the jetty with string. Pulling one up I found it had a number of small fish swimming strongly within. Duncan, who seemed to know everything, said that they were live bait for catching large roach and pike. I shuddered; the thought of live bait appalled me. "Bloody softy," scoffed Duncan who, apart from being the complete angler, also knew some swear words which he went on to list with great relish as he rolled them off, wrapping his tongue round each syllable in his soft Scottish accent. The conversation went on to the revelation of some extraordinary facts of life. These revelations, once imparted to me by my friend and mentor, completely changed the way I looked at men and women. Surely Duncan must be wrong this time! My Mum and Dad could not possibly do that!

As we cycled back through Wythop we paused to look at the old mill beside the tumbling stream. An elderly local gentleman told us a bit about the hundreds of small mills which used to grind corn and work machinery for making bobbins, spindles and shuttles for the cotton mills using beech cut in the local woods. The old man went on to tell us about small tanneries, spinners, weavers and iron smelters, where the villagers made their own charcoal up in the coppices. "In Langdale you can still see women spinning from their own sheep's fleeces and men making charcoal at Wabberthwaite." Duncan and I looked at each other. We were both thinking of the difference between this grand variety of life and the world we had left behind, the commuters setting off to business each day from the rows of neat suburban houses in North London, the gleaming shops, the spotless pavements and orderly parks. It was never going to be quite the same for us, even if Hitler never dropped a bomb.

Just before Embleton we stopped as a man with a red flag called to us. "Blasting, lads, watch theesen. The's a gay loc o styens coos fleein doon. Hey op!" A shrill whistle was followed shortly by a series of thuds. A dirty brown cloud drifted over Higham and a few fragments of granite could be seen rolling down the outspill from the quarry. "Oweh! Tha can gar by noow!" We went on. With time on our hands we wandered down towards the turning back to Higham. Passing a small farmstead, we paused to watch the farmer bring a herd of cows down from Watch Hill. He was followed by an old Clydesdale horse, drawing a tumbril loaded with bracken. At his shout we opened the gate and stood aside.

Most of the cows went across the road and down the farm track towards the buildings. An awkward cow set off up the road and the farmer started to give chase. Observing that the old horse was about to smash the tumbril's great wooden wheels into the gatepost, I dropped my bike and ran forward, grabbing the calm old horse by the bridle and pulling it to one side. The iron tyre of the wheel scraped against the slate gatepost and the huge wheel hub caught for a second, tilting the shafts into the horse's side; but the good nag paused and the tumbril was through safely.

Meantime, Duncan had cycled down the lane and eventually passed the wayward cow which had stridden ahead every time he tried to pass and threatened to put a hoof through his spokes. As he came back the farmer was mopping his brow with the largest red-spotted handkerchief we had ever seen. "Thank you, lads," he gasped. "By heck, I'se warum! Ista fra yon skyul fra Millil in Loonon?" We, who by now were beginning to understand the dialect, nodded. "We are not actually from Mill Hill School," explained Duncan, a stickler for accuracy. "We are from Belmont, the junior school." "Will tha help me doon t'lonnin wi' these coos? I'se not a real good fettle!" We helped him down to the bier where the farmer's wife was waiting. "Eh, what handsome lads!" she said to our embarrassment. "Wouldsta like a coop of tea when Dad's got t'coos settled?" As we were not allowed tea at school, Duncan and I were delighted to accept.

Duncan was not keen on farmyard dirt, whether it was clean dirt or dirty dirt. I had tried to explain the difference. While we waited for the promised tea, Duncan sat on the milk stand, dreaming about the day's events. I, meantime, was in the cowshed copying the farmer who was chaining up the cows ready for milking. I soon got the hang of it, passing the long chain over the neck and the short chain under before pushing the "T" piece through the ring to secure it. Edgar the farm lad came in with the gleaming milking machines, festooned with orange rubber tubes and chrome teat cups. I took a spare cloth from the udder-washing bucket and followed the lad's example, washing the cow's udders. "Don't do any more," said Edgar. "It sets the milk off flowing and I can only milk four at a time." He took a machine in between two cows and bent down to draw a few drops of milk onto the floor. "Why do you do that?" I asked. "It's to see if there's any mastitis clots in the milk. Mastitis is a disease cows get sometimes." Edgar, it transpired, was attending a Farm College and was working here for practical experience. He was now quickly and quietly slipping the rubber-lined chrome teat cups over the cow's teats, trying not to let too much air in at the same time. He was very quick and gentle. In what seemed no time, all four machines were clicking away and the clusters of teat cups rocked gently. "Time for your cup of tea, lads," said Edgar. "I've had mine."

The farmer led us over to the house and into the back kitchen. Here, a great wash copper was built into the corner with a fire grate below. A large galvanized iron dolly tub contained what appeared to be a small stool fixed to the end of a fork handle with double handgrips. "That's a wash dolly," said Duncan. "I've seen them in books." I thought of the laundry leaving the school as it did from my home, in large labelled bags or hampers. I thought all washing went away like that and came back nicely pressed in brown paper parcels. A gigantic mangle stood in one corner like a medieval instrument of torture. I looked at it and shuddered. I had heard some uncouth deliveryman at the school avow that he had "never laughed so much, since me wife caught her tits in the mangle." I shuddered again at the graphic scene which sprang up in my innocent young mind.

The cup of tea turned out to be a small feast for two hungry boys. The farmer's wife stood back, beaming. On the table stood a plate with an unbelievably long sausage coiled round and round like a ship's rope; but a sizzling brown rope, shining and giving off delicious aromas which made us very eager to start. The farmer said grace and I was glad we had not sat down too soon. Duncan and I sipped our tea politely and ate our way steadily (but with what we thought were fastidious manners) through sausage, bread and jam, gingerbread, apple cake and finally a currant cake of enormous proportions. Southern food had never tasted like this. "Reach oop, lads," said Bob Young the farmer. "Ther's nay need to be shy, it's a good bate shop here." He had taken off his cap and I was amazed at the contrast between his white scalp and ruddy face. He was dressed in a brown Harris tweed hacking jacket, corduroy breeches and a black waistcoat over a khaki shirt. Thick woollen socks led down to hefty leather boots which laced right down to the upward curving toes. Mrs Young the farmer's wife, noticing my curiosity, said proudly, "Them's Dad's shepherding boots! He's got clogs for milking and round the yard and a fine pair of brown boots and gaiters for market. Never wears wellies even in winter." I pondered this information. All the farm men seemed to wear wellies or clogs. Perhaps it was some kind of class or rank distinction.

The day's events had made a profound impression on me and I began to form a mental picture of a future lifestyle. Without a doubt, I made up my mind. One day I would have a tweed jacket, black waistcoat and corduroys. I wasn't sure what to think about the boots, but one thing was certain. One day I was going to eat Cumberland sausage at my own table. One day I was going to be a farmer!

* * * * * * * * * * * * * * * * * *

Uneasy days

The small group of boys who had travelled up to Cumberland in September 1938 returned to London after Mr Chamberlain's humiliating capitulation to Hitler at Munich. The two Czech new boys were heartbroken at this betrayal of their country. During the following months, Hitler occupied the rest of Czechoslovakia and a squadron of fighter Blenheims, a makeshift conversion of the light bomber, was hastily established at Hendon aerodrome. "Hitler wouldn't be so cocky if he knew what we'd got," said a local publican to my father as they watched the planes flying in formation. I, who knew all about the Luftwaffe's latest planes from reading flying magazines, was less impressed. Poland came under pressure to yield territory at Danzig, the Polish corridor, a strip of Prussia awarded to Poland through the Versailles Treaty which – although being Poland's access to the sea – now divided Prussia from Germany.

War seemed certain but the British Government rejected a Popular Front alliance with France and Russia against Hitler. Many leading Britons were uncertain who they feared most, the Nazis or the Communists. Colonel Beck, for Poland, negotiated with both sides and the snubbed Russians, ever fearful of attack from the West, signed a non-aggression pact with Germany, opening the way for Hitler's subsequent attack on Poland.

That fateful summer, our family were on holiday at Southsea near Portsmouth. My eldest brother George, a Territorial Reservist, joined us in army uniform, to his mother's grief. He was stationed at nearby Portdown Barracks. His conversation was of appalling food, greasy dishes and widespread constipation amongst the conscripts. "Lucky devil!" one conscript, straining in the latrines, had said on hearing three loud splashes from the adjacent cubicle. "Lucky be buggered!" came the hoarse reply. "That was my knife, fork and spoon!"

I thought George looked superb in his uniform and I was very proud to be seen walking with him on Southsea Common.

One day it seemed as if the entire Royal Navy was sailing in through the narrow entrance to Portsmouth harbour. I counted eight battleships, two battle cruisers, two aircraft carriers, six cruisers and forty destroyers in one day. My father and I watched in disbelief as flotilla after flotilla crammed into the congested harbour. "If Hitler wanted, he would only have to scuttle one big ship in that narrow entrance to put the whole lot out of action." I thought of the great German transatlantic liners, *Bremen* and *Europa,* both of which had sailed past during that week on their way to and from Southampton. Good job Hitler wasn't as smart as my Dad.

The rest of the seaside holiday was memorable to me chiefly for the amusement arcades, drunken sailors whistling at my sisters, and playing on the beach with my nephew Nigel.

There were also ice creams, warm sea and countless trips on the Isle of Wight ferries and the many pleasure boats which plied the Solent and Portsmouth harbour. These now had to dodge amongst the great grey warships, scurrying picket boats and tenders. Although I was sad when the seaside holiday came to an end, I looked forward to my return to Mill Hill. There was a lot of fun to be had round Mill Hill, especially at the swimming pool.

A few days later, the German Army swept into Poland. I helped other boys to fill sandbags to protect the Air Raid Wardens Post and Gas Decontamination Centre, which were being rapidly set up next to Mill Hill library. In spite of being big for my age I could hardly carry a full sandbag and soon tired. Next day I was sent off to an uncle's farm in the sleepy little village of Duntish in Dorset. Here I fell in love with pigs and loved feeding the frothy whey and meal to the pink piglets, which my uncle, Farmer Gray, kept outside on the dry chalky grassland.

I also fell in love with Marion, the blacksmith's daughter; but she, being a much older woman of fourteen years, did not return my youthful passion. It was an eventful stay. Several cousins arrived to stay at the farm and there was much rivalry between us. Political discussions occupied the adults who were shocked by Russia's apparent betrayal of the anti-Nazi allies by her non-aggression pact with Nazi Germany. It seemed to be the end of poor Poland. One Sunday, listening to a small bakelite radio in a farm worker's cottage, I heard the doleful voice of Prime Minister Chamberlain declare that the country was now at war with Germany. Coming out to share the news with my new friends in the village, I heard a roar. An Armstrong Whitworth Whitley bomber lumbered low overhead and the excited villagers swore they saw German crosses on it. My positive identification of the aircraft as a Whitley was an unacceptable anticlimax.

A few days later my sister Daphne came to take me back to London. The expected air raids had not taken place; and anyway, it was time to go back to school. It wasn't too bad, I supposed. At least it would mean going back to Cumberland while the war was on.

Unknown to me, my golden youth as a southern schoolboy was over. A few days later my mother and father, together for once, waved me off from the platform of Euston station as the train pulled away with its cargo of noisy schoolboys…

Cumberland was less welcoming this time. With the whole school in place and set out for normal schooling, there was no freedom to wander the lakeland countryside. Strict discipline was the order of the day as the staff organised the overcrowded boys. Cockermouth was out of bounds following unfortunate clashes between the London lads and the locals.

In the absence of proper playing fields, a cycling club was set up; and the boys were encouraged to achieve considerable mileages in competition. I was rather out of things for a time because I did not own a bicycle and other boys got fed up with lending me theirs... I started to do up a fearful old boneshaker when one day, while I was in detention for some minor misdemeanour (mine, I was sure, were all minor or misunderstandings), an excited boy came in to tell me that a crate had arrived for me from Gamages store in Holborn. I had made no secret of my father's financial problems and the shiny new bike inside the crate embarrassed me. "Thought your Dad was supposed to be hard up?" jeered an envious bystander when, my detention over, I joyfully broke open the crate. I was speechless: how could good old Dad have afforded this wonderful BSA Golden Key racer?

Equipped with this wonderful mount, I was soon one of the stars. For the first time, apart from a certain prowess at swimming, I had found a sport I could excel at. Around the lakes tours of an ever increasingly ambitious nature culminated in a hundred-mile circuit before winter conditions closed in. A twenty-mile race round Castle Inn, Bothel, Mootah and Cockermouth was organised and I was determined not to let my dad down in this race. We were set off at intervals and somehow I managed to ride up hills when the others had got off and pushed. One by one I seemed to be overtaking the earlier riders and so far, no one had overtaken me.

The hill from Castle Inn to Bothel was a killer but after that it was an easy sprint down to Mootah, Cockermouth and back to the school. The headmaster was clearly amazed when I rode up the long incline of Castlegate Drive. I had set up a new record. One hour and three minutes for the twenty-mile circuit. The first race I had ever won out of the water!

Now that things were settling down in the reorganisation of the school accommodation, I was put in Dormy 10, a huge room in the loft of the building in which one had to climb over great truss beams. These were a bit like the upperworks of an ancient ship and we had great fun scrambling competitively around them. By some oversight, there was no dormy prefect, and to my dismay, Peter Bennet Baggs, a long-time enemy and rival, was in the group of boys who shared the lofty room with me. After three disturbances we were summoned to the headmaster's room. We had no doubt that the cane was being prepared for us and the speculation was over how many strokes we would get... Arthur Roberts, our young and respected headmaster, eyed us seriously. "Why must we have this continuous trouble in Dormy 10?" There was a sullen silence which I ventured to break by saying that it was because we had no prefect to keep order and settle arguments. Arthur Roberts chuckled. "So, you are a politician like your grandfather, Lansbury!" He sat looking serious for a minute. "Very well then, I will make you prefect and see that you keep these brats quiet!" Later he confided that he had intended to cane me but decided to make me a prefect instead...

I enjoyed the new responsibility and endeavoured to do the job well. Indeed, I was enjoying being a senior boy; and real pride was added when my form master told me that I had been chosen to play Hamlet in an abridged version of Shakespeare's masterpiece. I learned to deliver the "To be or not to be?" soliloquy with great feeling but I was far less convincing in the duel scene with Laertes. The other boy was a much better and more elegant swordsman and must have felt very miffed at having to be slain by such a clumsy Hamlet!

After the performance I felt seedy and, for the first time ever, I could not eat my tea, which happened to be my favourite, sausages. "You must be ill," said Duncan. I was very ill indeed.

A perforated appendix festered undiagnosed for days before the school matron called a horrified doctor. By now I was green-faced and running with sweat. The doctor bundled me into his own car and we rushed to the Cockermouth Cottage Hospital. The matron and sister were called back from a rare dinner party at the Pheasant Inn and a surgeon was called from Carlisle. I lay on the operating table chatting to Sister Jessie Coulthard. The pain had long since gone away as fever took hold. She smiled reassuringly. "Just count up to ten," she said. I remembered reaching five, then a confusion of dreams with a voice singing "God save the King". I awoke to find my mother leaning over me, her face racked with anxiety. Seeing that I was awake, she smiled. "What a fright you have given us!"

The next few days were pleasant enough. The drip tubes in my arms, the drainage tubes and tales of my singing "God save the King" and spouting lengthy quotations from *Hamlet* while semiconscious had made me something of a star, with nurses and patients alike. Furthermore, my mother was well and happy. Each day Mother, who had by now been joined by my father, came to see me. I revelled in the attention and the pleasure of seeing them together. They brought me fruit, sweets, a model aeroplane which I was able to build on the bed table which could be swung over my bed. I made the room pungent with balsa cement which must have been heaven for the nurses who had had to tolerate the fearful smells arising from my illness. I also had the latest newspaper in which to follow the war news.

The war in France, however, was still at a standstill. Round Lake Ladoga, the heroic Finns had inflicted terrible losses on the Russian troops who had been sent into the Karelian Isthmus to secure the approaches to Leningrad in anticipation of German treachery – a treachery which was not to be confirmed until 1941. It all seemed very strange.

I got on well with the nurses who vied with each other to please the "posh lad from Mill Hill School". Complications set in, however, as peritonitis flared up; and I lost my appetite for both food and witty conversation as the fever took hold. There followed a second operation and I was aware of many long faces. In those pre-penicillin days, peritonitis was usually fatal. However Mr Munro, the surgeon, had done a good job, removing gangrenous bowel, creating anastomoses and inserting massive drainage tubes with great skill. I remembered cooling hands on my forehead but I kept slipping off into confused dreams.

When I awoke, I had a terrible thirst but was not allowed any liquids, other than brief mouth washes. Once in desperation I tried to drink the water from the daffodils beside my bed.

Watching the slow drip of the saline glucose, as it left the bottle suspended by my bed, I longed for sleep to forget my thirst. Slowly I was slipping into a resigned torpor. That night, Matron Gill came in to ask if it would disturb me too much if the men in the public ward next door had the wireless on for a Gracie Fields concert. I was past caring. Later on, Gracie's golden voice pierced my semi-consciousness as she sang "Jerusalem, Jerusalem, I heard the Angels sing!" I woke up properly for the first time and listened to her cheerful voice and chatter. I felt hungry. Matron allowed me a drink of warm tea and I sat up. Later she brought me my favourite treat: some tinned strawberries! Perhaps Gracie had saved my life!

I recovered quickly now and with such good nursing I was soon fit enough to leave. The family thanked the hospital staff who were lined up in the hospital entrance to say goodbye. I had fallen in love with Nurse Rutherford and I was sorry to leave the friendly little hospital.

It was a cold foggy day as the streamlined London Midland and Scottish engine *Coronation Scot* steamed round the bend into Penrith station to take the family back to a blacked-out, anxious London, which still awaited fearfully the coming onslaught from Hitler's bombers. The house in Mill Hill looked strangely normal, apart from the lack of passing traffic. It was only after dark, with the full blackout of all street and domestic lighting, that the grim fact of war became apparent.

Each day brought news of severe shipping losses as the U-boats and mines took their toll. Germany was winning the war at sea. From France came newsreels of our boys taking baths in canvas tents which served as mobile bath houses. It seemed as if they were constantly singing "Roll out the Barrel". Frozen-looking airmen tended Fairey Battle bombers and Hurricane fighters on snowy French fields. The Fairey Battle bomber had proved to be an underpowered, nose-heavy disaster. Daylight bombing raids by the RAF on North German ports and towns had been abandoned due to unacceptably heavy losses. The phoney war was at its height; or was it the trough?

I had recovered my appetite and was slowly regaining my strength and energy. I was enjoying the break from school and loved being with the family. Mother was at home and my old haunts around Mill Hill seemed little changed. Above all, there was a chance that my brother Billy might soon be home on shore leave. One evening the newspapers and radio gave news of an unsuccessful air attack on a British tanker in the Thames Estuary. It was Billy's ship, the oil tanker *British Officer*. Billy had much to tell us when he eventually reached home. They had had a calamitous voyage. The tanker had run aground going up the Mississippi to load oil near New Orleans. The Captain had shot himself and it was an unhappy ship. On the way home they had been bombed by a lone Heinkel in the Thames Estuary. Nonetheless, Billy was fit and cheerful, if a trifle drawn. I remained at home recovering from my severe abdominal operations and I enjoyed some happy times as I listened to my brother's tales of New Orleans, the bars, the jazz and the fights on the levees as drunken crewmen quarrelled over women and gambling grudges.

I learned from Billy to admire a pretty woman, to compare the calves of nubile girls and judge a woman's figure. I felt very grown up. It was not, perhaps, the best preparation for a return to prep school and I would certainly have done better to have studied some Latin and Mathematics, my weakest subjects! My other brother, George, had progressed well in the army and was an extremely handsome young officer. Both of my sisters were now married and my only sadness was that my dad was now alone. Mother was back in a nursing home after yet another slip back onto the bottle. Soon it was time for Billy to rejoin his ship. We waved goodbye as he set off down the road with his sea bag slung over his shoulder. He had developed from a scruffy teenager into a smart, broad-shouldered young man. Dad was delighted to see that he walked with a sailor's roll. Billy went back to sea and I went back to school. It was the last time that any of us were to see him.

It had been a bleak spring. Churchill's boast that he would sink every German ship in the Skagerak became a mockery as the combination of German air power and superior gunnery chased the Royal Navy – or what was left of it – out of Norwegian waters. The army was forced to flee north to Narvik prior to evacuation. Prime Minister Chamberlain, who said that "Hitler had missed the bus by invading Norway," had found to his dismay that Hitler had caught an aeroplane instead.

Churchill was now in charge and people hoped for better.

* * * * * * * * * * * * * * * * * * *

Summer term was a period of great readjustment for me. The mature criteria I had picked up from Billy did not fit in with the realities of schoolboy life. I found myself ogling the school maids and I was extremely jealous of a classmate, Peter Davies. Apart from being a star pianist who could thunder away at Gershwin's *Rhapsody in Blue* while making eyes at any passing female, "Flash" Pete, the lucky devil, had been seduced by a twenty-year-old local girl who had taken a job as a school domestic. According to Flash Pete, she received him in her bedroom every night. His stories of feeling her soft breasts and all the other things she let him do to her drove the dormitory of bored, adolescent lads wild with curiosity and envy. My own longings were not really sexual. I wanted someone of my own to love and be loved by. I was now too old for the boy-and-boy crushes common in single

29

sex boarding schools. I wanted a girlfriend. The signs and events of approaching adulthood were starting to appear. Over the next few weeks, I was to experience my first shave, my first kiss and my first bereavement.

The bereavement was not unexpected. My famous grandfather, George Lansbury, was suffering from cancer in Manor House, the trade union sponsored hospital in Hampstead. I had visited him there some years earlier when he broke his thigh at a political meeting in Gainsborough shortly before Clement Attlee succeeded him as leader of the Labour Party. Old George had been inconsolable ever since the war had ended his long crusade for peace. Now, as the German tanks rolled towards France, he gave my father his gold wedding ring, telling him to sell it for the Peace Pledge Union. Shortly afterwards he died in my father's arms. The great Christian Socialist leader of the Labour Party, Cabinet Minister and Privy Councillor had given his all for peace and died a penniless, broken-hearted old man.

The Common Entrance Exams of 1940 were coming up for the older boys when the disastrous news started to come in from France, overshadowing the news of the old man's passing. The report of my grandfather's death did not make the headlines as it would have done only weeks earlier. It was, however, on the front page of the *Times* newspaper as we sat at school breakfast one sunny May morning. The news was passed from boy to boy down the long refectory table until it reached me. I pretended to take the incident in my stride. After breakfast, Arthur Roberts called me into his study and expressed his condolences. It was too much; I broke down in tears.

The next day, we heard that the Germans had broken through at Liege and Sedan. A few days later Holland, shocked by the destruction of Rotterdam by dive-bombers, had capitulated, the Dutch Royal family leaving down the canals in a British motor torpedo boat. The British Expeditionary Force had advanced into Belgium to defend the canal lines but the German panzers drove through to Abbeville and the Channel cutting off the bulk of the French army in the south from the northern forces and completely outflanking the impregnable Maginot Line. Belgium surrendered and the poorly led and poorly equipped British Expeditionary Force was evacuated from Dunkirk in the "miracle of the little boats". An appeal for help had been responded to by all the small boat owners within reach of the south coast. An amazing flotilla of fishing boats, sailing barges, river cruisers and small launches of every description joined the paddle steamers and other odd craft which sailed for the French coast. This heroic operation snatched the helpless men off the beaches. Somehow Churchill had turned even this catastrophic defeat into a victory. Not long afterwards, France surrendered; and Britain stood alone.

During that summer, I met a nice local lass called Joyce Arrowsmith who, sitting up in the gallery of the Congregationalist church choir, had reminded me of Judy Garland. She wore a similar picture hat to one worn by Judy in the film *Babes in Arms*. Feeling bold and safe amongst the other boys in the rigid wooden pews, I winked at her and much to my surprise, she winked back. Joyce came from a nice friendly family and on the pretext of being friendly with her twin brother Hilton, I was invited – and more surprisingly, allowed by my headmaster – to go to Sunday tea. Although only thirteen years old we were good friends and puppy love was sweet indeed. The Headmaster turned a blind eye to this little romance and even seemed to encourage it. On Joyce's 14th birthday the family took me with them to Allonby where, after a picnic on the beach, we held hands in blissful ecstasy. One day I plucked up courage and kissed Joyce. It was my first kiss!

As I walked back up Castlegate Drive to the school, my feet did not touch the ground. In my elated mood, I did not at first take in the motley column of men marching down the road. Hardly any of them were in uniform; but a properly turned out sergeant was marching briskly beside them exhorting them to keep in step. They all carried broomsticks or what looked like broomsticks. I recognised Joyce's dad who winked at me. Also in the ranks was farmer Bob Young and many other adults whom I recognised; but the biggest shock was to see my History master, Jock Ayre, swinging along. One of the older men was in a 1914/18 officers' uniform. They were the local defence volunteers, as a black LDV printed on their grey armbands denoted. Later I heard that they had all turned up carrying what guns they had. Most of the countrymen had shotguns or sporting rifles and they expected to confront German parachute troops at any time. However, the local commander had feared some fearful accidents with all these untrained, armed men at large. Much to their disgust, he had impounded all the guns, which were then locked up in the drill hall. The broomsticks were for them all to learn arms drill before they could be issued with rifles and uniforms. Eventually they became the Home Guardsmen of *Dad's Army*.

I went home for the summer holidays in fine spirits. I had been told I was to be Head Boy in spite of my far from outstanding academic achievements which, having missed so much time because of my illness, prevented me from taking Common Entrance and going on to the Main School with the rest of my age group. I grew close to my father during this time. My mother was also home in relatively good health; but she lapsed and returned to a nursing home just as the Battle of Britain started. I watched the dogfights throughout August with youthful enthusiasm. Shrapnel and bits of Messerschmitt were the new souvenir currency. I also watched long-legged showgirls, Pat Kirkwood and Judy Campbell, raise money to buy Spitfire fighters for the RAF by appearing in their showgirl outfits in Hendon Park. I much appreciated their patriotic efforts, though with somewhat different feelings. Somehow the authorities had set up a shot down Messerschmit 110 in the park for the public to gloat over.

Later that same day, I found a Fiertag Birth Control catalogue lying on a bus seat. It confirmed all of my friend Duncan's amazing information on the behaviour of married adults. I found myself looking at people with new eyes. I asked myself many questions. Were all grown-ups really up to these rude games? Flash Pete assured me it was so. I wanted to know, if so, where and when? Sex was not, at that time, up for all to drool at on the cinema screens and it was not unusual for a fourteen-year-old to be comparatively innocent.

On August 30th 1940 I saw a rosy-cheeked telegram boy leaving the garden of my father's house. Somehow I knew that it was Billy. Dad was on the telephone talking to my Uncle Ernest who was in Churchill's War Cabinet, serving in the Ministry of Information. He was holding a yellow envelope. He did not tell me at once but suggested that I should go for a cycle ride in the bright sunshine while he finished his call. I resisted as obstinate boys do and went and sat in the dining room... Despite his efforts to speak quietly, I heard his words to my uncle: "Billy's ship has gone down." I cried a little but from my earliest days at boarding school, I had learned to hide my true feelings. When Dad came off the phone, he saw at once that I had heard; he put his big arm around my shoulders and said a few words about the possibility of survivors and tried to give me hope. Now in a time of real sadness when tears would have helped the shock and pain, I did not have the release, which should have come to a thirteen-year-old boy. Instead I swallowed the lump in my throat and tried to be a strong companion to my dad. I wondered how my mum would take it and how poor old Dad was going to tell her.

Billy's ship had been sunk off Cape Wrath. The U-boat commander had penetrated the destroyer screen and sank four ships. Billy's ship, the *SS Millhill,* had been struck in the stern and quickly sank with the loss of all hands; there were no survivors. The King thanked Billy's parents for their son's sacrifice for his country. Poor Billy, he had not really had much choice.

That night a furious artillery barrage opened up against the German bombers and the fury of the guns was somehow a comfort to my father and me. We did not know that Luton, where my sister Esme lived, was also being heavily bombed. The Luftwaffe was trying to knock out the Vauxhall works where tanks and lorries were being made. Esme was sheltering under her bed in Luton hospital giving birth to baby Kate as bombs burst nearby. Fortunately the birth went well; but the telephones were out of action and we did not get the good news.

Next day, unaware of the drama at Luton, my father and I went over to check Dad's plywood and veneer mills in Stratford. The mill was idle having been closed as a non-essential operation at the outbreak of war and Dad had just been awarded a contract to reopen, producing plywood bulkheads for the RAF's new and secret Mosquito aircraft. The previous night's bombing had been mostly aimed at the Poplar docks and the East End. As Dad and I walked down Warton Road, a local cockney woman called out to Dad, "You are in for a surprise, mate!" We were indeed. For as we turned into the yard of No. 48, Warton Road, we saw that the entire factory had been demolished. Two perfectly aligned craters were all that remained within the pockmarked walls.

All the massive machinery had vanished leaving only the office where, as a child, I had spent happy hours playing with the typewriter and office equipment while my dad worked busily translating orders into work sheets. Even the office was a shell when we got inside. An incendiary bomb had gutted the place leaving only an empty safe intact. In one day, he had lost his son and his business. It was typical of my dad that his first comment was, "Thank God none of the men were working."

When we got the news of Esme and Peter's new baby, it was a relief and great pleasure to travel to Luton and see them... My nephew Nigel was delighted with his new sister Kate and could not be persuaded to leave the side of her cot. It was a sad time for Kate to arrive; and seeing my little nephew so innocently rapt, I experienced my first jealousy of childhood's careless days. I was almost a man.

The next year at school was a very mixed-up time for me. I enjoyed being Head Boy, with all the responsibilities that that entailed. I worried a lot about my parents, especially as I had been with them in the heaviest bombing of the Blitz and knew what they faced.

In the Christmas holidays I was caught with Dad and my sister Daphne in dockland during a major attack. For the first time I huddled in a shelter. Dad had spread sheets of his *Evening Standard* newspaper on the dirty floor of the temporary shelter in a street subway. Daphne clasped me to her as the whistle of falling bombs got nearer and the thuds more shattering. Three times the whistle of the descending bombs got nearer and nearer but as we waited fearfully for the fourth and potentially fatal whistle, it never came. During a lull, we emerged thankfully but apprehensively into the brilliant glare of burning buildings. It seemed a mad world when, approaching the Thames embankment, we saw trams still running against a background of flame and shells bursting in the sky. We had to walk from Blackfriars to Euston station through burning streets, dodging from shelter to shelter in lulls between attacks. God! How I admired the firemen who carried on trying to quell the fires right in the middle of the target areas! At Euston we waited for my sister Daphne's train to leave for Glasgow. I shook with fear and wished it would go! At last it crept out of the station and Dad and I were able to go down to the safety of the underground railway. Here the once perky cockneys, refugees from the bombing, lay sullenly grey-faced with staring eyes. I wondered how long they could stand it. It was not easy to live in two worlds, this one and the haven in the Lake District.

The senseless yoyo to and from school went on. Having been sent up to Cumbria to be safe, we always seemed to come home for the holidays during particularly fierce Blitz attacks. After the Christmas holidays, I was packed off back to childhood and school. I enjoyed some rugby against Cockermouth Secondary School on Lorton Road, a pitch with a backdrop of great scenic beauty. We also played at Workington beside the hideous, smoke- and flame-belching steelworks on a full-sized pitch where little boys' legs ran out of steam. In spite of my enthusiasm for rugby, school seemed unreal and I hated my family being dispersed and so far away. In May, 1941, Easter holiday time, I returned to our home at Mill Hill just in time for the second

Great Fire of London, when the fires got out of control, burning out the city and ringing St Paul's with flame. The morning after the raid, my father and I picked our way over the fire hoses and rubble as we made our way down Ludgate Hill. There did not seem much left of the great city. Everywhere was broken glass, shattered, smoking buildings and running water, and yet chattering office girls were going to work normally. Buses were running albeit slowly as they bumped over firehoses and rubble. Heavy rescue gangs were digging in the rubble of offices, shops and houses, looking for survivors. In the bright May sunshine there was almost a holiday air as people compared notes on their near escapes or tales of vast damage to their workplaces. Once back in the comparative quiet of Mill Hill, it was hard to believe the devastation that was taking place the other side of the city.

Soon afterwards, I read in the newspapers of a great victory in the Western Desert. General Wavell was rounding up the defeated Italian Army in Egypt and Libya. Mother was home and Daphne and her new husband Alex, who was back from the sea, had come to live at home as well. At least some of the family were back together.

I went back to school in the summer of 1941 in higher spirits than for some time.

* * * * * * * * * * * * * * * * * * * *

That last term at Belmont, I cycled all over the Lake District with the Headmaster, who had become a good friend after Duncan had gone on to Oundle. We climbed crags, dipped in mountain tarns and cycled vast distances. Joyce Arrowsmith was a good friend, too; and our innocent romance remained that way. Most Sundays I managed to get out to the Arrowsmiths' house for tea or a short drive to some beauty spot. Joyce's elderly parents seemed to enjoy seeing us indulging in the banter of puppy love. Joyce too seemed to enjoy every one of my jokes, my little poems and satirical drawings of her friends and relations. I often thought about Billy and my parents' sadness; but up here the sun shone, the blue hills and shimmering lakes formed a wonderful frame for my romantic inclinations. Even cricket went well. I had developed into a reasonably accurate fast bowler and managed to wield the bat in a shockingly clumsy manner to "cowslog" a lot of runs. I also swam a great deal whenever possible. This was the only sport I had ever really excelled in, apart from cycling, and I was easily school swimming champion, not surprisingly perhaps as I was nearly a year older than most of the other boys.

However, a particularly florid outbreak of acne started to cover my body with lumps and boils. This got worse each passing month and I was quite unable to take off my shirt in public. Swimming was soon to be only a much longed-for memory. Despite the spottiness, I was, for a while, a very happy boy.

There were no plans for me to go on to Mill Hill Main School, which had been evacuated to St Bees on the Cumberland coast. It seemed a waste of money in view of my father's problems arising from the destruction of his livelihood. Everyone seemed enthusiastic about my wish to be a farmer. How that was to be achieved nobody considered, except that my father often spoke of "having a little farm of our own one day." I don't think anyone had really accepted that my father, once a very rich man, was now actually short of both capital and income, thanks to the German bombs which had wiped out his beloved veneer mills and so much of his life's work.

The idea of being a farmer appealed to me as my educational progress had been completely disrupted by my illness and the extra year I had stayed on at the junior school as a result... I had also fallen in love with the little farms of the Cumberland valleys, the smell of horses and barns full of fragrant hay. Even the smell of oil lamps and dry cow-muck had a magic of its own. I had no real idea of the hard work and the drudgery involved. I expected to be a farm pupil like Adrian Bell in his lovely but over-romantic book *Corduroy*. I pictured myself like him, acting as the farmer's right-hand man as we walked round prodding contented livestock, sniffing hay, riding to market in a pony cart or feeling the quality of soil between knowledgeable fingers... Only my headmaster, Arthur Roberts, expressed the view that there might be more scope for my artistic and theatrical talents on the boards, rather than on the land. For me, the memory of days spent on Bob Young's farm at Greenlands was enough. I wanted to wear tweeds and corduroys and eat Cumberland sausage in the smell of oil lamps like Bob Young; and besides, I wanted to be near Joyce in Cockermouth.

The end of term came and I returned to London, my schooldays over but my formal education barely started and very, very incomplete. The bombing had lessened as the German army turned its wrath on Communist Russia, who had now become our ally. However the great Russian Bear was in full retreat. Rommel was rampaging with inexplicable success in the Western Desert and Greece and Crete had fallen.

Arrangements were made through the local parson, who had taken services at the school, for me to join a Quaker farming family in Pardshaw near Cockermouth. Educationally I had burned my boats. There was no going back. It only remained for Dad to scrounge some coupons and buy me some gear. They did not sell corduroys in Hornes of Regent Street. They did fit me up with a nice blue suit and two sets of overalls. A grey Trilby, a blue beret for work and a pair of Wellingtons completed my kit. My old school grey flannel suits could be used for work under the overalls.

Dad saw me off once more from Euston. Mum, sadly, was back in the nursing home at Chertsey. She had seemed pleased that I was going to be a farmer, perhaps because her other two boys had been taken by the services and she did not want to lose another, not that at fifteen it seemed likely in my case. But clearly she had doubts about my having left school so young and uneducated to be what she so clearly predicted, a manual labourer. Dad – who had left school at thirteen, had sailed to Durban as an apprentice on a four-masted windjammer, had jumped ship and had trekked to Bulawayo by my age – was less concerned. Memories of warm happy summers on our uncles' farms in Dorset and Somerset made him confident that an equally friendly and enjoyable life awaited me in Cumberland.

The wartime train moved off from Euston, its windows grimy and the seats looking worn and grubby. It was not as crowded as most trains were, with unhappy servicemen returning from leave or clutching rail warrants to new postings. The stale compartment held only three civilians: a young couple and me, a rather spotty boy. I was sitting by the window, facing the engine, always the best way to travel according to my father because, he said, you saw the world coming towards you rather than receding. If you twisted your head you could see both ways, I had argued. Mum had always preferred the safety of sitting with her back to the engine in case of a crash. Strange thing, I thought, how there are always two sides to everything. Whenever I heard a statement, I seemed to hear or find an alternative argument.

I looked at the young couple sitting opposite: they were quite obviously on honeymoon. The girl was dressed in a brown costume suit with a pink blouse and wore scuffed court shoes. She had a small rose pinned to the lapel of her jacket and a bright new ring on her left hand. I, although still only fifteen, had a fair knowledge of these matters having two fashion-conscious sisters and access to my mother's romantic novels, which made much of honeymoon couples and such. I wondered why she had no engagement ring. Perhaps the young man in his shiny blue suit could not afford one. Perhaps this was one of their last few days together before he too went off to change his cheap blue suit for classless khaki.

I wondered if the war would still be on when I reached call-up age. It had been a pretty disastrous war so far. Hitler had driven the British out of every country where they had attempted to fight, from Norway, the Lowlands and France to Greece and the Western Desert. London as a port had been bombed out of existence, as had my father's business. Now the Russians were in full flight from Smolensk and the defeated French seemed to like the Germans better than us. Even the Royal Air Force seemed unable to fight over France the way it had fought over England. The war at sea was going badly and the outlook seemed bleak; yet Mr Churchill spoke defiantly and with confidence whatever disasters befell the remaining Allied forces. It was not a happy time to start my working life; but soon I would be back in my beloved Cumberland.

The young woman's voice broke into my reflections. "Are you on leave or going on holiday?" she said.

"No, I am only fifteen and I am going to Cumberland to start work," I said proudly.

"What are you going to do?" asked the young man.

"I am going to work on a farm near Cockermouth."

The young man sneered at me. "Not much of a job, that."

"Well, it's what I've always wanted to do and one day I am going to be a farmer," I replied, feeling very defensive of my chosen profession.

The young woman, seeing that I was discomfited, said, "I am sure he knows what he wants to do, dear." They fell into silence.

The young couple eventually started to guess where they were. "That's more like it," said the young woman as the train passed through a rocky cutting. She leaned forward and spoke to me, exposing a generous cleavage. Embarrassed, I averted my eyes. "We are going to Keswick and I believe there are some really wild mountains and big lakes there but we have never seen anything like that before." I smiled, remembering the first time I had seen those mountains round Keswick and had fallen under their spell.

"Well," I said, breathless with enthusiasm and the chance to display my knowledge of the Cumberland I loved so well. "It's a long way yet and you will see much more exciting things than the rocks in that cutting before we get to Keswick; there's mountains, lakes and some grand rivers full of salmon." I fell silent. It was impossible to describe the glories which lay in front of them. Then looking at the couple, sitting so rapt with each other on the opposite seat, I wondered what it must feel like to be married. I had yearned for a girl and the thought of anyone actually being allowed to make love to one naked in bed was almost too much to bear. I did not fancy the young woman sitting opposite but the young man must love her. Did he too feel incredible joy that tonight he could hold her with everyone's blessing? The young man was looking at me strangely. I hoped I had not been thinking out loud.

Gradually the flat countryside fell behind as the long ascent of Shap began. The train slowed and stopped and as a seasoned traveller, I explained to my fellow travellers that the railway men were taking on a second engine for the steepest part of the climb up to the summit of Shap. Soon we were climbing up the long valley east of Kendal, up past Tebay and out onto the bleak plateau of Shap. The speed increased as the bleak hills gave way to the kinder countryside of the Eden valley. The train rattled and swayed as the driver slowed for the run past Lowther, and round the curve into Penrith Station. The change of motion brought me back from my reverie about the past with a jerk. The young honeymoon couple started to get down their luggage from the rack. They had forgotten me, the rather spotty boy.

I wondered how I could get my trunk from the guard's van to the far platform from which the single track left for Workington via Keswick and Cockermouth, with many halts in between. A porter was a rarity since many had been called to the colours. When I got out of the train I saw that the guard had already started to put my heavy trunk and bicycle out on the platform. A friendly sailor who told me he was on his way to work at the Broughton ammunition dump, near the naval depot at Workington, took one end of the trunk while I took the other and wheeled my bike at the same time. The sailor had spotted some of his mates on the train and after helping me to load the trunk, he left to join them, kit bag on shoulder and walking with a cocky sailor's roll. I thought back to the last time I had seen Billy, my sailor brother walking away from us at Mill Hill. For a few minutes I felt sad, lonely and very far from home and family. I got into the warm compartment of the little train and I dozed off, dreaming strange dreams of home, the war, schooldays, and Joyce Arrowsmith waiting for me at Cockermouth.

I woke with a start. I had missed the scenic part of the journey as the train swerved along the shores of Bassenthwaite. We were already chugging steadily down Embleton valley past Cook's Strawberry Howe farm and slowing up as the church steeple above Kirkgate came into view. The little six-wheeler engine chuntered to a stop beside the open platform of Cockermouth station. I got out and reached for the long brass handle of the goods compartment. A tall figure, the Quaker farmer, was at my side as I wrestled my trunk from the van. "How do you do, sir?" I said. The farmer looked me up and down with an enigmatic smile. "Hello, so you are Terence? You are a big lad but I doubt if you will have much stamina for hard work," he said, swinging the trunk easily onto his huge shoulder. "You bring the bike."

My heart sank at the dour welcome. My natural, cockney friendliness and confidence were shattered by this austere greeting. Perhaps he was just shy. The car journey to Pardshaw thawed the silence a little but the farmer's questions were mostly about my religious leanings. When we got to the farm, the family seemed friendly enough and the farmer responded with a slow smile to their teasing. "Not used to being called 'sir'," he said to me in a deep drawl. "I am Eddie and I suppose you had better call me that. We won't expect much from you at first."

The men were coming in for their tea now and I went up to change into the working gear which I would hardly be out of for the next few months. I came down in the boiler suit provided by Hornes of Regent Street. All the men were in corduroys. They smelled of cows, warm milk and disinfectant.

The youngest giggled. "Sit down then, Long John Silver!"

I, who was proud of my height, sat down.

A dull green card above the hearth bore the text "Christ is the Head of this house, the unseen guest at every meal, the silent listener to every conversation". I shivered. The text seemed menacing and ominous, somehow devoid of the warmth and love which I associated with my dead grandfather's religious faith. Once more I felt flattened, awkward and out of place. The farm girl, Alma, smiled at me; she was pretty. She bent to open the oven door revealing pretty legs and a nice figure as she stretched over the kitchen range.

"What's for tea?" said one of the men.

She smiled at me again. "Coomerlan' sausage."

Chapter 2

Cold Porridge

Eddie the farmer had been right. I did not have the strength or the stamina my size had suggested. Neither had my years at a suburban preparatory school and life in the prosperous south of England prepared me for life with a particularly joyless Cumbrian family, whose absorption with the presence of Christ and the need to avoid sin had left little room for love, let alone joy.

Eddie, my farmer boss, had it seemed experienced the presence of Jesus, walking the fields with him. Now he was preoccupied with the devil's presence. In his mind, he saw the devil waiting to tempt his workmen into sin through levity, or pleasures other than hymn singing or chapel attendance. This situation, as I wrote to my friend Duncan, "leads to a pretty repressed atmosphere". It also manifested itself in the behaviour of my workmates. They, fearing Eddie's sarcastic and often deafening tongue, were sullen and rebellious behind his back. Swearing or drinking carried the threat of instant dismissal, unless the sin was followed by abject promises of repentance and reformation. Consequently the men had grown to be two-faced and suspicious of each other.

I, being "educated", was allowed to sit in the house after work with the family and occasionally travelled to chapel in their car with them. This earned me great opprobrium from the other men and I was soon the object of open hostility, a situation aggravated by my "posh" southern accent and the partly justified belief that I was a spoiled brat.

I was exhausted by the sudden change from the comfortable and easy life of suburban childhood; my soft hands were blistered and chapped, and my long overgrown back and unprepared shoulders ached constantly. Farmer Eddie, on the other hand, was an exceptionally fit, hardworking man and like many Quakers, was, without realising it, a very hard taskmaster. He rose at five thirty every day of his life and seldom rested from his farming labours before eight or nine o'clock at night, unless for some chapel or other spiritual activity. This was Eddie's life. Hard work, chapel and – from what the men said – a lot of activity in bed! I pondered on the latter. His wife, Madge, was certainly attractive, in the rather buxom manner of the village girls, but she had a sharp tongue with Eddie and was the only thing in sight he seemed to fear. I found it impossible to imagine them making love or even being in love.

The farm men who had grown up with endless drudgery had little sympathy for an overgrown schoolboy who could not, or would not, do his share of the work. Even Eddie castigated me when I was unable to lift a ten-stone bag of fertiliser straight up from the ground into a spreader. "You are abusing yourself and me by pretending you can't do it!" I was mortified by my weakness. At school I had been the strongest boy by far.

The youngest of the men, Binner Grayson, was positively aggressive, having up till then been the bottom of the pile. Now, finding himself with someone below him, he took a particular delight in ordering me about, often countermanding Eddie's orders. I who was used to obeying orders instantly and without question and indeed, having my orders obeyed as Head Boy of my school, attempted to obey both. The result was frequent clashes with Eddie over jobs not done due to my diversion onto other work by Binner. The other men would also put their oars in; and this multiplicity of bosses together with language difficulty due to the West Cumbrian pride in dialect and their tendency to go broader when speaking to offcomers made me, by trying to serve a host of masters, confused and ineffective. I failed to stand up for myself at least partly because the men could not understand my southern twang, any better than I could follow their Nordic patois. By the end of the first week I began to experience the threat of physical violence from some of the farm men. Eddie, too, was clearly disappointed in my potential, both as a worker and as a Christian. Unlike my famous grandfather, I did not have strong faith or pacifist convictions, nor did I take a keen interest in the family prayers.

To add to my misery, Joyce, my schooldays sweetheart in nearby Cockermouth, who was now approaching the School Certificate Examination, seemed strangely indifferent towards my overtures. I, uncharitably, thought it was because I was now an incompletely educated farm boy, rather than Head Boy of a posh school. I had misjudged her; for Joyce was no Estelle. More likely it was because I was constantly tired out, grubby and very depressed company. Later on I discovered that she did have another boyfriend at Brigham, a nearby village; but basically, she was just very determined to concentrate on her studies. She was under great pressure to make up to her parents for her twin brother's unappreciative attitude to school and his home. Perhaps it served me right. During my last term at school I had tried to make Joyce jealous by flirting with a pretty but flighty girl from the Moor district of Cockermouth and had flaunted her at Joyce despite having no real interest in the girl. Now it seemed that my world had collapsed.

I could not even find comfort by satisfying my enormous appetite. Food there was indeed in plenty but it was not the delicious cooking of my mother or even the school cooks. My misery was complete when I found that at the farm, winter breakfasts began with cold porridge: cold, salted porridge! Dishes of the cold spludge were placed on the kitchen doorstep to cool. I dreamed about my mother's steaming creamy porridge and the sugar sparkling on the milky surface. I remembered her warm presence, when she was well, presiding over happy family breakfasts at Mill Hill. Even the farm bacon, salted and hung up on hooks from the ceiling, tasted rancid compared with the delicious smoked rashers my mother found in the shops at Mill Hill. Now I appreciated what it had meant to be in the family bosom. Feeling cold and lonely in the farm kitchen, I looked sadly at the sweat-stained wool of Alma's armpits and the contours of her nicely rounded figure. I was fascinated by the swell and sway of her breasts which moved as if they had a life of their own beneath all that wool, as she busied herself around the kitchen. I suppose Alma's breasts were my only comfort; and even that was only in my mind!

By the end of the month however, things started to get better. I got used to the cold porridge, the coarse, rather stale bread, the absence of such luxuries as toast and the drear atmosphere when the family were about... I even began to quite enjoy the rough food and rougher humour of my cowmuck-smelling tablemates. I had even managed to get a laugh out of one or two of them by dint of my gift for mimicry. I could reproduce Eddie's sanctimonious drawl intoning some homily or other about sin, followed by a reasonable imitation of a rasping Louis Armstrong scatting "The good Lord said sit down, sit down, sit down, you're rocking the boat" in reply. The men thought I was completely mad but at least they had smiled.

One day I was astonished to hear that Stan the horseman had been chosen to drive the new tractor. It was the very first tractor to arrive in the parish and was, though none of us realised it at the time, the start of the mechanisation which was to revolutionise British Agriculture by the end of the war... I was not allowed to look at it, let alone touch it. It was a bright orange "Utility" Fordson, a very simple machine which was being mass produced at Ford's factory at

Dagenham. How the factory had escaped total destruction during the Blitz was a mystery to me but it had somehow kept in production and one of the little yellow tractors had been allocated to Pardshaw.

Leslie Abbott – a very bright young farmer from Corner Croft, a tiny holding across the village street from Eddie's farm – knew a bit about tractors. Eddie asked Leslie to teach Stan how to drive the machine. It was hard going. The crash of gears and backfiring could be heard all over the village. Stan was having difficulty in starting the tractor. He was unable to grasp the simple sequence of the starting procedure. Twice I saw him kick the tractor in frustrated rage. He had now tried to adjust the fuel mixture by unscrewing the simple needle jet and was going round in a cloud of black paraffin smoke and sporadic explosions. He later overfilled the sump with oil causing the plugs to oil up resulting in further smoke and misfiring. The transition from horse to tractor was not going to be smooth... Eddie complained that Leslie was having a full-time job, putting the tractor right.

Stan's Waterloo came one bright day when he was ploughing up grassland. All was going well. Leslie had set the plough for him and the furrows were turning over nicely with a cloud of seagulls following the tractor. The gulls swooped and squawked as they examined the neat slices for worms and other goodies in the fresh damp soil. It reminded me of sea trips I had had with my father when the seagulls planed along in the wake of the ship and my father had spared some of his sandwiches for me to throw to the screaming gulls. I chuckled as I remembered a gull bombing my dad's black homburg hat. "Never mind, Bill," my mother had said. "It's supposed to be lucky!"

My reverie was shattered by a warning cry to Stan from Leslie. Stan was fast approaching a low stone wall. Forgetting that he was not driving a horse, Stan panicked and went through the wall in a shower of rocks shouting, "Whoa! Whoa, tha black booger! Whoa!" The ever-patient Leslie sorted Stan out. There was no lasting damage to the robust little Fordson tractor, apart from some minor dents and scratches... Fortunately the wall was not one of Lakeland's dry stone masterpieces and Leslie was able, with my unskilled assistance, to make a modest attempt at rebuilding the fallen rocks. The terrified Stanley did not want Eddie to know and swore me to secrecy. My sealed lips won me a friend!

Leslie and his wife Mildred, a fine tall girl, who had striking grey streaks in long curly dark hair, were a bright friendly couple and were most helpful in making me feel less of a fish out of water. They often lent me a bike when my own thoroughbred racer had broken down yet again under the punishment of farm life. They owned a pair of "Him" and "Her" Raleigh Golden Arrow machines, the nearest thing to self-indulgence I ever saw from them, apart from the hot cup of cocoa which they sometimes shared with me on cold winter nights.

Whenever I saw Mildred striding up the village in her grey coat and wellies, usually carrying a couple of full buckets as well as an ever-growing lump on her tummy, I felt more cheerful. When the "lump" arrived, it was a baby boy. Leslie was a very proud father. He encouraged me and gave me helpful tips about the tractor and even hinted that Eddie was far from perfect, both as a farmer and a man. Somehow I felt better whenever I had been with the Abbotts.

One breakfast time in late autumn, I was gobbling down my food hurriedly. Eddie had told me to set the milked cows off walking down the lane towards Pardshaw Hall, nip in for my breakfast, then cycle down the lane to turn them into Kingsland field. I reckoned this would give me about ten minutes to eat my breakfast. Gulping down my hot tea, I was eyeing Alma's figure and listening to the men discussing the coming threshing time. Threshing, although hard work, was a pleasant break in the dairy farm's routine drudgery. I heard that all the lads from neighbouring farms went off to whichever farm the threshermen were visiting. While listening to the men, I was absently continuing to ogle Alma when she turned and became aware of my stare. She sniffed and left the room... Hearing hushed and scandalized tones coming from the front parlour, I immediately thought that I must have done wrong and prepared myself to face Eddie's wrath. However, it transpired that the threshing gang had been threshing on a Sunday up at Mockerkin. This had utterly outraged Eddie and his wife as being an affront to all decent Christians.

In my childish imagination, I began to visualise the threshermen as horned demons with barbed forks and flashing red eyes. They were red-eyed all right when I did see them, but it was from constant work in dust, smoke and soot. The threshermen arrived in a cavalcade of bright pink wagons and a threshing drum, pulled by a smoking, steaming traction engine which hissed and clanked up the village. They stopped first at Salkeld's farm at the end of the village. Manoeuvering the great threshing machine into place through the narrow gateways took some time and I got a rare break to stand and stare. However I soon had to start work, helping to carry water, in ten-gallon milk churns, to fill the great engine's tanks. This done, I barrowed out several loads of coal. For once I felt I was a useful lad!

Later on, I helped strip the thatch off the little round oat stacks in readiness for the day's threshing. The chief thresherman was a tough old man, grimy with coal dust, oil and soot. He clearly loved his great engine and was constantly tending it with oilcan and cloth as the great machine throbbed and wheezed under his loving hands... Quite suddenly, I found myself a valued member of a happy gang. Men swore good-naturedly and told doubtful jokes; but there was much innocent laughter and many smiling faces. Old Mr Salkeld showed me the proper way to fork sheaves from the stacks layer by layer without trying to lift myself by pulling at the sheaves I was standing on. I learned to keep in time with the man cutting the string bands of the sheaves and feeding them into the threshing drum. Mr Jackson, another neighbouring farmer, showed me how to stack straw bottles and after a time, called me a good lad. I positively glowed with pleasure. Soon I could carry sacks of oats and do every job round the thresher and was treated as an equal. A special source of pleasure was the thrice daily arrival of the tea hamper. Great cans of hot tea were brought out by the farm girls who gave us all big bright smiles. One even blushed when I helped her over some fallen sheaves which lay across her path. My eyes fell on her bouncing figure and her hands crossed involuntarily over her bosom. "By lad! Thaal have to watch thissen or ole Mossop'll rattle thy shanks," Mr Jackson said to me; "he's gay particular wha gars near that lass o hiss'n!" I felt rather proud that a mature famer had addressed me in such an adult way. However I was soon fully occupied by the tea hamper. Meat rolls, gingerbread and apple cake were handed to me in generous portions by smiling men. I was in heaven.

Returning that night to Eddie's farm, the atmosphere of tense intolerance swept over me like a black wave. I had always, in the past, been able to extricate myself from unpopularity by being, or pretending to be, something of a jester. Alas, my jokes and gift for parody and satire fell on stony ground in that tense humourless atmosphere. My popularity reached its nadir when, tired and confused one night, I began washing cows' udders at the wrong end of the byre. The head cowman, Billy Nicholson, swore mildly. "Godammit, lad! Don't you know which end to start yet?" Eddie overheard Billy swear and ordered him to apologise or be sacked. Billy took umbrage and asked for his cards. The other men were slow to forgive me for Billy's departure and the increased workload which resulted.

Eventually I learned to play the parts both Eddie and the men required. I hated the hypocrisy, but I attended Thursday night chapel with the men and adopted their rough speech and crude humour. My talent for acting stood me in good stead. Meantime I learned to snag mangolds and turnips, being careful not to cut the mangolds lest they bled and went rotten in the clamp or pie. Turnips, it seemed, were less tender; but I was not. I cut myself and bled many times before mastering the awkward sickle favoured in the district. Later as winter came on, the cows needed green fodder to supplement their indoor diet of hay. Whatever the weather, we had to go out and cut marrowstem kale which grew taller than myself. We often worked soaked to the skin and frozen to the bone. Binner exhorted me to "work to keep heat" and for once Binner was right. The work did indeed generate enough heat when my aching back allowed me to keep going.

I loved working with horses and I learned to harness up the great Clydesdale mares and geldings. It was all that I could do to lift the massive collar and hames over the horses' heads. I caused great derision amongst the men by trying to take off a horse collar before rotating it round on the horse's neck to bring the wide base over the broad forehead of the patient nag. Most of the gentle giants would stand quietly with anxious eyes and twitching ears as I strained to turn the collars and slide them down onto their muscular shoulders. Next came the heavily padded saddle which carried a bridge upon which the heavy shaft chain would rest. Uneasy iron-clad feet stamped as I reached under huge bellies for the girth strap which always seemed to be just out of reach. Swinging the leather breechings with all their buckles and dangling chains over the bulging rump and threading the swishing tails through the strapping was supposed to be the work of moments. I must confess it took me time. Perhaps I was too particular about the horses' comfort in my desire to gain their trust and friendship. I had not been too successful with my workmates in this respect... Sometimes the horses were unappreciative and caught me across the face with irritable sweeps of their tails. Once buckled and hooked together, the harness was complete apart from the bridle. Getting the bit into the fearsome mouth and the head straps over the brow of an upheld horse's head took some doing. Yoking up was also an adventure. One had to back the clumsy carthorse between the shafts of a cart and pull the shafts down so that the chain fell into the saddle bridge. Then the hames were hooked to the wagon chains and the rope girth strap secured. Only then could the breeching or croupe chains be hooked on. The correct sequence was vital or the horse moving forward prematurely could rip a set of harness to pieces. Once yoked up and aboard an empty cart, one was a charioteer and I used to drive proudly along the village street. For a few precious minutes, this was the life! However, the empty carts were not for my pleasure. Muck, wet kale, mangolds or potatoes were waiting to be loaded by hand or by shovel. Whichever, it meant more backache; usually it was sloppy slurry from the cowsheds.

Most of my work with horses was done after the daily drudge of milking and mucking out. Milking time was not too much fun. I loathed carrying the full pails of milk from the biers to the dairy across cobbles made slippery by rain and wet cowmuck, a job which strained my long back and punished my aching feet. I envied Binner who sat warm and snug on a three-legged stool between the warm cows, stripping out the last drops of creamy milk which at that time we believed the milking machine left behind. Meanwhile, I washed udders with icy water. I never understood why we used cold water. There was always a kettle steaming in front of the house fire and I was sure a warm udder cloth would have stimulated milk flow a lot better than the shock of near freezing water. Certainly I would have been happier. I dared not ask Eddie; he would probably have thought it soft. Most of all I envied my school friends, who were probably still in bed while I wrestled overloaded wheelbarrows over the cobbles and through the mud to the midden.

Throughout that winter of 1941/42, I was never really well and longed for some time off in daylight to walk round the village or simply stand and stare. It was hard to remember that the beauty of the fells and lakes was just over the rise of Mosser Fell and down the steep road to Loweswater. Colds and flu were not an acceptable reason to stay in bed in this harsh world of wartime agriculture; and a combination of both hung round me for weeks, causing even more backache and depression.

On the rare occasions when I was in the house long enough to hear the news, it was equally depressing. One Sunday night on a rare trip to Cockermouth, I was sitting with Joyce's hospitable parents while she studied – or, as I thought, avoided me in another room – when the news came that the Japanese had bombed Pearl Harbour. Over the next few weeks, the United States' forces in the Pacific, deprived of the shield of the sunken Pacific Fleet, were driven out of the Philippines. The triumphant Japanese cycled down through Malaya chasing a poorly led and disorganized army of British and Australian conscripts. Their bombers with incredible skill sank the pride of the Royal Navy, *HMS Repulse* and *HMS Prince of Wales*. Hong Kong, the great fortress of Singapore, Rangoon and Mandalay, the bastions of Empire, had all unbelievably fallen to the little yellow men. In the Middle East, the war in the desert was going little better as Rommel with great dash and skill turned the tables on superior British forces time after time, forcing retreat after retreat from what seemed like certain victories. It seemed the Germans' versatile 88mm anti-aircraft gun could be used against tanks and was proving an almost insuperable obstacle to the poorly designed and lightly armoured British and American tanks... From the Russian Front the news was no better. After recovering from Red Army successes outside Moscow, the Nazis turned aside from the capital and swept down to the Dnieper, the Don and beyond. The need for a scrap of good news was desperate and it came when the RAF put 1000 bombers up for the first time over Cologne. It was to be the Royal Air Force's high water mark for many dark months to come.

Just before Christmas 1941, I got some good news from London. My sister Daphne had given birth to twins. Little Patsy and Billy Day were doing well and my mother was back from the nursing home, recovered, and helping with the new arrivals. The house was full of baby gear and adoring in-laws from Scotland. My father sounded happy.

Farmer Eddie at last realised that I was abnormally tired and not well. To my surprise and pleasure, he gave me a week off to spend Christmas at home. It was wonderful to be with them all but already the family home was changing. There were shortages which were not just due to wartime rationing. No one had much time to listen to my stories of farm life. The babies kept my sister busy and fraught. My dad was beset by family problems due to my grandfather's lack of provision for his eldest daughter Annie. George Lansbury, unlike many politicians, had never thought of amassing wealth when in a position of great influence and power. He died leaving no debts but just a few hundred pounds which were bequeathed widely. Annie had been George's housekeeper since his wife's death years earlier. Although at one time she had been promised a pension in recognition for her services, the authorities reneged. Now she was destitute. If

50

Dad's factory had not been bombed and had been earning, it would have been easy for Dad to support his sister, but now he was existing on diminishing capital. Some, but not all, of my father's sisters agreed to help. I went back to the farm very concerned for them all. My dad's money and family problems as well as the constant danger they endured in London made my discomforts at Pardshaw seem trifling.

As the spring warmed up I enjoyed the field work. I had shivered in the icy helm winds which swept down past Penrith and Keswick from the snowy Pennine hills drying out the saturated fields and blowing dust and soil into the hedge bottoms. Now I could savour the warm breezes which swept in from the sea across the West Cumbrian plain. Occasional black showers drifted up from Egremont and hid the gentle rise of Dent but most days they petered out and the warm soil felt good beneath my hands and knees as I crawled side by side with my mates, up and down the endless rows of turnips, mangolds and kale. We were singling and weeding the newly germinated root crops with what had by now become horny thumbs and forefingers. As the ground grew harder, we tied pads of sacking round our sore knees; then, as the young plants grew stronger, we forsook our hands and knees and worked up and down the rows wielding hoes as we chopped at the eager growth of weeds which threatened to overwhelm the precious crop. I pondered on the battle between man and nature. It was hard to take in that this was an annual battle which had been going on for centuries and would repeat itself next year and again and again.

Binner, in spite of his affectation of boorish ignorance, seemed to have a natural appreciation of the inevitability of the seasons and the recurring problems they brought with them. "Nowt's the syame and nowt's different! Just a loc a bloody wark every bloody year!" A few months earlier, before Pardshaw rendered me inarticulate, I would have murmured *"plus ca change"*; but such sophistication had been knocked out of me...

As April passed into May, my brother George prepared to join the 8th Army which was now struggling in Libya. Before joining his troopship, George paid a brief visit to Cockermouth as a smart young Lieutenant in the Royal Tank Regiment. I felt a bit of a rustic oaf as we met in the Globe Hotel on Cockermouth Main Street. George, who bore a striking resemblance to Errol Flynn, was resplendent in tunic, Sam Browne leathers and shining pips. By chance we met Joyce on the street. This temporarily restored my prestige with Joyce, for brother George was undoubtedly an officer and a gentleman and a very handsome one at that. After a few happy hours we parted and went on our very separate journeys: George to North African sand, sunshine and danger while I, his strangely altered young brother, with some forebodings, went back to the Pardshaw farm with its overtones of religious guilt. I was greeted at the farm with sceptical comments from my workmates. "Thy brother will ha had 'is commission bowt fer him!" This time I was angry. George had had no help at all from my family; far from it. Indeed the family name with its association with socialism and pacifism would have been an obstacle to promotion rather than a help. Our dad could and would not have been able to buy a commission in 1940. The gulf between the reality of my family and the Pardshaw concept of it was too great to explain to either these cynical Cumbrians with their preconceived ideas or to Eddie the farmer.

By now I had realised that Joyce's preoccupation with examinations was real. When she had time, she was as friendly as ever, but the romance was over; I was ready, as Joyce said laughingly, for "fresh woods and pastures new". Soon after this new understanding, Eddie gave me a "weekend off". This rare treat was to stretch from after milking on Saturday night until milking time on Monday morning. The joy of this freedom in daylight hours was too good to be true. Joyce's parents kindly arranged a lodging for me with a postman's wife who lived on Rubbybanks, a one-sided pot-holed street on the bank of the river Cocker. As I was back in civilized society for the brief break, I had to borrow some pyjamas from Joyce's dad. The Saturday night out was fabulous. I danced with some of the shoe factory girls from Yarmouth who were very kind and ignored my awkward feet. I also tried to dance with some of the older girls from the secondary school, who were less patient with my inexperienced dancing.

Two of the maids from my old school were there. One of them, who as a fast-developing schoolboy I had lusted to kiss ever so badly, danced with me twice, before a flushed and angry local swain took her away. I was amazed at the way she had strained against me. I could feel her breasts against my chest and her thighs sliding against my own. She smiled at me knowingly as my arousal became evident and I pressed myself eagerly and obviously against her. I felt incredibly stirred and manly. It was a shock to me later in the evening when I saw my former headmaster dancing with the girl.

On fire with approaching manhood, I fell in love with several young ladies in Cockermouth during the winter. I preferred them to the girls out in the village who, apart from Alma, the house girl at Eddie's farm, were a dull lot. Too much work, chapel-going and fear of the devil had taken their toll. The Cockermouth girls had been livened up by the arrival of the shoe factory from Yarmouth and the uninhibited East Anglian girls had brought great life to the Saturday night dances.

After that first glorious evening at the dance I returned to the postman's house. To my surprise and discomfort, I had to share my bed with a fierce-looking soldier. The remnants of a Commando company, survivors of the Dieppe raid, had been sent to Cockermouth with their leader, "Carpet Slipper Webb", for rest and recreation. Sten guns and a captured German machine gun were propped up in the hall as I went in. A tough-looking sergeant was tending a series of nasty cuts on his legs where German barbed wire had sliced the flesh. I learned from the commandos of their part in the disastrous raid. They had climbed a sewer which passed up the cliffs in order to get behind and into shore batteries with demolition charges. They had been successful; but other groups of men had suffered heavy casualties, although they had penetrated the town. The main force of Canadians had been stranded and slaughtered on the shingle beaches. The supporting Churchill tanks had mostly been unable to climb the shingle beaches or had been stopped by simple concrete road blocks. I, who had heard the raid described as a successful reconnaissance on the official news broadcasts, was flabbergasted.

When I returned to Pardshaw the men who had seen me enjoying myself with the girls at the dance were full of jokes and good-natured leg-pulling. Eddie the farmer had given up trying to convince me of the evils of the town. I had even gained the other farm men's respect by using my easy manner to charm girls many years my senior into dancing with me while the other lads clustered shyly round the wall of the Public Hall. "He's got neck for ought bar syap and water," commented Binner, himself a braggart on the farm but a shy mumbling oaf in the town. It was June before I actually enjoyed some time off in daylight again. The double summer time, introduced as a wartime effort to increase the hours of daylight, resulted in daylight almost to midnight. As haymaking had not yet got into full swing, the farm lads enjoyed the long summer evenings free of toil. I could not persuade the other lads to cycle over to the nearby lakes of Buttermere,

Crummock and Loweswater. Indeed I was astonished to find they had never been further than the next couple of villages and Cockermouth. None had climbed the high fells and they refused to believe that I and my schoolmates had cycled round all the lakes and climbed many of the peaks.

One mellow June evening, just before my sixteenth birthday and before haymaking put a complete stop to all leisure, I sat sketching Mosser Fell and the Buttermere Fells just visible beyond. Alma the farm girl walked down to see what I was doing. I swore inwardly; I was fed up with the critical downtrain attitude of almost all of Eddie's household. To my surprise the girl – or young woman, since she was a mature twenty-two – sat down beside me and expressed astonishment and admiration for my work. I fairly glowed; I loved Alma in a way because she alone of the Williamson household seemed not to fear Eddie's critical tongue. She always had a pleasant smile and had once winked at me during one of Eddie's tirades against sin. I did not consider myself a gifted artist and was always surprised to meet people who could not draw. It always seemed so simple to me. "By, it's turning cold," said Alma, edging closer to me. Intent on my painting, I had not noticed the chill evening air flowing down the hillside. Her presence close beside me became disturbing but I did not want to break the spell, in spite of the shivering which now beset me. The shivering, I realised, was not just due to the cold. The girl's body radiated a gentle heat which I was aware of even though we were not touching; and she gave off a faint womanly scent which was comforting and reminded me of my mother. It was also strangely exciting. Alma said she must go in and got up. With a last look at my painting and a friendly smile, she set off for the house. I remained a few moments before I too got up and wandered after her. As we walked by a clump of nettles a rabbit scuttled out, its white tail bobbing brilliantly in the evening light. Meg, the farm sheepdog, appeared from nowhere and went dashing joyfully after it, appearing and disappearing in the long grass of the orchard. "Hope it gets away," I said to the girl. "You're too soft to make a farmer," she said, mock-scornfully but with kindness in her voice.

That night I dreamed romantic dreams of nights with Alma and woke desperately disappointed to find she was not with me. Sex was becoming an obsession in my waking hours and was not helped by the boastfully described erotic fantasies of my workmates. I began to believe that I was the only virgin left in the village and I wondered what was wrong with me. Eddie's wife started to complain darkly about the bed linen and sin. I, who was suffering frequent wet dreams, was mortified.

During the early summer, there were moments of great hilarity and pleasure. One warm evening there was a barn dance in nearby Ullock. The farm lads had got hold of some drink and pairs of boys were clumping round the floor, red-faced and shining with all the spirit of young cart horses loosed out for the first spring grass. They wheeled, jumped and curveted until they collapsed into a heap of flailing limbs. The girls and matrons looked on with frozen disapproval until one lady, wiser and more tolerant than the rest, got the band to play a "Paul Jones". At once the whole floor was a gay kaleidoscope of scampering girls in coloured dresses and white-shirted men. Round and round went the contra-rotating circles, slowing down and breaking up as the music dictated the formal ritual of change to partners and back to rings, then speeding up to a hilarious race before once more the hopeful lads prayed the music would stop leaving them opposite a comely lass rather than a formidable matron.

Later in the evening, Alma sought me out. She was supposed to be engaged to a sergeant in the Royal Signals but she did not wear his ring and on the rare occasions he came on leave, he seemed to prefer the company of village lads or the hard men who drank in the dark kitchen of the Beehive Inn at Eaglesfield Cross. I danced reasonably well by now and was pleased to waltz her round the floor in spite of the semi-scornful comments and whistles of my workmates. Besides, they were becoming good-natured in their rough way. Alma danced close to me, but without the flirtatious pressure of the town girls at Cockermouth. I did not dare dance cheek-to-cheek; that was considered outrageous behaviour in this chapel-shadowed community. It was enough to have her in my arms, absorbing her warmth and smell. When the music stopped she thanked me and as she turned away, she squeezed my hand. It was nothing, perhaps; but to me it seemed a great deal.

I noticed Alma was not in the hall after the interval. Her boyfriend had long since gone off to the pub with his "marrers" and had not returned. On impulse I stepped outside and wandered along the path beside the river Marron. A small humped bridge rose in front of me and I paused on it to stare into the water which was shimmering in the bright moonlight. I was fascinated by running water and was admiring the rippling reflection of the clouds scudding by the moon when I was startled by an altercation nearby. "Of course I love you!" came a loud voice. "But tha's sok a cold bitch! Ah long t'tak tha in my arms." "Ugh! you stink of beer an' smoke," came a girl's voice along with muffled sounds of courting. The band could be heard playing the "Anniversary Waltz" and I felt a sudden wave of loneliness sweep over me as the plaintive melody wound on.

"What are you doing out here?" said a small voice beside me.

"Nothing, I just like to be alone sometimes," I replied, recognising Alma with surprise.

"No one should be alone tonight," said Alma sadly.

I looked towards the pub. Alma caught my glance. "Oh him, he doesn't care about me or he would be with me now."

She started to cry softly. I was taken aback; it was the first time an adult other than my family had cried alone with me and I didn't know what to do. Hesitantly I put a hand out to comfort her. She did not draw away, even when I put an arm round her. I looked down and noticed the neat parting in her dark hair which shone slightly in spite of the now clouded moon. She had stopped crying and stood with her head nestled against my chest. Suddenly she lifted her face and kissed me. It was not just a friendly kiss and I was shocked by the trembling intensity of it. I shifted my position to take her properly in my arms and smothered her in a passionate embrace which she returned. I was suddenly aware that unlike my previous experiences, she kissed with her mouth open. It was at once a shocking and exciting feeling. I felt for the breasts which I had feasted my eyes on and daydreamed about for so long. Alma let me hold her trembling for a minute or two but as my breath grew agitated, she drew back. "Behave!" she said, smiling up at me, and then she turned from my arms and went back into the dance. I stayed on the little bridge for some time, reliving my moment of joy. Could it really have happened? Alma was twenty-two and I was only just sixteen. What would it be like tomorrow and in future when I had to face her in front of the Quaker family? The other men would never believe me; but in any case I couldn't tell them, could I?

Shortly after I returned to the dance, Alma's boyfriend came back from the pub to collect her. "Get tha coat, lass," he said brusquely. Alma got her coat and went out with him, her face radiant. I stood pale and shaken watching them go. I did not dance again that night.

The rest of my farming year in Cumberland passed quickly and for the most part happily. The work was still hard, harder indeed than I would ever be asked to work again in my life. Throughout hay time, we worked from dawn right through to the small hours of the next day with monotonous regularity. The horses sweated and snorted as they pulled side delivery rakes up and down the hillside fields. The mower chattered and clattered as it felled the tall but badly tangled grass crop. Soon there was too much hay down but not gathered to risk cutting any more and farmer Eddie set all hands to clearing what hay was fit to cart. It was a wet hay time in 1942 and the gang turned and turned again the mouldering hay. Most of the gang were suffering from summer colds by now, brought on by inhaling the mixture of pollen and mould spores which rose in clouds each time the hay was disturbed. Wheezing and sneezing they sweated on, making haycocks and shaking them out again and again, before finally loading the dusty hay onto tumbrils which lurched drunkenly back to the hay mews in the great barn. Here, the long-suffering horses stamped and slipped as they leaned back in their breeching harness, backing the great loads up the steep ramp to the stout floor over the byres below. I appreciated the skill of the builders who through the centuries had sited these barns below the hillside road level so that hay could be stored above the beasts, and horse and wagon gain access to the first floor in safety. I loved throwing hay down the "fothergang" and carrying great armfuls to the bellowing cows. I learned to carry more loose hay in my arms than I would previously have believed possible and always without leaving a trail which might cause Farmer Eddie to roar and shout a reprimand.

Some nights, if bad weather had interrupted the work, I joined a few young villagers at dances. One Saturday some girls and farm lads from Mockerkin cycled into the village. They were on the way to a dance at Lorton. Binner, Alma and I joined them. I was at ease again with Alma. Neither had ever mentioned the incident on the night of the Ullock dance. The sergeant had returned to his unit without becoming engaged to the girl. Eddie, whom I suspected had an eye for Alma himself, advised her to forget him. I didn't think she had.

As we cycled through the villages, we picked up more and more lads and lasses. As the cavalcade of bicycles grew, so did the shouted chatter."Howista min? Ower they hinging? Hasta got t'hay in yit?" "Nay, wiv bin turning t'bugger." "Twill only be fit fer t'midden!" "Aye, likely will howiver." By the time we had passed through Brambling Gill the party had grown to fifty bicycles or more. The "crack", apart from the difficulty of haymaking, was of the great Russian front battles around Kiev and Kursk. The Germans had crossed the Dnieper and then the Don after stout Russian resistance at Voronez. Moscow, Leningrad, Rostov and Stalingrad were all besieged and suffering unbelievable hardship but "the bloody Roosians were giving Hitler some socks". In Cockermouth there had been an "Aid to Russia" week in response to an appeal by Mrs Winston Churchill. Remembering Churchill's hatred of the "Reds", I considered the strangeness of this.

I had registered for National Service on my sixteenth birthday in a small building on Bridge Street. The registration officer had asked me where I worked. I told him. "You may not leave your job except to move to another farm," said the man sternly. I pondered this. It meant I could not go back to school even if I wanted to, not that I did. Would it mean that I couldn't go to agricultural college? I asked. The registration officer had no idea. That week, Eddie had taken me to collect insurance cards. I was now a working man.

As the chattering, laughing bicyclists streamed down through Rogerscale to Lorton, the evening sun fell on Grassmoor and Whiteside. Lorton, which lay at the foot of Whinlatter Pass, was bathed in warm light. To me, this valley always seemed a warmer, more welcoming place than Pardshaw; I wondered if it was just the people. There were a fair number of offcomers living in the valley and they seemed to smile and laugh more easily than the rural West Cumbrians.

However, laughter seemed infectious that night; everyone was in festive mood as we paused outside the Wheatsheaf waiting for the landlord's daughter Eunice to join them. The dance was in the Yew Tree barn, a great stone building which had once been the malt house of Lorton Brewery. From within, I could hear the unmistakable sound of Billy Bowman's accordion. Billy's band was much loved in Cockermouth and the surrounding villages. A violinist, a pianist and a drummer completed the band which though small produced a wonderful richness of sound and rhythms. The latest "forces' favourite" tunes, fresh from the BBC, were belted out side by side with the old country dances. The concrete floor, once deep in malting barley, no longer echoed to the soft scrape of wooden malt shovels. Instead it was dusted with talc until it was "as slaep as ice". The dancers held out their wrists obediently to have them rubberstamped with blue ink to prove they had paid to go in. I had learned to do the military two-step, the Canadian one-step, the barn dance and the graceful Valetta. They were more fun than the waltz and quick-step but not as agreeable as a slow foxtrot with the right girl. I was fast learning which were the right girls.

That night I waited near Brambling Gill for a long, long time. It was past one when the last nosey cyclists had gone by; more than one wanted to know who I was waiting for. I wondered if someone would tell Eddie that I was hanging about after a girl. Ginny Rogers had agreed to meet me as long as no one saw us. I was almost ready to give up by the time she eventually came out of the roadside house where she lived with her brother. She, like her cadaverous brother, was a bit of a mystery to the curious locals. They were obviously not poor yet lived alone quietly without going to work. Ginny threw herself about wildly at dances and most of the lads were afraid of her. I sensed a fellow outsider in the lass and went out of my way to be pleasant. I was rewarded. Ginny would dance closer than the other girls. She was well aware of the effect she had on me and she enjoyed it. In the interval when Billy Bowman and his band went for a beer, she persuaded me to go along to the Horseshoe Inn.

I stood at the bar shyly as I ordered a drink for the first time. It was only a half of mild for me and a sherry for the girl, which I could ill afford, but I felt I had crossed another threshold. Eddie would certainly have sent me back to London in disgrace if he had discovered this fall from grace. As I went to meet her, the now familiar trembling started and I moved quickly to hide my nervousness. She matched my movements silently and silkily, rather like a cat, I thought. Unspeaking, she took my hand and led me off the shadowed street and into a low-beamed byre. Turning quickly to me, she hissed, "Come on then! Don't be all night!" I hesitated, slightly put out by her bossiness which reminded me of my mates at work. Then with a shrug I followed her up into the hayloft, giving her legs a more than passing glance as she negotiated the vertical ladder above me.

For several hours we lay and cuddled in the darkness as we explored each other's thoughts and bodies. The girl had told me that there was to be nothing more than that. Her mother had fallen pregnant to an Australian soldier and her father, a ship's officer in the Merchant Navy, had kicked her out before going back to sea. She had not come back; and now Ginny and her brother lived alone, he hating women and she determined not to fall like her mother. I respected her wishes and was happy to hold her young breasts while she chattered incessantly. I sought and found those parts I had been mystified by and she let me feel my way without a protest. She did not respond to my fumbling but let me lie between her legs as my passion grew. I grew hot and sweat stung my young eyes. I did not press the girl for – much as I had started to regret my promise – I had made a bargain and I was still young enough to think that I was bound to stick to it. Eventually, my curiosity satisfied and kisses having grown stale, I felt sleepy and was glad when she said she must go in.

The ride back to Pardshaw seemed endless and the first streaks of dawn were painting the sky over Grassmoor as I wearily climbed the backstairs to my bed.

Somewhere a cock was crowing.

It was not mine.

Next day farmer Eddie's wife looked suspiciously at me when I came in for my breakfast. I looked back boldly; I was a man of the world now, even if I was still a virgin! Eddie, evidently prompted by his wife, had started a sermon on the evils of late nights and dances held during hay time. I winked at Alma who left the kitchen choking back laughter. Suddenly a mood of revelation came over me. I felt compassion for these sad, sad people whose love of God had deprived them of so much happiness and joy. I felt a new sense of power and freedom. I was my own man. I was also lucky that morning. It was my turn to take a horse and cart to Armstrong's timber mill at Cockermouth for a load of jute sacks full of sawdust bedding for the cows.

Armstrong's yard lay between Cockermouth's beautiful tree-lined Main Street and South Street. I had left Pardshaw as soon as I could get away from the breakfast table. The sun was shining on the fine steeple of the parish church as I guided Bobby, a fine old chestnut gelding, down the hill from the station and round the corner of the fine grey stone market buildings. The top entry to Armstrong's yard was through a low stone carriage arch beside what had been a gentleman's residence. Bobby jibbed at going into the noisy yard, but a blue overalled lad helped me get him through the arch. I was a little resentful of the lad's interference but I knew him to be a friendly chap. He had once diverted an angry soldier who had objected to me dancing with his girl at a Public Hall dance one Saturday night. The soldier had gone away grumbling about bloody civvies and I had gone away without the black eye I expected. The lad offered to watch Bobby while we waited my turn to be loaded. Great trees were being sawn for building timbers, pit props and fencing posts. By the saw pits there were rows of jute sacks, full of white curly shavings and golden sawdust. As Bobby was in safe hands, I hurried round to Birketts Bakery cafe where farmers visiting the market could, for one shilling and sixpence (7p), eat as much as they wanted. The long tables were loaded with meat rolls, pies, teacakes, gingerbread and apple pasties. It reminded me of the wonderful feasts during those happy threshing days at Salkelds. I sat down and scoffed happily as the red-cheeked waitresses joked good-naturedly about my clothes. I had taken my latest ration of clothing coupons to Willie Fletcher's, purveyors of fearless clothing, as proclaimed by a huge painted sign on the riverside wall of his shop by the Cocker Bridge. Joyce's uncle, who owned the shop, had fitted me up with the brown corduroy breeches I longed for and a tweed cap which I wore at a jaunty angle on the side of my head in the fashion of the country lads... Although I could not yet afford a black waistcoat or tweed jacket, I still felt right.

When I had eaten my fill, I returned to Armstrong's yard. My turn for loading had come while I was eating and some lads who knew me had already half loaded my cart. "Oweh, me lad! Hasta filt thissen? Hasta browt ought fer thi marrers? Weer's ower bate owiver?" I laughed loudly at the leg-pulling and climbed up to finish loading the jute sacks which were now forming a nice square load eight courses high. One of the lads threw me a rope and I supervised the process of placing the ropes properly. When I was satisfied, I slid down and tightened the ropes with a spricket hitch, a knot which Leslie Abbot had patiently taught me. The exit archway from the yard onto the main street was high enough for the load so I went out that way.

As I turned into Main Street, I saw Miss Hardbutt, one of the lady teachers from my old school. I touched my new cap politely but she turned away rudely. "Old cow," I thought angrily. "Probably thinks I am letting the school down by working on a farm." As the horse and cart overtook her, I shouted, "Now then, Hardy! Ow's tha garn on then? Ista fettle?" As people turned to look at her I blew her a kiss, and lifted my cap with a flourish as a bubble of exhilaration welled up in my chest. Miss Hardbutt tried to hide her embarrassment by ducking into Luchini's Ice Cream Parlour but I was by now gleefully out of control. "Have a nice ice for me, Miss!" I bellowed.

"See yer agen syean!" I drove the old horse on, laughing at the sight of her snobbish face, purple with mortification.

Exultation – like pride – cometh before a fall. As I turned up Station Street, I saw Joyce looking very attractive as she came out of Jim Bewley's County Fruit Stores. Anxious to impress her, I urged the willing old horse into a trot. Alas! The swaying load caught a lamp post and the front corner bags came tumbling down onto me in a shower of sawdust and shavings, knocking me down on my knees. Old Bobby, being a wise old nag, had stopped. I got up, both my pride and body bruised. Joyce was nowhere to be seen, having bolted from the scene of my disgrace, for bad horsemanship in town was just about the worst offence.

Alma, who had been shopping in town, appeared from Mr Drummond's doorway. "Terence! Whatever will Eddie say about this then? He'll bless you for this!" She smiled, sarcastically, I suspected. Bad news travels fast in a small town and the lads from Armstrong's yard were already running round the corner. "By the heck, Terry lad, tha's made a right cow's arse o' this loc!" The lads quickly pulled the sacks from the road and Alma bravely directed cars and wagons round the incident. Fortunately, thanks to petrol rationing there was little traffic. I got up on the cart and climbed the remaining layers of sacks. The lads under Alma's direction threw up the fallen bags and directed my efforts to rebuild the load. Once more I slid down and tightened the ropes. "Now take care and watch where you are going this time," said Alma. There was no doubt: she was the woman in charge and I felt like a small boy again. A thought flashed through my mind. Had it really happened, that breathless moment on the bridge at Ullock?

That night, Eddie the farmer said nothing about the battered-looking load as I returned, other than to comment, "Tha's bin awa' a gay long time!" For several anxious days, I expected a thunderbolt of wrath to fall upon me; but Alma was kind and said nothing…

Harvest arrived before the haymaking was finished. This was a farmer's nightmare. Day after day the farm team struggled to clear the fields between showers. The saturated crop of oats lay as if steamrollered and the old horse binder which had been crudely adapted to be towed by a tractor was inadequate for the job. The binder was intended to cut standing crops of corn and bundle the stems into nice tidy sheaves, ready for stooking in clumps of eight to finish ripening in the sun before being carted to the stackyard. In the summer of 1942, the laid wet corn proved too much for it. Farmer Eddie grew more and more frustrated and his furious shouts could be heard at Mockerkin three miles away. Much of the corn had to be cut by hand and the backbreaking job of scything through wet laid oats went on hour after steaming hour. The younger men, including myself, were set to tying up armfuls of loose oat stems into sheaves and stooking them in such a way that the tractor and its ramshackle binder could get at the corn from the one direction it was able to function, that is, with the laid corn facing the knives. Eventually, the fields of corn were cut and the sheaves stooked in moist steaming rows. Load after load of damp corn and fusty hay left the fields for the outside stackyards on creaking and swaying tumbrils. Tempers grew short from lack of sleep and fatigue. Even the normally placid Clydesdale carthorses grew tetchy and awkward.

Gradually the weather improved, the weak September sun evaporated some of the moisture and the damp crops were clawed in. By the time the first rime appeared on the meadows, the first loads of muck were being carted out for spreading on the stubbles. Another farming year was about to begin and I was due to move on to a different type of farm.

Two weeks after the last stacks were thatched and the ploughs had started turning in the stubbles, I, now brown and bursting with health and good spirits, was packing the last of my gear into my trunk. When I had finished, I swung the heavy trunk easily up onto my strong shoulders and took it down to Eddie's car. My year on the Cumberland farm was over and it was time for a move. I went into the kitchen for my final meal with the family and my workmates. Eddie said grace and they sat down. I had got up again to fetch the large brown teapot from its keeping warm place by the open fire of the great black-leaded range. The men came in from milking, reeking of cows, warm milk and disinfectant. "Sit down, Long John Silver!" said Binner, repeating the words he had used a year earlier. I, who was even more proud of my height, sat down laughing. Eddie laughed; then his wife joined in and they were all relaxed and laughing. "Must be 'cos I'm going," I thought. "I hope we are parting pals," said Eddie with a great beam. Looking round the smiling company, I wondered who had changed.

The war news was much better. There had been some terrific battles in Russia, where the terrible winter stalemates before Leningrad, Moscow and down into the Dnieper basin had given way in

63

the spring and summer to attack and counter-attack on a vast scale. The Germans were held before Stalingrad and the scorched earth policy was slowing down their advance towards the oilfields of the Caucasus. In the Pacific the hitherto invincible Japanese had suffered defeats at Midway Island and in the Coral Sea. Most memorable for the British was the success of Monty in the defeat of Rommel at El Alamein. Winston Churchill had ordered the church bells rung to celebrate the great victory.

"This is not the end," said Churchill. "It is not even the beginning of the end, but it is the end of the beginning."

Somehow, this summed up my new mood and confidence.

Alma stretched over the stove and I noticed, as I had done on my first day at the farm, that she had pretty legs and a nice figure. Alma caught me looking; and lifting up her chin, she winked, a long, deliberate, conspiratorial wink.

Nice tits, too, I thought…

Better than cold porridge!

Chapter 3

Bedfordshire Clanger

My return to London and Mill Hill proved noisy and chaotic. Before leaving the Cumberland farm, I had agreed to indulge in a last wrestle with Binner. My new strength and confidence had made me almost invincible at schoolboy-style wrestling. I could slip a "cowgrip" headhold, survive a sweeping kick behind the knees and even when down rolling under a potential conqueror, I could usually twist quickly astride my opponent's chest and kneel on his shoulders to claim victory. Thus Binner was quickly disposed of as I got him on his back and sat laughing on his chest. Farmer Eddie had followed the lads out onto the little lawn behind the Pardshaw farmhouse and said that he did not think much of the catch-as-catch-can style of our almost "all in" wrestling. He challenged me to a bout of formalized Cumberland wrestling and showed me the starting posture and grips from which the opponents sought to throw the other off balance. Although inexperienced and outclassed by the older farmer, I was able for a considerable time to keep on my feet. It could not last; and with a quick movement, Eddie had me lifted from the ground in a great hug and the grass came up to meet me with a resounding thud. A sharp pain went through my shoulder and I knew at once I had broken my collarbone. Silently I cursed my luck. There were so many things I had wanted to do before I left Cumberland, including finding a few minutes to say goodbye and make my peace with Joyce.

My injury caused great consternation among the farm women but I was, in spite of considerable pain, determined to catch my train to London. A quick visit to Dr Abraham, the same Dr Abraham who had helped save my life only two years earlier, soon had my arm strapped up in a sling which I considered very glamorous.

I had always wanted a good sheepdog of my own, and had been presented with a young Collie pup by the Bowness family at Pardshaw Hall a few days earlier. Now I was faced with the problem of making the journey south with a large trunk, a bicycle, one arm in a sling and a dog! In spite of wartime regulations, the trunk and bicycle were dispatched as luggage in advance, a wonderful service available at the station of departure in those spacious days when the railways delivered luggage to the door of one's final destination.

Thus I set off for my homecoming. I thought that I was very different from when I first arrrived in Cumberland as a pale but primly dressed prep school boy. I was only sorry that I would not be able to arrive home as I had planned: sun-tanned, fit and muscular, with my trunk on my shoulder and a dog at my heel! Every inch a farmer!

The train journey was pretty chaotic. I watched my beloved mountains drift away as the train sped southwards from Penrith. High Street and Kidstye Pike were grey silhouettes as the climb up Shap swept them behind the nearer fells. As the train rolled out of the hills down to Morecombe Bay I had a last sight of the Langdales, purple against a bright blue September sky. There were glimpses of Crinkle Crags, Wetherlam and the Old Man of Coniston before all were lost behind the trees and hedges of rural Lancashire.

I was tired and hungry by the time the train ran into darkness somewhere near Rugby. My broken collarbone was aching dully and the Collie pup became very restless. I thought about my mother's kitchen with its brown velvet Victorian tablecloth and earthenware teapot, round which the family would gather as the light faded and curtains were drawn. Homesickness had not troubled me much in Cumberland as I had been too busy or too tired to think much about a world so different and so far away. I suddenly wished I was back in the secure warmth of my parents' home in Mill Hill. All those tough hard months in Cumberland seemed like a bad dream. The lighter, happier moments were forgotten. A kindly ticket collector must have noticed my tiredness and distress for he took the restless pup along to the guard's van and I fell into an exhausted sleep.

I was awakened suddenly by the noise of gunfire and excited voices. The train was somewhere near Watford and the carriage was lit up by the pale blue glare of searchlights. Anti-aircraft fire was perforating the black sky with dull orange flashes. It was a far more intense display of gunfire than I remembered from the earlier Blitz. Slowly the train ran on through Willesden Junction and into Euston. Here the noise of escaping steam and slamming carriage doors mingled with the sounds of battle as guns crashed in nearby Regent's Park. I could hear the clanging bells of fire appliances and ambulances as they raced down Euston Road towards Marylebone and West London where most of the bombing and fires seemed to be concentrated. My dog and I drew many curious glances from the other passengers as they made their hurried way towards the entrances to the Underground railway.

Down in the ticket hall it was suddenly peaceful and strangely unchanged from my peacetime memories. The dog and I negotiated the escalators with some difficulty and emerged onto the Northern Line platform. It was a very different picture down here as we made our way between sleeping families. Here there were hastily erected screens round crude toilets. There were some first aid cubicles and uniformed voluntary helpers who had not been there in the early Blitz; but there was still a smell of sweat and urine mingled with dust and the ozone smell of electric trains.   I thought of the clean Lakeland air and bustling farm folk, so far away and unknowing of the war and these grey, haggard people lining the platforms as the war raged over the burning streets and houses above them.

The journey out to Hendon was mostly underground and it was not until the train emerged at Golders Green that the flashes of the train's electric brushes as they crossed the points reminded me that we were once more exposed to the perils of the night. At Hendon I got out and dragged the now exhausted Collie pup up the stairs to the bus queue, the drone of German planes and the crack of gunfire making both me and my dog flinch. I found an empty telephone box and got through to my father.

Eddie the farmer had not managed to contact my family and they were astonished to hear me say that I was at Hendon with a broken shoulder and a Collie pup. At first, I was not allowed to get on a bus to Mill Hill with the dog. Fortunately my father soon arrived and I felt wonderfully reassured by the sight of his familiar walk and confident manner. "Well, son, you have really done it this time! Let's see what we can do." My father gave me a hug and I felt the familiar warmth of his cheek and the scratch of his ever-present stubble. It was good to be back. Apart from my odd encounters with the girls in Cumberland, it was the first physical expression of affection I had experienced since leaving London. My admirable dad soon persuaded an inspector to intervene on my behalf and allow the "injured" boy and his dog to board the double decker bus, which was about to leave in spite of the crash of gunfire and occasional thud of bombs. Fifteen minutes later, I was sitting at that beloved table with a cup of tea, answering a thousand questions about my life in Cumberland, the broken collarbone and the journey home. The Collie pup was already asleep under the table, ignoring the raised excited voices and the continuous tattoo of gunfire. My mother was cuddling me like a young lad. I wondered what the men on the Cumberland farm would have made of it all. I had so much to tell, so much to remember and just a few manly secrets to treasure.

I was growing up fast.

The weeks it took for my shoulder to mend flew by. It was soon time to seek another job and I found one with a Scottish family in Bedfordshire. My interview was brief and took place on the steamy platform of St Pancras Station on a fine frosty morning with the sun striking silver and gold on the multitude of barrage balloons which hung serenely in the clear blue winter sky. Few words were exchanged, as my new boss was hurrying to a farmers' meeting in London. The farmer had told me to tuck a white handkerchief into my belt to identify me on the busy platform full of hurrying soldiers, sailors and airmen. Mr Hope was a short, aggressive-looking Scot with a balding head and a prize-fighter's nose. He spoke in short bursts of guttural Scottish English. His wife stood back, inspecting me and looking worried. In spite of his formidable appearance and aggressive manner, I found him easier to talk to than Farmer Eddie had been. Clearly he had not heard of my famous family name and therefore he had no expectations of saintliness or of other difficult virtues to live up to.

There was only time for a rapid negotiation. It seemed an ideal arrangement. The farm was at Thurleigh, about eight miles north of Bedford. I would be within travelling distance of my home, if and when I got time off, and I was not too far from my other married sister Esme, who lived near Luton. This was a special attraction for although she had been a stand-in mother to me as a small boy, I had seen little or nothing of her for years and I looked forward to seeing her and playing with my nephew and niece. I also hoped that I would be able to join the local Air Training Corps as I was now sixteen. The farmer was a bit non-committal about this, doubting if I would have much time for off-the-farm "hobbies". My new job would be as assistant cowman working from six in the morning to six thirty at night. There was no work between milkings on Sundays and once every two months I would have a "weekend" off from Saturday lunchtime to Monday morning. This seemed comparatively generous after the seven day weeks of the Cumbrian farm.

A few days later I set off for Bedford. I emerged from Bedford Station on a lovely January day in 1943. An elegant American Air Force Captain was waiting in the spring-like sunshine for a taxi. I admired his Hollywood good looks, his superb gold-trimmed cap, smart tunic and knife-sharp fawn gabardine trousers. It was my first close encounter with an American serviceman and I was impressed by his confident smartness which reminded me of the heroes in many American films I had seen. Suddenly I felt scruffy and insignificant beside this magnificent figure, so different from the drab khaki of the few Tommies who were hanging round the station yard waiting for transport like poor relations at a posh wedding...

"Hello! Are you Terry?" said a friendly voice; and I turned to meet a strong-faced young man in blue dungarees who had got out of a battered Hillman Minx car. The car was attached to an even scruffier farm trailer containing pigswill bins, which even at a distance gave off a noxious smell of stale vegetables and mouldy scraps. "I am Tom, the boss's son." He had a friendly lopsided smile and I felt at home with him at once, in spite of the smell which clung to his clothes. I glanced back at the splendid American officer, then back to Tom. The farmer's son caught my expression. "All cock and well-pressed trousers," he said. "We are drowning in the buggers up at Thurleigh. All they do is scrounge eggs and sniff round our women! They think a few Chesterfield cigarettes will buy anything."

We drove out of Bedford town chatting busily about farming in Cumberland and in Scotland from where Tom's parents had moved to Bedfordshire bringing their herd of Ayrshire cattle down with them. I mentioned that I had worked with a herd of Friesian cattle in Cumberland and was astonished at the vehement reaction this invoked. "Bloody walking water carts, that's all they are," pronounced Tom. "No looks, no legs and no butterfat in the milk. Can't compare them with Ayrshires. You have to run a few Jerseys in the herd just to keep the milk fat level legal! Father says they are bloody useless things!" Thus Friesian cattle, which were to become the nation's premier breed, were summarily written off by the doughty Scots family for whom I was to work. I kept quiet. I had learned not to argue with dogmatic northern folk whether they be Scots or Cumbrian. Neither breed was good at admitting the possibility of another viewpoint!

The ancient Hillman car in which we were progressing slowly through the Bedfordshire countryside was being passed regularly by large American trucks, some of which were carrying men wearing olive fatigue overalls; and to my surprise, many were smoking large cigars and waving enthusiastically at female bystanders. Without doubt they had an air of confidence, prosperity and glamour that the girls responded to. "Bloody Yanks," said Tom. "They think they own the place already." More and more lorries passed in both directions. Many carried aircraft spares but most seemed to be carrying liquid concrete or were returning empty for more. I could not help noticing the number of Negro drivers with their shining white grins and jaunty baseball caps. I had not seen any Negroes in town and had not yet learned of the colour bar, which operated even in the armed forces of democracy. White Americans from the south were not prepared to tolerate the sight of English girls dancing with black men. Trouble had broken out at village dances where "uppity niggers" were mixing freely. My liberal upbringing was to be outraged time and time again by the extreme conservatism of even the lowest-ranking white American Servicemen; and I was far from alone in my resentment of this arrogance.

The car slowed as we approached an elegant but obviously derelict windmill and turned past Thurleigh, a very pretty village of thatched Tudor style cottages grouped round a beautiful church. "Here we are at Manor Farm in the mud," said Tom. I was horrified to see that a superb avenue of lime trees which led up to the redbrick manor house had been cut off halfway up their silvery trunks. Tom did not comment but a gigantic shadow passing over the sunlit road preceding a descending bomber gave me the answer to the appalling tree butchery. The farmyard was at the end of a vast runway and the roar of many aircraft engines swept into the car. "Yes," said Tom, seeing my surprise. "They only just miss the cowshed when they are taking off loaded with bombs; and the planes kept touching the trees so they came and lopped them down." I was delighted that there would be the added excitement of an airbase at my place of work.

Lunch was a huge lump of savoury suet containing pieces of meat and sausage called a Bedfordshire Clanger. I enjoyed the meal and meeting the Hope family. There were three boys: Tom, who, had collected me, Bill, a heavily-muscled but very short young man, and Jimmy a rather ferocious-looking schoolboy.

Talking over my duties, it was soon obvious that the job was far less demanding than the work in Cumberland. I was expected to be up at five forty-five each morning but I had a whole hour off for both breakfast and lunch and finished at six thirty at night. In addition I was not expected to work in the fields between milkings on Sunday and had Saturday afternoon off between lunch and milking time. This was undreamed-of luxury after the endless drudgery of the Cumbrian farm.

70

I was soon into the swim of things. I was by no means the bottom of the pile here. There were several odd-job boys and landgirls below me in the farm hierarchy, though only the dairy staff worked as long hours as I. I was also able to indulge the interest in pigs which had been stimulated at my uncle's Dorset farm, by helping the pigman feed and muck out during my time off.

Once more I found myself something of a curiosity amongst my workmates. Joe, the horseman, was convinced that I must be the disgraced son of a well-to-do family. "Did you get expelled from a posh school for browning someone?" he asked, with engaging frankness. I was shocked by the suggestion and hastened to assure Joe of my heterosexual inclinations and experiences with girls in Cumberland, unfulfilled though they were. Joe in turn was shocked and warned the young landgirls that I was a "dilly man". I, who had not heard the expression before, now understood why French letters were called "dillyhats".

1943 was a year of optimism and victories in the Mediterranean theatres of war. The Afrika Korps surrendered to General Montgomery in Tunisia, Sicily was invaded and later the Italian mainland. Even the news from the Pacific looked better. The Australians were repulsing the Japanese in the wet, wet jungles of New Guinea, as General MacArthur and Admirals Halsey and Nimitz started to roll back the extended Japanese front, island by island.

The Russians too were striking back, emerging from Stalingrad and Voronez to win the greatest tank battles in history at Kursk. The Wermacht was in retreat from the Volga to the Neva.

Spring passed into summer accompanied by the constant roar of aircraft engines, busy bomb tenders and Jeeps. The 8th Air Corps was preparing to take on the Luftwaffe in daylight. Meantime I got to know the rather eccentric ways of the Hope family. Father Hope was a total despot who brooked no argument as he was quite unable to see any merit in other people's views. Many a salesman or Ministry official left the farm shaken by an encounter with him. I found him amiable enough as long as he wasn't crossed. Many times I had to bite my tongue listening to Mr Hope's views, which exposed a woeful lack of education and appreciation of history or current affairs. The boys, apart from Tom, the eldest, were equally ignorant. However they were good farmers and very good workers. Little Jimmy, who had inherited all his father's bad genes and none of his mother's gentleness, was the worst of the lot. Although only thirteen, he bossed all the men and did his best to wrong-foot me. Fortunately I did not come into too much contact with the little fiend because Jimmy was mad on tractors and hated cows. Jimmy could start some of the enormous American tractors long before the men had mastered the techniques. Being fresh from horses, they had to learn the art of decompressing the engines before swinging the heavy starting handles.

I was curious as to how Mr Hope had got his start into farming. It transpired that he had been a milk lorry driver and had married Mrs Hope, a local farmer's daughter. There had always been an oft-repeated tenet to aspiring young farmers that the only way into farming was by "Patrimony, matrimony or endless bloody parsimony!" Mr Hope had got his start by matrimony. He had served on the Western front in the First World War before being wounded in the arm. This had made him something of a hero amongst the Ayrshire farming community and he never failed to bring up his "bullet through the elbow" when called upon to help with real work. He would have loved to have been able to be a "gentleman farmer" and could be seen most days, going off in shooting clothes with a game bag, shooting stick and shotgun. He frequently invited officers to join him but I noticed that they seldom came twice. Mrs Hope was a tiny "wee body" with a constant expression of kindliness overlain by worry. She cared for every person or animal on the farm and was a most compassionate woman. Her workload was immense as she cared and cooked for her demanding husband, sons, daughter-in-law, grandchildren and the men who lived in as family. Outside on the farm, she fed pigs, tended hens and supervised the rearing of young stock.

One day as I was putting the cows out to graze, a large bulldozer burst through the hedge trailing reels of power and telephone cable. A swarm of olive-clad GIs followed amongst Jeeps and trucks, concrete lorries and diggers. In minutes, a temporary fence was up and the US 8th Air Force took possession of most of Manor Farm. Mr Hope was choleric with rage as he had not been consulted. He paced up and down berating the sweating GIs like an angry bulldog but they simply carried on despite his threats and pleas. New aircraft dispersal points were established close to the house and the whole farm operation was virtually within the base. To all intents and purposes Manor Farm, the farming family and I, were now part of the American Air Force. Exuberant GIs were ever at the door cadging eggs and milk, giving away candy, cigarettes and cigars and PX supplies. The landgirls soon succumbed to transatlantic charm and the glamorous uniforms. I, now sixteen and feeling my oats, was envious but watchful.

I learned a great deal and in time became very friendly with both air crews and ground crews. The work was hard and demanding of all my skills and stamina but by now I had a man's frame and strength despite my tender years and, most important to me, I had the respect of my workmates. Moreover, my American friends took me to the camp's film and stage shows. I saw Bob Hope and Glenn Miller in the flesh and heard real American jazz; but I was always uncomfortable about the strict colour segregation throughout the camp.

Sex was becoming a real problem. Gangs of landgirls from Milton Ernest and Colmworth were working on the farm and several delighted in tantalizing me. My army air force friends spoke glibly of their nightly conquests in Bedford and it seemed everyone was enjoying carnal bliss except me. One night a girl slightly older than I was staying at the farm. As usual, I had retired to bed earlier than the others, due to my very early start in the morning. The girl came and sat on the blanket chest in my room as I lay reading in bed. She was chatting sensibly and smoking a cigarette but kept crossing her legs and adjusting her skirt. I was not very interested in either the girl or her long legs. I was reading Margaret Mitchell's novel *Gone with the Wind* in the few precious moments before I fell asleep. The girl got up to leave and put out the light. In the darkness, I saw the glowing end of her cigarette coming back across the room towards me and I felt the girl's arms go round my neck. The cigarette went down and I felt her warm lips cross my cheek till they found my lips. In spite of my disinterest in the girl, I found my body trembling and an awareness of my loins as I responded and clutched at her. The girl slipped away and left me in turmoil. I lay for a long time wondering if it had really happened.

The next day was a busy one. After the morning milking the whole gang turned out to get the hay in. Milking, that morning, had been disrupted by one Flying Fortress bomber after another taking off over the cowshed causing the terrified cows to kick and struggle in their stalls. By breakfast time huge squadrons were assembling in the perfect blue skies to show the Germans how much better the USAFF could do the job than the night-flying RAF.

The day passed in a frenzy of dust and hayseeds as the gang sweated to get the fine crop of green hay baled before it was bleached or spoilt by rain. In spite of the toil there was not one of the gang who was not thinking of the bomber crews or what they were experiencing over Germany. I had heard the nervous crews anticipating the German fighters. "I can't tell a goddam Spitfire from a Messerschmitt," said one to me in the Jackal, a Thurleigh pub, "but if anything points its nose at me, I shoot the motherfucker down." About three o'clock in the afternoon the first bombers returned. There were gaps in the formations but as they broke up into individual squadrons, it was clear that most of the Thurleigh planes had returned. One aircraft swept low over the haymakers, streaming smoke and with shattered sections of wing and tail fin. The aircraft's name *Maryland my Maryland* was clearly visible and I knew it was from the nearby dispersal point. June, one of the landgirls, was in tears with worry. She was pregnant by one of the crew and desperately in love.

That evening after milking, I visited the dispersal site where the ground crew were busy patching the aircraft and replacing one huge Pratt and Whitney engine. June was already there. Her boyfriend was chatting to the ground crew master sergeant nonchalantly; but I thought he looked strained. The squadron had only lost two aircraft but other groups had suffered severe losses. June went off with the flyer in his Jeep and I heard the ground crew marvelling at the damage. *Maryland* was to be stripped of her guns to become a "Hangar Queen" and would fly in anger no more.

I returned to the farmhouse, feeling tired from the day's work and the tension. As I went up to my room I met the cigarette-smoking girl who deliberately barred the way to me. I laughed and jostled her to get past. Somehow I was holding her with her cigarette-bearing hand stretched out and her face upturned to mine. Without knowing quite why I did it, I kissed her and all my yearnings flared up. I felt very mature and brave. "Come to my room later," I said. "Okay," said the girl, and laughed as she turned and ran downstairs.

I took great pains to wash myself carefully that night, with particular attention to my underarms and teeth... I found some fairly clean pyjamas and got out a buff packet of American service issue condoms. Carefully, I took one out and placed it under my pillow. The anticipation of lovemaking was making me shake and I had difficulty setting my alarm clock for the morning milking. Without a glance at my novel, I settled down to enjoy the wait for the girl to come to my room and, I hoped, into my bed. Alas! My dreams were shattered by the ringing alarm; the room light was still on but I could tell from the light outside that it was morning and time to milk the bloody cows again... She had not come. I almost cried with frustration. I had boasted to the head cowman of my prospects for success and now I would have to face the older man's mocking leers. I had been so proud of my likely conquest but now pride had indeed come before a fall.

After breakfast I grabbed the chance to question the girl. She explained that Mrs Hope had met her coming upstairs and had stood talking till she dared not come in. However, she promised to come to my room that night; and I went to work a little happier.

There was more hay baling that day and once more the Flying Fortresses took off in great droning formations. This time they spent the day practising tighter and tighter formation flying in order to concentrate the firepower of the gunners. There was a sprinkling of a new type of Flying Fortress with additional gun turrets bristling 0.5 inch machine guns above, below and behind. During that morning we heard two enormous explosions. Two Fortresses had collided near Wellingborough. Five members of the two crews had managed to bail out.

The mood of the flyers was much more subdued that night when they came into the village pub. It was clear that they were not having it their own way with the Luftwaffe. However, the talk was of bigger squadrons, better flying and better armament. I went back to the dispersal tents with the ground crew and enjoyed listening to them boasting and singing as they played cards and smoked enormous green cigars. I had hoped to hear legends about America's great jazz musicians but found to my disappointment that few GIs had heard of the New Orleans jazzmen whom I worshipped. I wondered if it was because the musicians were mostly black. The GIs were quite unlike the Americans I had seen in films or the smart officer I had seen at Bedford station with his Anglo-Saxon good looks and Hollywood appearance... Many had what seemed to me, a relatively inexperienced English boy, to be foreign accents and Mediterranean looks. They were not the "Englishmen with American accents" I had expected.

Going back to the farmhouse as the early summer evening grew chilly and with thoughts of the girl once more welling up, I met the farmer's wife, Mrs Hope, getting out of the old Hillman car, a frown on her normally friendly face. "I've packed that creature off home," she said; and I realised with a sinking heart that she was referring to my intended lover. It was the end of my hope to enjoy life's great experience for the first time.

Hay time passed into harvest. My mother, who had been in poor health for many years, contracted flu and developed pneumonia. I went to visit her in hospital and she seemed in good spirits and was delighted to see me so tanned and well. It was a shock a month later to find her still in bed and a worse shock to be told by my father that she would not be getting better. I took the news badly but concealed my hurt with the impassiveness I had developed to conceal my feelings amongst my schoolday tormenters and the bullying farm workers of my early apprenticeship. My mother's death came not as a surprise but a total unreality. I had seen so little of her during my adolescence and working years that it was as if someone other than the mother I had loved as a child had died. It was some weeks before I fully realised I had lost my mother; and even then, much of my sadness was on my father's behalf. The real loneliness of missing that familiar face and warm embrace came slowly and deeply.

The summer days as a motherless boy were filled with work and the roar of bombers. At night the sky reverberated with the straining Merlin engines as wave after wave of overloaded Lancaster and Halifax bombers climbed up from Lincolnshire and Cambridgeshire. By day the Fortresses roared off each morning and every afternoon the ground crews watched anxiously as the survivors came back: sometimes in smart formation, sometimes ragged with many stragglers. Worst of all were the days when huge gaps appeared. Every day, the news was of successful night raids by the RAF and equally successful daylight raids by the USAFF.

I noticed a great number of new faces amongst the young aircrew officers who now came to the farmhouse door seeking eggs and milk. They had a seriousness which had been missing from the laughing, swashbuckling young men who had come earlier. Only my ground crew friends were familiar faces. The turnover of air crews seemed, even to the insensitive farm lads, to be ominous. The losses given out in the news bulletins and the dismissal of German fighter successes as propaganda did not match the demoralization I could detect in the American camp. A week or so later, a massive raid on Schweinfurt resulted in such severe losses amongst the American flyers that USAFF generals spoke of treachery and German foreknowledge. As summer passed into autumn and the harvest was successfully hauled in, the roar of engines seemed to lessen. October brought clear skies and a brilliant harvest moon. The month also brought major raids on Germany to a standstill. Unescorted bombers had proved too vulnerable to fighters in daylight despite heavy armour, tight massed formations and heavy firepower. It was to be many months before the arrival of long range Mustang fighters made the resumption of large scale daylight raids possible. The RAF saturation raids on Berlin and other great cities were proving similarly expensive and eased off. It appeared that the Luftwaffe had, for the time being, won the Battle of Germany.

One night when work finished early, I took a delightful twenty-one-year-old landgirl, Hilda, to see Humphrey Bogart and Ingrid Bergman in *Casablanca*. She had no idea that I was only just seventeen and she had ditched a very put-out GI to go out with me. One day she asked one of the girls on Manor Farm if I had been out with girls before. I was mortified when this other girl laughingly told me my technique must need improving. I had only thought of romance, not technique! Before I could remedy my courting methods, Hilda, who had really won my heart, was sent to work in another part of Bedfordshire; and for a time, life seemed bleak for a girlfriendless farm lad.

Later in the season, two schoolgirls from Luton came to work on the farm. Both seemed very small and weak but in no time they had made themselves useful and Farmer Hope, who had always wanted a daughter or two, was delighted to have them about. I, at first, was less than comfortable with them. The girls recognised the residues of proper speech in my conversation and one of them knew my sister Esme, but both were appalled at my lack of education and prospects. How could a Mill Hill schoolboy be working as a manual labourer here? Both were tomboys and loved to play practical jokes and indulge in horseplay. Neither were goddesses like Hilda the departed landgirl, love of my life, but they were good fun and I eventually began to feel happy in their company. Doris, a well-rounded fluffy blonde, had a serious boyfriend in Luton, under whose direction the other girl, Jean, a tall athletic girl, acted as chaperone to the more flighty Doris. Both were trembling on the brink of womanhood and loved to speak darkly about sex, the wickedness of men and the need to remain virgins. I had my doubts about Doris. She had a very knowing look and often talked about how experienced her boyfriend Rex was and how far they went.

One night, after a stimulating evening at Bedford fair, I cycled the eight miles back to the farm with them. I was tired after the bike ride on top of a hard day's work. Before going to bed I had a quick look round the cows as the farmer was out for the evening. Thankfully there were no problems and I ambled off wearily for bed and a good night's rest. On going upstairs I met Doris coming out of the bathroom clad in a large white towel. For a moment she reminded me of Dorothy Lamour in a sarong. I stood and looked at her, noticing a mischievous twinkle as she pulled the towel tight across her budding bosom, an action which caused a rose pink nipple to pop out. She gave a snort of laughter and let the towel drop away momentarily, revealing both breasts and a pink tummy, in a flurry of adjustment. I blushed and went into my room. Later, coming out to brush my teeth, I bumped into her again, this time wearing pyjamas and a hairnet. To my surprise she did not rush by but seemed to be hesitating in my way. I brushed past and felt her lean against me. Taking her arm, I expected the usual mock fighting and horseplay. Instead she rolled round into my arms and kissed me.

I, never one to miss a chance, kissed her back. To my surprise she opened her lips and used her tongue quite vigorously. I was at a disadvantage. I had heard of "French kissing" but had not experienced anything as deliberate as this. Was this the technique Hilda my lovely landgirl thought was missing? I felt a very different warmth rising up my neck and prickling behind my ears. I grabbed her to me and pushed back with my tongue, knowing she must be able to feel my body reacting to her as she pressed against me. "Bloody hell, a schoolgirl!" I thought as I slid my hand inside her pyjama top. The smooth warm skin of her soft stomach and budding breasts was like silk in my hands and I gasped as if in pain. Doris stepped back with a mocking smile: "You are getting in a state!" Just then, the door opened and Jean's head popped out. "Come on you two, behave yourselves." Doris gave a laugh and went in. I, flushed and pleased with myself, brushed my teeth and went thoughtfully to bed.

Two days later coming back from the pub after a couple of pints with the American ground crew, I mounted the stairs quietly. I opened the girls' door. Both were lying on top of the bed. Neither had changed into pyjamas and I drank in their semi-nakedness. Jean snapped up into a sitting position pulling the coverlet round her; and snarling, she hissed, "What do you want?" Doris continued to lie voluptuously on the bed, smiling enigmatically. "Come for a walk,

Doris," said I. "Don't go," said Jean. "You know what I told you." Without a word Doris got out of bed and pulled on a pair of slacks and a checked blouse. We went out together, ignoring Jean's protests.

The October moon was superb and I led her down the farm drive and across to the corn stacks where there was a heap of long clean thatching straw waiting for Mr Clarke the thatcher to use next day. I lay down and Doris, with a show of reluctance, joined me. I, with a pint or two inside me, was thoroughly roused and determined not to be fobbed off. I roughly opened Doris's blouse and put my cold face against her warm breasts. "Enjoying yourself?" said Doris as she pulled back and snatched her blouse together. I pushed her down and kissed her fiercely. I thought I felt her responding and slid my hands down to push at the waistband of her slacks. "No you don't!" said Doris. "Not like that!" I paused, then wrestled her slacks off. Doris went limp and let me feel her secret parts without moving. She made no movement or comment as I sat up and reached in my pocket for a condom. Neither did she comment on my first bungled attempts to fit the wretched thing. Very clumsily I tried to make love to her. Somehow – I was never sure if she had helped or not – it was happening and I was pushing fairly gently. I did not rush but I did not ask if she was ready; I did not know I should have. Instead I pushed on till I welled up to a climax then sank, panting, onto her shoulder. In my ignorance I asked her if she was satisfied. "No," said Doris. "I didn't want to do it in the first place." Taken aback and far from at my most perceptive after a few pints, I kissed her again. She seemed wooden.

As I was embracing her, we were bathed for a moment in the brilliant lights of a passing bomb truck. For a moment I felt caught, as if a master on dormitory rounds had shone a torch and caught me at something improper. The truck passed by without slowing and I came back to reality. "Anyway," I said, "you will always be my first woman." Doris did not reply but she did squeeze my hand and I felt better. As we walked back to the house, I threw the used condom into the hedge. I remembered a Cumbrian farmer's words: "Bloody things! Laak washing tha feet wiv thi socks on!"

We embraced again, very gently this time, outside the farmhouse, the magnificent October moon shining in her eyes. I was in love at that moment but I could not say it. We embraced again outside her room and I went proudly to bed.

Next morning, I, a jubilant boy, went out to help milk the cows at five forty-five. For once I did not feel tired. As usual the cowman chaffed at me and I, an immature and foolish youth, could not resist telling the older man of my success. I did not see Doris that morning but coming in for lunch I met Jean; her face was thunderous. "You rotten pig!" she said. "Doris has been in tears all morning because you had to boast of your conquests!" I went inside with a sinking heart. I had never expected the older man to betray my confidence and humiliate the poor girl. Doris sat in stony silence throughout the meal and it was not until evening that I got her to talk and apologised. We eventually resumed our friendship but she would not let me touch her again.

I had made my Bedfordshire Clanger and it tasted sour in my young mouth.

The rest of harvest went by very quickly. The girls avoided me as much as possible although there was no obvious rancour. Jean was obviously – and very wisely – determined to keep us apart. When the last corn was carted and harvest's attendant works were over, the girls went back to normal life: school, home and town friends. I missed the girls for a while but the goddess, Hilda, was back; and for a few rapturous weeks I worked happily knowing that I would see her for a quiet evening's chat in the canteen of the landgirls' hostel at Milton Ernest. I did not know if the other girls had told her about Doris but my experience had chastened me and I never once attempted to do more than kiss her goodnight in a brotherly way. The relationship was doomed to fizzle out as I had completely lost confidence in my relations with the opposite sex and she had by now realised the disparity in our ages and experience. In any case, I was getting itchy feet. I had been on the Bedfordshire farm for a year and in view of the farmer having three sons, I could see little chance of advancement.

I pondered once more the old agricultural adage that the entry into farming is by parsimony, patrimony or matrimony. There was little chance of saving on my tiny wage; so parsimony was out. I was far too innocent and principled to think of marrying a farmer's daughter to get a farm but there was just a possibility that my own father's plans might come to fruition and we would one day have a family farm or smallholding if and when he was ever compensated for the bombed family business.

Thinking of my widowed father alone at Mill Hill, I decided to try to find work nearer home where I could keep in touch with the

80

family and perhaps enjoy a less isolated life. Mr Hope did not accept my notice graciously and threatened me with instant call-up to the army or exile to the coal mines as a Bevin Boy. He like many others had forgotten that I was still, at seventeen, some way off military age. The farmer also poured scorn on my naively disclosed wish to seek a job with a fifty-two hour week, which would give me time for life off the farm. "What sort of a farmer will you make if you only want to work fifty-two hours?" he roared. I stood my ground. For the next few days I was ostracized as some sort of a villain for wanting to leave. However, by the time my month's notice was up, the farmer was praising my work and offering me more money to stay on. I thought this was a bit late in the day but in any case I was ready for a change and a taste of normal living. I went to say goodbye to my American Army Air Corps friends. They loaded me up with green cigars, Lucky Strikes, Camels, Chesterfields and giant Dunhill cigarettes. Not to mention candy, "V" packs and other goodies.

My homecoming this time had a mixed reception. For one thing, I was a very large, uncouth youth smoking ridiculously large cigars and flashing black market cigarettes and goodies. The highly principled family were shocked by my hardness and boastfulness. In addition, it was as if I thought I had invented sex, and my braggadocio shocked the broadminded but reticent family. I even boasted of drunken escapades, which did not go down well with a family which had had more than its share of drink-related problems. Somewhat to my surprise, I found I was not as popular as I had expected. Furthermore my sister was now overworked and fraught with worries as she had inherited the running of my father's large house on top of her own family work with two young children. I was shocked at the decline in the family fortunes. I had left home with my mother in charge, with a maid and gardener and a part-time chauffeur from the works. Now it was austerity and near poverty at a stroke.

I was not too long finding a job and with my father's support I managed to persuade my sister to let me live in the family home. The job on a Totteridge farm paid three pounds a week for fifty-two hours plus overtime. After tax I took home two pounds ten shillings (250p). Of this I gave my sister one pound ten shillings rent (150p) and used the rest for bus fares to and from work and modest lunches in a workman's dining room. With a bit of overtime, I still had a little cash to spend. I loved the new farm job. Although the land was scattered round semi-urban areas, the farm was modern and very well-equipped. I had my own Fordson tractor and was treated as a man indeed.

Once again, fast promotion was blocked by the farmer's sons. There was a farmer's daughter but she was a manly virago devoted to horses and of a very imperious nature. The sons in contrast were amiable if erratic young men, happy to pass on their skills and knowledge, unlike the rural closeness of the Cumbrian and Bedfordshire workmen who seemed to want to preserve their skills as trade secrets!

Teddy, the younger son, had a short temper and was liable to flashes of violent rage. He had worked with Bertram Mills' Circus and impressed me with his tales of West End life in London. If he could be believed, he had once come between two lesbian lovers who had fought violently over him with torn hair, torn clothes and severely scratched cheeks. As a very young seventeen-year-old I could not believe Teddy's stories of threesome love sessions involving a strap-on dildo. This was something I could not even believe existed until Teddy took me up to Charing Cross Road one Saturday night and showed me one in a backstreet chemist's shop. Teddy also introduced me to the sleazy world of streetwalkers, many of whom, in a Lisle street cafe, seemed to know him. Teddy boasted that he never had to pay, as they all wanted him to make love to them for nothing. I was fascinated by the girls, but they were all too hard-looking for me. I still believed in romance; and anyway, there was no way I was going to risk getting the clap.

Freddie, the elder brother, had been a successful National Hunt jockey and was a thoroughly nice if simple guy. He seemed genuinely interested in me and in helping me to learn as much as I could about the farm. Freddie did not know much about the business side of the farm as his father held the reins as well as the purse strings; but he managed the operations very well. The farmer, Fred Ensten senior, was seldom seen on the farm, arriving for short visits in a large American Packard car. He was also a butcher, a market grader and a keen race-goer. Rumour had it that he was a great ladies' man in spite of his bulging corporation and advancing years. The landgirls avoided him in confined spaces and he was rumoured to have a fancy lady in the flat above his butcher's shop in Burnt Oak.

The relatively short hours gave me time to go to a few parties organised by the parents of some of my former schoolmates. They all questioned my choice of career, my lack of schooling and my prospects. In spite of my roughness, they and my former friends accepted me back into their circles, though not without reservation and quite a few snubs. Few, for instance, would acknowledge me if they met me in the bus on the way home, as I sat reeking of paraffin and cow muck. However once I was clean and in reasonable clothes, I got on well with most of them. Despite this, I found my interest and loyalties drifting back to the men I worked with. They lived in what seemed to me to be the real world. Soil, sky, green growth and golden cropping.

I met some nice girls at the youth club. One even knew quite a lot about farming; she did not treat me as a freak and could talk sensibly with me. We went about together for a bit but she fell badly in love with my best friend who was home from Mill Hill School for the Easter holidays and that was that. In time I was friendly with many young people around Mill Hill, but my real life was on the farm.

Teddy, the farmer's younger son, at first seemed to see me as a threat to his position in the farm's social hierarchy or pecking order. In spite of my obvious roughness, he regarded me as a Mill Hill toff. I, who was being at least partially ostracised by these same toffs, was angered and on several occasions I came to blows with the much older man. Eventually we had a serious but inconclusive fight in which I ended up bloody and more damaged than Teddy but sitting victoriously on the man's chest as I pinned him to the ground. I was not streetwise in regard to fisticuffs but my wrestling strength was too much for Teddy who, despite his dire threats, never bothered me again. After this violent display the other men christened me "The Mill Hill Mauler", a title which was to stick and embarrass me for many years.

At night there were still air raids and an occasional stick of bombs on the farmland. The bomb craters would disrupt operations or, more seriously, ruin the field drains and cause flooding. At least they were not falling on the houses! There was considerable tension in the air as rumours and denials were everywhere about the impending invasion of Europe by the Allies. Certainly every lane and byway seemed choked with lorries and equipment. Huge tank transporters and armoured vehicles laboured up Bittacy Hill from the REME depot and there were endless convoys of men and materials down the Barnet bypass southwards. One very wet June morning, with the clouds barely above the trees, the farm men and I broke off from a dusty job rebaling a stack of straw. We went into a little pub in Aldenham for a glass of watery beer to drink as we ate our meagre sandwiches. The pub was quiet and two old men were discussing the news. I could hear snatches of their conversation. It seemed that General Eisenhower had announced that landings had been made in Normandy. They had established an 11 Divisional beachhead front and this was being rapidly reinforced. My God, thought I, this is it. It was nearly five years since I had listened to Mr Neville Chamberlain declare war on Germany while I was staying on my uncle's farm in Dorset. Now the real struggle for Western Europe had begun.

The day passed slowly for the farm gang who continued trying to bale up an old stack of straw which had got wet and mouldy. The fungus spores made their eyes and noses run and their lungs sore. No one had any thoughts other than for the desperate struggles that must be raging at that very moment on the beaches, in the water and among the sand dunes. That night, crowding round the radio, the family and I listened eagerly for news.

Already the British beachheads at Gold and Juno beaches were secure. The American landing at Utah beach was also successful but there was a sad story of muddle, accident and great losses on the Omaha beachhead where strong defences had not been sufficiently softened up by bombardment; and the strongly-fortified German positions had allowed their gunners to wreak fearful slaughter on the exposed GIs. Bad seamanship had sunk landing craft full of infantry and amphibious tanks before they could engage the enemy. At one time a Royal Navy destroyer had risked grounding as it came close in, to silence a German battery which was causing much slaughter on the beach and in the sea. Only sheer courage and determination had secured the exits from the beaches, and allowed the overwhelming numbers and firepower of the American troops to secure a proper foothold.

As the days passed into weeks, the anxiety of the public grew. Caen had not fallen and Monty's generals were having a tough time getting their troops through the bocage country. The famous Seventh Armoured division of open desert warfare fame were stalled in the high hedgerows where they could only see short distances and fell easy prey to concealed 88mm guns and the odd Tiger tank for which they had no match. Repeated attacks by massed tanks and infantry were failing to make real progress into and beyond Caen itself; and burnt-out tanks littered the Normandy countryside.

I came home one night to better news. An excited friend shouted that the Americans had gone fighting mad and had broken out of their lines near St Lo and were motoring through open country to outflank the Wermacht... Allied air superiority was wreaking havoc behind the German lines and British and Canadian forces were pushing south to close the trap on the retreating Germans at Falaise. The next few days were a succession of advances and counter-attacks but it was clear that the battle of France had been won and the great pursuit was on. The Falaise gap was not quite closed. A large part of the Wermacht escaped across the Seine and fought a rearguard into Belgium leaving strong pockets of resistance in the channel ports, thus denying them to the Allies.

Paris fell, bringing with it huge logistical problems for the Allies in feeding the vast urban population. Sheer exhaustion of men, petrol and supplies slowed down the Allied armies and the Germans were able to withdraw in some order to strong positions along the Scheldt, thus denying the port of Antwerp to the Allies. Meantime a new and terrifying threat had appeared over south east England as Hitler unleashed his secret weapon, the V1 flying bomb. The first bomb had fallen on a railway crossing near London. It was mistakenly reported as a plane loaded with bombs having crashed and the location was mentioned on the BBC news. This gave the Germans an accurate ranging shot and a massive and accurate attack on London developed.

All the city's air defences were moved south into Kent, so that they could intercept the flying bombs. Many were shot down by gunfire and by the RAF's new Meteor jet aircraft. Only the very latest and fastest piston-engined aircraft, the Tempest, could catch the V1s as they droned their way across the Kent countryside. In spite of the balloon barrage, the guns and the RAF, many were getting through and the disruption was enormous. South London was fast becoming a devastated area and the effect on morale was frightening. The noise of the approaching bombs was long drawn out, followed by a terrifying few seconds' silence as the engine cut out and the bomb fell. Sometimes in a silent spin, sometimes in a whistling flat glide and sometimes in a shrieking dive. The public cheerfully nicknamed the death-dealing machines "Doodlebugs" but the flippant name belied the dull fear they engendered. The damage and loss of life were becoming serious. Once more the children were evacuated, this time in even greater numbers than in 1939. Churchill's government, unknown to the general public, seriously considered abandoning London.

Meanwhile, back on the farm, work went on as usual. Despite being outside the main target area, everyone had bomb stories. Poor

Ron, one of the tractor drivers, had been blown out of his house. We had seen a friend's house disappear in front of our eyes and had been close to death or injury several times as bombs fell nearby.

Harvest proceeded slowly with a wet start and the first casual workers appeared as the schools and colleges broke up for the summer vacations. There were fewer helpers than usual. Many had gone to work in more peaceful areas! I was enjoying the work on this farm more than all the other places I had been. I enjoyed the company of the men and especially one romantic tramp called Brocko who lived in the hedges but was kept fed and clothed by the nuns at St Mary's Convent. No one knew why he was a tramp. Brocko was a highly intelligent cockney who had served in the Royal Navy and on the North West Frontier of India as a soldier. Despite a severe injury which made him lame, he was a good worker. Perhaps he was on the run from East End gangsters. One day the Mother Superior at the convent had asked him why he did not work at a regular job. "Work, Sister? Work?" he had replied. "I ain't got time to work! I got me livin' to get!"

There was one revolting fellow in the gang, Old Ballie. He was an unshaven and unwashed local man with a Geordie wife, whose strange accent only I with my northern experience could understand. They had inevitably managed to produce a horde of snotty-nosed kids who cluttered every corner of the farmyard and were constantly in trouble... Ballie was obsessed with sex and was always looming behind people, both men and women, with suggestive comments and leers. I managed to avoid the fellow most of the time but felt very sorry for his wife and family. We were all very alarmed one morning when one of Ballie's kids was carried round by his sister, white-faced and unconscious with blood streaming down his neck. His older brother had swung a pickaxe over his head and spiked the little lad who was standing behind him. Despite the serious wound, the mother said, "What have you done, you little bugger?" and rushed him under a tap. Cold water brought him round but no medical aid was sought. The little lad appeared next day with a huge lump on his head and extremely crossed eyes. The lump eventually subsided leaving a conical crater in his skull. He seemed all right but the whole family behaved so oddly anyway, it was hard to tell if his brain was affected. Life was tough for farm children!

Things brightened up still further for me when the latest gang of casual workers arrived. One was a pretty girl who glanced demurely at me from time to time but did not say much until one day when we were getting some temporary stacks threshed to meet an urgent order for corn. I was dreamily thinking about threshing days in Cumberland when the girl spoke and interrupted my reverie. "Too busy to talk, then?"

I looked at her, her small trim figure bent over as she rolled out the rat wire towards me. She looked at me appraisingly and I, embarrassed, stared at my feet. "Stuck up are we?" she said. I scowled.

It was a long time since I had felt stuck up about anything.

Chapter 4

Plum Colic

"You remind me of Seth," said the girl laughingly, "Seth in *Cold Comfort Farm*. Yes, I think we should call you Seth: it suits you!"

I looked at her suspiciously, wondering what *Cold Comfort Farm* was. I had a vague memory of hearing of a book title like it; or was it a song the farm labourers used to sing up in cold wet Cumberland? No, that was "Down on Misery Farm" sung surreptitiously behind farmer Eddie's back when he was in a sarcastic or critical mood. I sighed; I missed the mountains and the clipped Cumbrian accents of my many good friends up there, if not the rain and the dourness of the farming community, who, as if hardened by climate and poverty, seemed to regard open cheerful friendliness as weakness, or weak-headedness. I thought of the farm girl, Alma, her friendly kind face, her slim waist, long legs and gently swelling figure. I chuckled; no savage breasts for music to charm! No beauty queen, Alma, but I had loved her in a way.

The girl turned; then, snatching a barley straw from my hair, she brought up her face with laughing, teasing eyes. "Yes, Seth!" She paused. "It might be fun falling for you!"

"Buggered if I know what you're talking about," I said, squinting at the girl in the bright Hertfordshire sunlight which reflected off the golden straw stacks surrounding us in the bustling stockyard. I was intensely proud and sensitive to ragging and hated to display literary ignorance. I pondered over her presence in the harvest gang. They were a mixed lot. Some posh school and college kids from Mill Hill, some right little roughs from Barnet, Brocko the colourful tramp from the Totteridge hedgerows, and the regular farm men. I looked at the smiling girl again; she wasn't bad-looking in a rather prim way. Perhaps she was from Hendon or Mill Hill Broadway or some other North London suburb. Maybe a teacher or student; some sort of a nob; certainly not one of the workers? I chuckled at the thought. Students and lads awaiting call-up to the forces often came to help on the farms, showing off their lack of muscles and their ignorance of country skills, always excusing themselves with snooty comments like "Oh well, I work with my brains!" I chuckled again. Work with their arses more like!

It had been a catchy summer so far in that desperate year of 1944. The haymaking had been a miserable struggle between downpours. The Allied forces had at last gone into France under leaden skies and, after the bitter fighting in Normandy, were now streaming across Western Europe, seeming to stop only when petrol and ammunition failed to keep up with the fighting men. Every day, I studied the morning and evening newspapers poring over the maps with their arrows and lines with news of advances and reverses. The war and its consequences were never far from my mind in spite of my tender years and open, carefree manner.

"Now what are you laughing at?" said the girl curiously, looking over. "You are always grinning at something."

"Better than bloody crying, isn't it?" My thoughts drifted off again. I thought about two old ladies killed in Mill Hill the previous night by a stray flying bomb behind the railway station. Old Ron (he was barely 21 years old), with his nerves shattered by a near miss from a flying bomb which had fallen at the bottom of Milespit Hill, killing one of his next door neighbours. Poor old Ron, who would now leap from his tractor and run for the ditch every time a passing motorbike or plane made a sound like an approaching flying bomb. Yes, I thought, There's plenty to bloody cry about what with Billy dying at sea and all those poor bloody Russian Jews the advancing Red Army had just found in the death pits of Baba Yara at Kiev.

"Dreamy, that's what you are," said the girl, and she wandered off to where the great stationary baler had just started up again after a cast drive belt had caused a much appreciated breakdown, which had given the chance of a few minutes rest for the sweating harvest gang.

The sun had broken through a few hours earlier drawing steamy air from the damp stacks; and clouds of choking mould spores were issuing from the threshing machine which thundered and shook with a throbbing whine as it had done every year since those far-off days when Ransomes of Norwich had made ploughs before guns and threshers before tanks. An oval plate, riveted to the pale pink painted wooden side of the fairground machine-like monster, informed that the thresher was made in 1912. God! I thought. How many poor buggers have been wiped out for nowt since this bugger was built? Still, the bloody Jerries had to be stopped. My train of thought was interrupted by Fred's voice. "Come on, Mauler! Show these townies how to bash the corn out of this outfit!"

89

Determined to show what I could do, ignoramus or not, I spurned the ladder which danced precariously against the side of the vibrating thresher. I jumped to grab the edge of the threshing platform and with a swinging jackknife of my body had one leg up and over the side; another convulsion and I was up on the top. Beside me the great roaring opening in which the huge drum spun, pulverising the loosened sheaves of corn as my knife slashed through the bands of coarse twine which bound them. Above me on the stack, the farmer's son, Fred, tossed the barley sheaves down to me with the relentless yet seemingly effortless regularity of a metronome.

Sheaf after sheaf was forked down as layer by layer the stack shrank and the heaps of corn sacks grew at one end of the machine and the great stack of bales went up tier by tier at the other. Occasionally the machine gave a coughing grunt of protest if I let an uncut sheaf slip through, the clattering tractor giving an answering bellow of rage as the engine's governors responded to the increased load. "Watch it, Terry!" shouted Fred. "You'll have the belts off again!"

Through the dust and stinging sweat which clogged my eyes, I was surprised to find the girl had appeared at my side.

"Can I do that? It looks easier than what I'm doing!"

I looked up at Fred enquiringly. The threshing platform was no place for inexperienced or careless workers. "Okay, but keep an eye on her," he said, with a not unkindly smile. The girl took a spare knife and slashed sharply at a sheaf, narrowly missing my hand.

"Watch it! And don't go mad at it," I said. "Just keep a regular rhythm and don't for God's sake get your fingers in the drum or it will take your arm off!"

"Don't be so serious all the time," said the girl.

"It is bloody serious and we want to get this stack finished tonight," I replied, attempting to assert my authority on this pushy townie.

She was a bright lass, though, and soon got the idea; so I jumped down from the drum onto the base of the straw bale stack to give the bale stacker a hand. This was a job I loved, mauling the great wire-tied bales onto my back and climbing up a staircase of bales to build a perfectly symmetrical stack, each layer tied in like brickwork, yet done in such a way that the bales could be easily taken down in vertical tiers with minimal effort and waste during the long winter to come. I chuckled to myself again, thinking of the red-faced efforts of unhappy helpers before they got the knack of handling bales.

Glancing up, I realised the girl had caught me smiling to myself again. As she bent back to her task I looked a little longingly at her lithe body and tight check shorts.

"Fancy a trip up the Rhine with that, do you?"

Ballie, the leering married farm worker, whispered in my ear, so close that I could almost feel his unshaven jowl and could distinctly smell the lunchtime intake of beer, cheese and the inevitable onions. I flushed with anger, not so much at the words, but at being caught out by such a coarse ignorant bugger as Ballie. How could his wife –or any woman – allow a disgusting brute like that to touch her? I had not yet realised what a coarse and ignorant young man I myself had become during my three-year descent from prep school boy to manual labourer!

The rest of the day passed quickly, helped on by a couple of bouts of near hysteria as the stack neared its brushwood base. Then the hiding rats, no longer feasting thieves but terrified fugitives, broke cover and fled. A low fence of chicken wire, as demanded by wartime regulations, surrounded the stack and thresher. As each new rat emerged, the threshing gang pursued it as if old Adolph Hitler himself were incarnate in the unfortunate rodents. Unable to pass the wire, the rats ran back to the stack if they survived the stabbing forks, hurtling stones and flailing thatch pegs. Eager terriers and a watchful sheepdog ensured that none who escaped the wire netting got far. I joined in with the others but I did not relish the killing. My mind always carried pictures of fleeing prisoners being hunted down and slashed at and bayoneted by grinning pursuers.

"Bloody softy, I suppose," I thought aloud.

"What's that?" said the girl, who watched these bouts of hunting fever with distaste.

"Nothing," I replied, feeling thoroughly discomfited. I spoke gruffly, to hide what I saw as my lack of manliness, and I went back to my bale stack, angry with myself and the work and – quite unreasonably – angry with the girl.

Once the stack was finished, the rat wire rolled up, the corn sacks sheeted down securely and loose straw thrown over the bale stack, the gang broke up and walked tiredly to their respective homes. I found myself waiting for the single decker bus back to Mill Hill.

"My name's Jackie," said the girl, who had come out of the yard unnoticed behind me. "I know you don't like me, but as we are going on the same bus, we might as well talk."

"Who says I don't like you?" I mumbled, lighting up with pleasure at finding myself alone with the girl and away from the enquiring leers of my mates.

Jackie smiled back with new confidence. "It's just that I thought I had made you cross this afternoon when you looked so glum after smiling such a lot."

The bus chugged to a standstill beside us. Its noise and fumes cut off further conversation until we were seated. I noticed with pleasure that the only empty seats were a pair together. I would not have dared sit with her otherwise. The girl chatted comfortably about her job as a Botany demonstrator at Hendon Technical College. She is a bloody nob then, I thought, far out of my reach. But anyway, it's nice squashed up in this seat beside her and she smells much nicer than the hefty landgirls from the Totteridge hostel. Most of them seemed to wash in carbolic, which while admirable, was hardly romantic. There were a few nicely-scented, glamorous landgirls; but they were – for me – unattainable exceptions. Smart American servicemen in Jeeps or other military vehicles always seemed to be hanging round the hostel, waiting for the prettier girls.

All too soon the bus was swinging round into Mill Hill Broadway, and it was my getting-off stop. "'Bye, see you in the morning!" I got off and started to walk up towards my father's house. As the sound of the bus retreated I thought I heard the steady pulse of an approaching flying bomb. Christ, I thought, I'm getting as jumpy as old Ron. The unmistakable sound grew louder and then ceased abruptly, to be replaced by a soft whistling as the winged missile glided downwards in a shallow dive. A strident bell clanged a warning from the fire station tower as the roof watcher warned the firemen of an imminent explosion. I lay down on the neat suburban pavement in the approved fashion with my hands behind my neck and my elbows and knees braced to take the ground shockwave. "Keep going!" I muttered. "Keep going, don't bloody well drop here!" An almighty blast and crack denied my prayer and I jumped up to see a black ball of smoke rising from the lower end of the Broadway.

I could see my father at the gate of our home calling something to me but there was only one thought in my mind. The bus! The flaming bloody bus! Somehow I was running down the road with the strength of my legs sapped by the shock and fear I was feeling. Glass shimmered and crackled under my feet and men with black steel helmets seemed to be everywhere, blowing whistles and shouting.

George Lett was already sweeping up the broken glass of his toy shop window. Yet only seconds before I had been happily listening to the girl's chatter, posh though it was. "God, let her be safe," I panted to myself as my heart thumped, partly from the running but mainly through my fear.

The bus had stopped on the wrong side of the road and a small crowd, mostly passengers, were standing round an elderly woman who was bleeding badly from a glass splinter wound in her scalp. The girl Jackie was comforting her and had got a pad of white material from somewhere and was pressing it to the woman's head. Another woman was weeping quietly over a prostrate figure on the ground.

"Make way, make way! I am a doctor." The frail figure of Dr Morley, who in more settled times had tended me and the family through our childhood ailments, was now on his knees by the body on the road. He quickly got up, shaking his head, and went to the girl who was now crying softly as she tried to find a dry patch of blouse to stem the woman's bleeding. Ashamed of my reaction, I felt a quick surge of excitement as I realised the girl was covered only by a thin aertex vest through which the shape of her youthful breasts was clearly visible. A familiar warmth and pressure at my loins caused me to blush with shame that such a thing could come into my mind at a time like this.

A uniformed man took Jackie's bloodstained blouse from her and applied a dressing to the woman who was now cheerfully appreciative upon realising that she was both alive and the only slightly wounded centre of attention. Two other men had lifted the body from the road and the crowd was already drifting up to the smoking hole on the Station Road allotments where the flying bomb had expended most of its energy and souvenir fragments were to be gathered.

"Come here, lass," I said. "You can't go about like that. What would your mum think if I took you home like that?"

I slipped off my shirt and threw it to her. She smiled and pulled it over her head and I caught a glimpse of upstrained breasts, once more feeling guilt at my own pleasure.

The walk to her home was full of nervous chatter. How matter of fact, I thought, in the face of what must be drama. Yet it all seems so ordinary: bloody bombs, death. It's a rum do.

My dad was very curious as to why I had run off when the flying bomb had exploded. I explained that a girl from the farm was on the bus and that I had wanted to be sure she was safe. My dad was intrigued about the girl but I was non-committal.

"Just a part-timer; I thought I had better see she was all right and I walked her home, that's all."

Later, before going to bed, I searched through the books until I found what I wanted. There it was: a battered copy of *Cold Comfort Farm* by Stella Gibbons. I skimmed through it. The farm and family sounded much like the one where I worked. The family were a bit strange. There was an old granny who kept mumbling about something nasty happening in the woodshed. A strange girl who flew aeroplanes and a dark, gypsy-like young man called Seth who she wanted to turn into a film star. Seth was dark and handsome – whereas I had mousey hair and irregular acne-plagued features. I could not see why the girl had called me Seth from *Cold Comfort Farm*.

The following day, I went to work on the early bus. My head was full of the previous day's events. The girl Jackie lived with her parents in a small semi-detached house on the way to Edgware. Her mother had looked very oddly at us as we arrived at the house. I suppose we had looked a bit odd: Jackie wearing my shirt, and myself, a spotty youth in a grimy singlet. She had become more and more agitated as her eyes took in first her daughter in a man's shirt, then the traces of blood, and finally the fact that I had no shirt on and was clearly not the sort of young man to live in The Grove, as their genteel road was called. Jackie cut short her mother's querulous interrogation with the bare details of the bomb and the loss of her blouse. She had introduced me, emphasizing that I lived in Uphill Drive, the right part of Mill Hill, and was going one day to be a farmer, or so I had told her as we walked along Hale Lane. Jackie's father turned out to be a nice old boy. He was an easy-going Scot who, after a life at sea as a ship's engineer, had become a Lloyds inspector. He had a twinkle in his eye and some rare tales of his temporary work round the coastal ports on contraband control. "Nice lad," he had said, while ostensibly out of earshot in the kitchen. "Better than some of the Persian ponces she sometimes brings home." Jackie had been desperately embarrassed but was obviously pleased with her father's judgment.

Next morning, Jackie came to work on a later bus and I had already gone to help assemble the "new" combined harvester and thresher, which the farmer's son Teddy had been to fetch from Norfolk. This enormous machine was pretty ancient, having been built

94

for use on the Canadian prairies. A vast, seventeen-foot-wide cutterbar and gathering platform extended like the wing of some ancient aircraft, on one side leading into a totally inadequate peg drum powered by a small petrol engine. The whole heap of machinery had to be towed round the fields by a protesting crawler tractor. I had read enough in my treasured agricultural magazines to realise that this machine was intended for light crops of bone dry wheat on the Canadian prairies and would be in difficulty with the heavy crops of damp laid wheat which the 1944 English harvest promised to produce.

Both Fred and Teddy agreed with me that the small motor would need to be replaced and the drum speeded up to cope with the heavier crops. I remembered the many cars laid up and valueless due to wartime petrol shortages.

It did not take long to find a big rusty American car. It had not been stored on blocks and the tyres were flat and ruined; but it had a sound engine and was fairly cheap. Old Monty, the Potters Bar blacksmith, made a mounting bracket and fitted a bigger drive pulley onto the motor and a smaller one onto the drum, thus increasing the drum's rotational speed. A modest flywheel was added to the far end of the drum axle to ensure plenty of inertia as the uneven flow of straw reached it. In no time the machine was ready.

"It seems a bit hit or miss," I said doubtfully.

"It's shit or bust!" said old Monty. "Good luck." I pondered on this strange expression; I did not really understand what it meant but somehow it seemed to fit the moment.

The morning spent working on the "new" combine had been fine and the fast-drying straw was popping and crackling as the gang came down to the harvest fields. Teddy had been missing all morning and Fred asked if anyone had seen him. Alf Pratchet, one of the many urchins from the Mays Lane council houses who did odd jobs round the farm in the holidays, piped up. "We seen 'im guv, 'e were down the long field bottom wi' the new tractor girl, weren't 'e, Titch?"

Titch, another Barnet urchin, nodded so vigorously that the huge flat cap, many sizes too big for him, slipped down over his eyes. Pulling the cap up and brushing the peak round to the back, he said, "Yer, an 'e were givin 'er it!"

Freddy's eyes narrowed. "What do you mean, Titch?"

Before Titch could answer, Pratchet joined in. "We seen 'im guv, 'e 'ad 'er under the 'edge givin' 'er a good feel round, then 'e dun 'er, 'onest 'e did, good and proper! We both seen 'im, din 'e, Titch?"

Freddy looked at me and shrugged. He was used to Teddy's peccadilloes. No more time was wasted on the subject and we set to on the job in hand. Freddy took Teddy's place on the crawler tractor and with a warning shout to me, the outfit set off in the cloud of dust which signifies that the corn is dry enough to combine. Soon a steady stream of chewed-up straw was issuing from the back, leaving a bleached wake behind the swaying, roaring giant, which now resembled some great battleship sailing on a golden sea.

I sat perched on a metal seat, no different from those attached to the horse-drawn implements of the previous century. Beside me was a huge metal lever with which to raise and lower the vast cutting platform according to the state of the crop. By clambering up and standing on the seat, a precarious process, I could just see into the collecting tank, which was already filling with golden grain. The modification to the machine was a success! Soon it was time to empty the tank; and an old coalman's dray with an improvised box was drawn alongside. I pulled another lever opening the slide to let the corn grains run out into the box. Old Ron, Ballie the licentious married man, Teddy, who had come back from his romantic interlude with an expression of total innocence, and the girl Jackie were soon busy. They were soon sweating and grunting as they filled eighteen stone sacks with grain as it ran down the sloping floor of the box and through a slide at the lower end. It was jolly hard work.

Round about tea time, a colossal explosion rocked the whole district, followed by another less close. "Bloody hell! What was that?" The gang, white-faced and shaken, looked at each other, nervy and on edge. At Teddy's command they got back to work with anxious glances at the sky. Soon Teddy's wife came down to the fields with the tea cans and the news that a new secret weapon, a giant rocket called a V2 as opposed to the V1 flying bomb, had fallen by the garage at Potters Bar and another had fallen on a crowded Woolworths store at Kingsbury. The gang talked in hushed tones about this new menace. Surely, when the war was going well at last, Hitler had not found yet another way to foil and disappoint the Allies?

I didn't get another chance to talk to Jackie that afternoon and I did not like the way Ballie was hanging round her. Freddy took her home that night in the farm van while I sheeted down the precious corn and combine. "It's your responsibility now," said Teddy. "You are the 'Combine Kiddo' so you must see to it that it is covered up at night and thoroughly greased in the morning, so see it gets done." I

96

sighed. I had hoped to see more of the girl; but at least I had been put in charge of the combine: this must be worth something. Still, I didn't even like the thought of steady old married Freddy being with the girl, and a strange feeling of loneliness came over me.

During the night our sleep was disturbed many times by the wailing of sirens as fresh waves of V1s chugged their way into London. Most fell long before reaching the northern suburbs; and South London was in a desperate situation. My brother-in-law, Alex, was home on leave; and as one bomb could be heard approaching, the entire family crammed into the "Morrison Table" shelter. This was an amazing box of sheet metal, angle iron and wire net, which had saved many lives. My brother-in-law swore in disbelief when I insisted everyone took cover. The bomb's motor cut and it whistled past the house to explode somewhere past Apex Corner. Alex lit a fag; his hand was shaking. "Bugger that," he said. "Let me get back to France; I would rather be shot at by Jerry tanks I can see, than sit listening to those bloody things coming." By now, we had all got used to jumping in fright when V2s crashed down without warning. We all agreed that these rockets, though devastatingly destructive, were not half as frightening as the V1s which could be heard coming and took so long to arrive.

When I got on the bus next day, Jackie was already on board and we managed to sit together listening to everyone's bomb stories. It was nothing like as bad as the Blitz, said some. Others who had been to Dartford and other South London areas were not so sure. Jackie and I spoke very little. A soldier sitting opposite eyed us speculatively, wondering perhaps about our relationship. I certainly looked a bit of a gypsy, whereas Jackie looked what she was, a slightly posh student or teacher with an almost Oxford accent.

When we got to the farm on Totteridge, we were surprised to see an army truck in the yard. Standing in the barn were three rather sullen-looking men in dark brown battledress with large blue circular patches on their backs. All three were darkly handsome and when they spoke, it was obvious that they were Italian prisoners of war. I looked at them grimly. There had been a nasty incident when I was working on Mr Hope's farm in Bedfordshire. A party of Italian prisoners of war had been set on, gathering the dried stems of mangold seed heads at a local plant breeders' holding. One of the armed soldiers guarding them – for all POWs were escorted in the early days – had squatted in a ditch to relieve himself. Seizing the opportunity, an Italian prisoner had beheaded the unfortunate soldier with the hedging knife which he had been using to cut the seed heads. The prisoner had then stolen the dead soldier's rifle and made off. For two days the countryside had been in fear of the desperado who, having killed once, was unlikely to show mercy to anyone who got in his way. Several cottages were broken into but only food was stolen. Eventually, the fugitive had been found asleep on a bed by a cottager. Two Home Guardsmen had shot the sleeping fugitive repeatedly in their nervous excitement; and the chase was over. Later it transpired that he had gone to the cottage where his English lover lived but she had not been there. He must have fallen asleep through sheer exhaustion while awaiting her return. It was a dramatic little incident, and tragic, as most wartime deaths were. Compared with the scale of slaughter occurring daily, on land and in the air, it was insignificant; but it had made a lasting impression upon me.

Now at Ensten's farm, two young Land Army girls were sitting with a young soldier in the lorry cab, giggling and snorting as they exchanged badinage. When they saw Jackie and me, they explained that Fred and Teddy had gone to Potters Bar in search of a better corn trailer for the combine. Old Ron was taking the two girls, the POWs and their soldier guard to stook sheaves in a field which had been cut with a binder and was to be threshed later for seed. This old-fashioned procedure was because the peg drum of our combine cracked the grains and made them unsuitable for seed.

Jackie had been allocated to help me to service the combine while the corn dried as the morning dew evaporated in the warm sunshine. The unshaven and disreputable Ballie leered meaningfully at this news. "Gonna give 'er a good greasin', are yer?"

Both landgirls giggled at my blushes. "Come on, girl," I said to Jackie, covering my embarrassment with rudeness.

"Not so much of the girl, thank you," said Jackie. "I am at least three years older than you."

I said nothing but set off, head lowered, down the lane, carrying a grease gun and a keg of grease. Jackie took the second grease gun proffered by old Ron and set off after me. "Have fun!" shouted one of the landgirls. Neither of us looked back; and as Jackie strode past me, there was an eloquently angry tightness about her receding back view suggestive of angrily pursed lips.

Greasing the combine proved harder than had been expected. Canadians were evidently a race of dwarf proportions. At any rate, there was no way I could get through the small hatches to grease the main bearings on the straw walkers, which carried threshing waste from the drum to the rear of the machine where it fell to the ground. Jackie was laughing at my muffled curses when I emerged, red-faced and angry, from the hatch where I had been hanging upside down, trying in vain to reach the grease nipples. My flushed face darkened. I could not bear being laughed at, and by some snobby teacher at that. "You come up here and try it then, clever breeches." The girl's chin tightened. "All right then, I will," she said. Thoroughly angry, I got down and prepared to help her up onto the machine. "I can manage," she said. "Just tell me what to do."

I blushed, embarrassed for the second time in close succession. It was too much for a teenager. How was I going to tell her to find the nipples and give them a good greasing? I stammered, "Find the little projecting bits and try to get the mouth of the grease gun onto them."

The girl looked straight into my eyes, mischievously. "These little projecting bits, don't they have a name?"

By now, I was beside myself with embarrassment and the suspicion that I was being teased. "Nipples," I said. "Grease nipples." A voice came from the open hatch, so strangely distorted, I could not tell if it was from the effort of climbing into the machine; or could she possibly be laughing at me? Through the opening I could see her shorts drawn tightly across her nicely rounded bottom, but little else. "Did you say 'nipples'? Did you say get the mouth on the nipples?" followed by a snort of pain or laughter. I once more felt a warm tightening and a flutter in my loins. Could she possibly be making sexy jokes?

Was this how posh birds went on? The girl's tousled head, slightly soiled with grease and well-sprinkled with barley awns and chaff, emerged from the hatch. If she had been laughing, her face was straight now. "I think I've made a good job of that," she said. I went to help her down and this time she accepted my help, laughing with her eyes as she slid down into my arms, resting against me perhaps just a second too long. Or did I imagine it? Flushed and confused, I got down under the cutting platform of the great harvester and started to check the mechanism.

"What are you doing?" asked a voice, very close to my ear. I lifted my head quickly, banging it on the suspension. "Oh, Lord, now you've bumped your head, just when I wanted you to get some straw out of my eye!"

I rolled over and found Jackie close beside me on the warm ground. I reached into my pocket for a handkerchief, noticing an alertness within, which I bent to conceal. "Can't see anything there," I said, amazed to find such depth of cornflower blue in eyes which looked into mine with disarming innocence.

"I think it's better now. What about your poor head?" she said, putting a gentle hand on my brow and drawing it gently down my cheek, brushing my ear. I groaned and as I moved away she held me with my hand trapped against her breast. "Don't go," she whispered. "I am sure I can hear one of those 'doodlebugs' coming and I am so frightened." I fell back next to the girl, not sure whether my adrenalin was flowing because of the approaching flying bomb or the warm softness of her against the back of my hand.

It was no flying bomb. The noise of a passing motorcycle receded but I stayed where I was, scarcely daring to breathe. Slowly I moved my hand, turning it until it rested round her breast, and I felt a nipple pressing into the softer skin in the cup of my palm. She had not moved back and it had been a deliberate feel. I held my breath and began to squeeze just hard enough to really feel the joyful softness; when in a rush of movement, she was holding me close to her body, her lips seeking mine. I was suddenly aware of her rapid breathing and the bland softness of her tongue. Time seemed to stand still. Over her shoulder I could see a weevil climbing a corn stalk and a silvery streak where the paint had peeled from an aluminium bolt. I seemed to see every mundane object with incredible clarity. Bloody hell! I thought; could it be going to happen? Fearfully I pressed my knee between hers and felt them part slightly. A little more pressure and she moved them apart, lifting her head away from me to look into my face as I moved my leg slowly between hers. Jackie sighed and I wondered if I dared to put a hand on her stomach. I did, and she smiled gently as I edged it so softly downwards until there could be no doubt it was over forbidden fruit.

I paused. This was heaven! It was all so different from my fumbling attempt at lovemaking with Doris in the Bedfordshire moonlight. Should I risk losing this sudden but oh so gentle experience of near paradise; or should I stay where I was? Jackie was moving slightly and it was with shock that I recognised the age-old rhythm: ever so gently, her pelvis was thrusting. My hand now turned until it was cupping the whole of her secret parts through the cottony material. Jackie moaned and I felt for the fasteners of her shorts. At once she pulled back and pushed me away. "Do you really think I am like that?" she said in a hostile voice, trembling with what I took to be indignation.

I was speechless; my experience of girls had not yet included the lessons concerning the contrary nature of a woman's immediate reactions. When did "no" mean no? When did a certain cadence to "no" mean "yes" or "maybe"? To increase my confusion, an aching knot had developed somewhere at the base of my stomach and I suspected it was the "lover's nuts" I had heard older men joke about. "Do you? Do you think I am like that?" She was staring at me with such emotion on her face that I was frightened for a moment that she might scream or become hysterical. I was silent; then, very gently, I kissed her forehead, and holding her upper arms I spoke softly: "I didn't really think at all." I paused. "It just sort of happened. I wasn't looking for it. I never have looked for it but if adventure comes my way, I would not refuse it." I paused again, reflecting on my own words which, in my imagination, a screen hero might have used.

"Lord!" said the girl. "You really are innocent!" I smiled to myself. Not really, I thought; not if she knew what I think when I look at her breasts and wonder what there is hidden under those shorts. I suppose I am just as filthy as Ballie, only I keep it to myself... "No hard feelings then?" said the girl, smiling up into my face. "No," said I ruefully; the ache in my lower belly was now acute. "Let's finish servicing the combine, then," said the girl cheerfully; and she got up, brushing a few crumbs of soil and chaff from her long legs, on which I noticed a fine covering of golden hair which shone in the sun against the shiny brown skin. Hell! I said to myself, not from frustration or self-reproach for the missed opportunity; I was not really an opportunist. It was just that my whole lower abdomen seemed to be contracting into a ball of pain. I hobbled round the machine. "Good heavens, what's wrong with you?" said the girl. I mumbled miserably, "I don't know, maybe I've got guts ache from too many bloody plums or something." Turning away I walked back up the lane to the yard.

The farmer's wife was just coming out of the house, shouting at the dogs. She always shouted in her high penetrating voice; and as I turned into the main farmyard, she could see I was in pain. At once she loudly diagnosed colic from eating too many plums and packed me off home. I, who had not yet eaten a single plum that summer, was gobstruck. However, the prospect of an afternoon off with a hot water bottle on my belly did not seem too bad.

Jackie returned alone some time later with the grease keg and guns. On hearing that I had gone home early, she asked what was wrong. "Not a lot," said the disgusting Ballie with a fruity leer. "It's 'is plums, 'e's got plum colic, used to happen to me when I was young." He paused to leer at her again. "Should've thought you'd know how to cure him."

After lunch, Jackie was sent to join the landgirls and the Italian prisoners of war. She later told me she had missed me, but there was work to be done; and she was soon busy stooking the soft but itchy barley sheaves which the binder had left in tidy rows. The Italians were working busily and had already finished one field. Jackie later told me that she had gone to look for a spot in the bushes for a pee. Pushing a low branch aside she almost stepped on one of the landgirls and the young soldier, who were lying partly undressed in the long yellow grass. "Mind where you tread," said the soldier grinning, and making no attempt to hide what he and the girl were doing.

Jackie flushed and hastened away. By now she was desperate for a pee but the other girl had come across the field to talk to her. Crossing her legs, she made polite conversation until the girl went back to join the Italians. At last she was able to slip down her shorts and relieve her bladder. "Feel better now, ducks?" It was the disgusting Ballie getting up from the bole of a tree where he had crouched, watching her. "What about a little feel round then?" Ballie continued with a toothy leer. Crimson, Jacky hurried over to join the other girl and the Italians. The handsome men had all discarded their shirts and she could not help looking at their shining olive skin, drenched with sweat as the muscles rippled and shone. "The whole atmosphere was charged with sex!" she told me later. What she did not tell me then was that she had felt very turned on by all the day's happenings and would have been desperately frustrated if the work had not been so hard.

By about six o'clock the barley was all stooked and as there was no other work planned for the evening, they all opted for a night off. Jacky had been very relieved. She did not like the way Ballie was hanging round. She had hastily collected her belongings and caught the bus to Mill Hill. She had, she told me, wondered how I was!

Chapter Five

Eve's Pudding

I enjoyed the afternoon in bed with a good book. There were no flying bomb alarms or rocket explosions and it was, for an hour or two, like those glorious school holidays before the war when I had been spoiled by the maids and my mother, when she was well, and my sisters when she was not. My father brought me some lunch in bed and commented, with a twinkling eye, that my stomach pains had not affected my hearty appetite.

In the evening Jackie called to see how I was and with her usual enigmatic smile asked how my "plum colic" was. I did not know how to answer. I was now sure that my affliction was linked to my amorous adventures earlier that day and that I was, indeed, suffering from what I had heard the farm men refer to as "lover's nuts". No doubt my workmates would have fun completing my education and discomfiture next morning. I hoped that Jackie would not be there. Somewhere in my mind a doubt was growing about her innocent smile.

I decided that I was fit enough to get up, having enjoyed the brief respite from heavy work. I joined my father, Jackie and my sister Daphne downstairs. As they talked about the previous night's bombs and damage, Jackie and my sister were busy making what passed for an omelette from the wartime dried egg and dried milk. As she put the chewy yellow pancake down in front of me Jackie said, "Mind you masticate well!"

"Golly!" said my sister. "I wondered what you said just for a moment!" The girl Jackie looked at me and went back into the kitchen, shaking with suppressed giggles. My dad looked over his spectacles, shaking his head reprovingly; but was there just the trace of a smile at the corner of his lips? I was astounded. I could not believe that a posh girl like Jackie could have heard about, let alone laugh at, something my masters at school and the farm men regarded as a shameful habit! Especially as it was a shameful but extraordinarily pleasant habit which, I thought, I alone had failed to grow out of. Why does God always make the nicest things wicked? I had asked myself this many times as I grew up. I had not yet learned that growing up was learning what to reject and what to hang on to, of what other people taught, thought and said.

The subject of "mastication" was not pursued but it was obvious to me that Jackie had established an intimate friendship with my sister, which placed them on a more mature plane than me. Once more despite my assumption of manliness, my maturity seemed to be undermined by the almost telepathic conspiracy of superiority shared by young women. "Let's go out," I said to Jackie.

We helped clear away the supper things, said our goodnights and went out into a balmy September evening. Dad, who was due on firewatch duty at the air raid post, walked up the road with us. We passed a house where someone was playing an Artie Shaw record of "Stardust". Shaw's soaring clarinet and Billy Butterfield's trumpet seemed to reach up to the scudding harvest moon creating a totally unreal feeling of romantic peace. My dad looked up at the sky. He loved to talk about his days at sea. "It's the same moon I have watched from the decks of sailing ships and tramp steamers all over the world," he reminisced. "I never expected to watch it wearing a tin hat in Mill Hill with half the world in flames round us." I knew what my father meant but it was so peaceful at that moment that I was embarrassed by the seemingly melodramatic little speech.

Almost at once, the far-off wail of sirens grew louder as one by one the nearer air raid posts set off their alarms. "Time you two were off home," said my Dad. I put my arm round the girl's waist and we set off to walk across the railway bridge towards her home. As we rounded the corner a policeman stepped out and asked what we were doing.

"Just going home," said I.

"You can't go down there. They haven't cleared up the mess from last night's bombs and there's a body or two not found yet."

The girl shuddered and we made our way back round the park towards her parents' house. Life is so funny, I thought, and so out of proportion. All the adults seem to worry about is whether their children are behaving; and are their daughters still virgins? Sudden death and desperate danger to their own lives and property don't seem to worry them. Funny thing, war, if it were not so bloody bloody. I thought of Billy, my brother, dead and fishfood somewhere in the Irish Sea; of my three pals from the youth club, dead under the rubble of the flat on Watling estate, minutes after leaving me. I thought of the poor old mums who never stopped grieving. I wondered why mothers always seemed to be the worst affected. My dad had loved Billy dearly, but could already reminisce about Billy's exploits with pleasure rather than grief.

"You've gone off somewhere again!" said Jackie, bringing me back from my reverie. I realised that I was not fulfilling the attentive and protective role I imagined for myself.

Before I could reply, Jackie told me about her embarrassment in the barley field that afternoon and her revulsion at the disgusting Ballie. She also told me about the landgirl and the soldier. She mentioned the sexy atmosphere without indicating approval or disapproval. She seemed to dwell a lot on the Italian prisoners' bodies and the effect of their brown torsos. Seeing that I was once more in deep thought about what she had told me, she spoke again. "Let's take the short cut across the park," she said. I, ever hopeful for more romance, agreed readily.

I held her small hand diffidently, not quite sure what to expect after the morning's events in the cornfield at Totteridge. Her hand felt warm and friendly enough and her thigh brushed mine as we walked along. She did not seem to be distancing herself from me and even seemed to press closer when I allowed my hand to slip upwards towards the swell of her breast. My mind wandered back to her laughter at supper and her risqué remarks earlier. Her matter-of-fact description of the rural amours she had witnessed during the afternoon puzzled me too. I really did not know where I stood with her and I did not want to spoil our friendship by moving too fast.

As we passed the tennis courts, I saw the hexagonal shelter where, in daylight, old men sat on the benches chatting and discussing the war news. At dusk the well-worn benches were the scene of much groping and giggling amongst my friends from the church youth fellowship, especially on Sunday nights after Evensong. For a brief period the romance of high church Anglo Catholicism had ensnared several of us. An able and charismatic vicar had inspired many of the local adolescents with a need for organised faith, after so many of their young friends, older brothers and even fathers had been killed or maimed in the bombing or on the distant battlefields and oceans.

I myself had fallen under Father Redcar's spell; but that which convinced the nicely brought up young suburbanites did not stick long on a partially brutalised seventeen-year-old, who had seen and lived in a very different world. I was suspicious of and hostile to "Christian morality". Hitler was a "Christian"!

My thoughts returned to the more pleasurable subject of petting on the benches. I chuckled. "Now what are you laughing at?" said the girl. I told her of the Christmas midnight service when the stalwarts of the youth fellowship had been organised into the "production team". Most of the lads had been up at the Rising Sun on Highwood Hill, an ancient pub of great charm, run by the Halifaxes. Mrs Halifax was a bustling, outspoken lady who loved the gang of young lads who, underage or not, supped huge quantities of the weak wartime ale as they sang, played darts, boasted of conquests and were generally full of good-natured exuberance. The lads gave no trouble when the hollow-cheeked and sadly chesty Mr Halifax called for order or time, and the lads were treated with indulgent respect by the local ancients who made up the rest of the clientele while the real men were away at the war.

This particular night, some of the lads were the worse for wear when they arrived at St Michaels, our parish church in Mill Hill. Tom Cochrane was the picture of innocence as he led the choir down the nave in his black cassock and white surplice, followed by well-scrubbed, cherub-faced choirboys, one or two of whose rosiness owed at least something to the skills of Taylor Walker the local brewer.

The illumination was reduced to the glow of candlelight in preparation for a spectacular flood of light and great ethereal chords from Mr Footit at the organ on the stroke of midnight. A reverent hush fell. Young Roxborough had been put in charge of the lights and instructed to cut off the power. An even younger lad, Billy Towle, was pumping the organ bellows manually to allow a gentle organ voluntary to continue in the near darkness. Flickering candles, a smell of incense and gentle strains of Bach generated an atmosphere of peace and goodwill to all men. Unfortunately, Billy was unable to contain his ale and being trapped in a tiny space behind the organ consul, he was forced to pee in the metal fire bucket. Perhaps if it had not been a metal bucket, perhaps if Bach had not been so gentle, perhaps if the acoustics of the building had not amplified the tinkle into a tattoo, clearly audible to the congregation and to Mr Footit the organist, things might have gone differently. Perhaps Mr Footit might not have struck a mighty chord to drown the apparently endless flow of Billy's bladder; but he did. Young Roxborough, hearing the crash of music, pulled down the power switch and the lights flooded back on, revealing a terrified Billy trying to stop the flow and wrestling to replace his still streaming widdler with one hand, while attempting to resume pumping the organ bellows with the other.

Roxborough, appalled by the scene his action had revealed, shut off the power again. The organ chords subsided with the despairing wail of a drowning elephant and the building was once more plunged into darkness. Billy, fearing retribution, scrambled damply from the scene of his crime and fled. Someone had the presence of mind to turn on the power; Roxborough had also fled but the resourceful Mr Footit was belting out good Christmas jollies. The vicar, however, screened from these dreadful sights and having a poor ear for music, apparently took the strange sound and lighting effects to be an intentional if unusual programme. After all, Bartok's new violin concerto had recently been played in the church hall and it had certainly sounded "unusual" to both himself and his wife. "Modern stuff, I suppose," he thought to himself, before launching into a Christmas homily on the virtues of Christian youth. I, who had seen Tom Cochrane revering or attempting to roger a willing girl chorister on the very benches which Jackie and I were now passing, had not been able to contain myself on hearing the innocent vicar's words. Wild visions of the congregation following Tom's example of virtuous behaviour flashed before me. A desperate attack of *fou rire* forced me to leave the church, hiccupping and clutching myself to avoid wet trousers.

When I had finished my partially true but no doubt exaggerated story, I peered anxiously at the girl in the dim light of the moon. She bent and stroked the park bench with a flash of white teeth and a tinkle of laughter. "I must meet this Tom," was all she said... Taking her seriously, I felt a pang of jealousy. We walked on in silence and she detected my mood. "You are a big booby," she said, squeezing my hand. "No one's going to roger me on a park bench!"

I was amazed yet again at her frankness. I had never heard a "posh" girl talk like this about sex, although the tough landgirls and camp followers I had mixed with on the American air base in Bedfordshire had left little unsaid. Indeed, my concept of the act of love had been badly tarnished by their trivialization of the great mystery. I felt at once hot, cold and breathless at her words. She smiled at me. "You really are a big softy, aren't you?" She reached up and kissed me softly but hungrily on my trembling lips. At once a warm flood of relief and happiness was released as I held her soft and enveloping body close. Close, and moving against me. A pang of pleasure welled up and thrilled me, broke suddenly and left me weak, twitching and ashamed. As if she sensed my loss, she became gentle and said quietly, "We'd better get on home. The sirens have gone and Mum frets if she doesn't know where I am when there is an air raid on. Anyway, we've got a busy day working the combine in that corn tomorrow." A little uncomfortable and damply cold, I agreed.

We were soon at her door. I, fearful that the stains of my "discomfort" might be visible, did not go in but kissed her tenderly. "Goodnight," I said, "and thank you." The girl smiled at me. "I can't imagine what for," she said with a rather wicked smile, and went indoors quickly. As I walked home I wondered if she knew what she had done to me. I felt embarrassed but at the same time pleased with myself. When I reached home I went straight upstairs.

"How is the tummy?" called my dad.

"Okay," said I. "It seems to have cured itself."

I thought I heard a snort of laughter from my sister's room.

I climbed wearily into bed. It had been an eventful day and I was a long time dropping off. Images of the girl kept flashing before me. Had all those things really happened? A slight ache at my loins assured me that they had. Did the girl know she had made me come? My "plum colic" had gone.

Was the disgusting Ballie right when he said she should know how to cure me?

There were several air raid alarms during the night but I, once asleep, heard nothing. My dreams were full of work, harvest fields and bomb site rubble. When I did wake up, I was disappointed to find I had not dreamed of Jackie.

The next day dawned bright and sunny. I went off to work in a brown boiler suit and had swung my toolbag on my shoulder in case there were problems with the combine harvester. Jackie was on the bus and chatted cheerfully about her work at Hendon Tech. She had only a few more days' holiday and was not looking forward to going back and teaching "the brats". I was silent and gave no hint of my thoughts. These "brats" she spoke of would be of my own age but educated. I did not yet know the difference between "qualified" and "educated". Not for the first time, I bitterly regretted having left school before taking Common Entrance, let alone School Certificate. It seemed to me that there was an insurmountable hurdle between myself and civilized people. I was at real low ebb and cursed my stupidity. It was not possible to go back to school and my lack of qualifications barred me, even from agricultural college; but in any case, these were all closed for the duration of the war.

The bus arrived at Totteridge Post Office and we got off and walked into the yard. We were soon swept into the maelstrom of dust, chaff and smoky engine fumes as the gang rushed to make the most of a fine hot day.

There was no opportunity to talk until the dinner break when I was relieved at my post on the dusty smoking combine. I gulped fresh air and threw myself down on the stubble headland of the field along with Jackie and the others whose turn it was for a break. To my chagrin, I found Freddy the farmer's son on one side of Jackie and the disgusting Ballie on the other. Ballie was leering at her and making suggestive remarks, which, to my annoyance, seemed to amuse her.

A tremendous roar of aircraft engines drowned out all conversation as squadron after squadron of American Martin Marauder bombers swept over on their way to Holland or Belgium where the advancing British armour was pushing for the Rhine. "All those lovely men up there," sighed Betty the landgirl. Jackie laughed her agreement. I felt diminuished. For the first time I realised that I was probably regarded as less than other young men because I was not in uniform. I had, in fact, haunted the recruiting office at Edgware Drill Hall, only to be told that my classification under the notorious Essential Works Order prevented me from escaping the underpaid and at times hungry drudgery of my farm job, and exchanging it for what appeared to me to be the glamour and possible glory of the Forces. Indeed, it seemed that when my call-up eventually came due, I would have to be a Bevin Boy and go down a coal mine, so short was the country of essential coal and the men to dig it.

At last Freddie and Ballie got up and went back to work. I was shy of moving too quickly; but Jackie slid next to me and looked closely into my face. "You seem very grim today," she said. "Have I done something wrong?"

I smiled. "No. It's just that I don't like being your bit of holiday fun."

The girl's eyes filled with tears. "Oh, Terry! You are so silly. Don't you know I love you?"

I was filled with mixed emotions. I did not know what to say. I did not yet love the girl. I knew I wanted her badly and I was very jealous of the other men being near her; but love was an emotion my tough peers scorned as weakness. It had never really occurred to me that she might really love me. She was "posh" and educated, apart from being several years older. I was flattered but a little afraid.

"No, I didn't know," I said, gruffly pulling her to me. "Love is a very big word and I don't think I am ready to honestly say I love you. But let's be friends and enjoy what time we have left together before you go back to your own sort of people."

Jackie's face was blotchy and puffed but I felt very tender towards her. We sat holding each other until I had to go back to the great dusty combine harvester. The rest of the gang left us alone for once, as if sensing the mini-drama between the boy and the young woman.

That night we missed the bus and walked across Belmont Farm to Mill Hill Ridgeway. We passed Belmont, Mill Hill Junior School, where I had once been one of the posh kids and eventually, Head Boy... I did not tell her. It would have taken too long to explain how I had become a rough farm worker; and I wanted to enjoy my last few hours with her. Diverting onto Millfield, we sat on the damp grass and looked down across the valley between Mill Hill Ridgeway and Harrow on the Hill. I thought back to the night in September 1938 only five years earlier when, as a twelve-year-old boy, I had first been evacuated with the school to the safety of Cumberland. How bright the valley had been then, bejewelled with brilliant lights. How happy and secure my family had been. In the moonlight, the blacked-out valley looked deserted and almost rural. A lone aircraft throbbed overhead. Almost casually, I commented that it sounded like a Jerry. We watched with interest as first one then a second searchlight started groping for the intruder. A sudden brilliant light broke out in the sky as a great cluster of parachute flares lit up the whole of the suburb below them.

From the Colindale side of Hendon aerodrome, a Bofors gun barked, sending a string of red tracer shell up at the flares which continued their lazy descent downwards. The groping searchlights now caught a tiny silver shape which turned and weaved in a cone of light as other searchlights joined the search. A shattering roar seemed to rip open the darkness around us. It was the battery of 4.5 anti-aircraft guns behind the Rising Sun on Highwood Hill several hundred yards away. I was familiar with these guns as I had danced with the young ATS girls who worked the range-finder predictors. Once I had walked back to the camp with one of the girls and she had kidded the guard house to let me in for a hot drink and biscuits. I had felt very proud to be her escort and behaved like a perfect gentleman. It was only next day that one of my workmates, who was younger and much, much scruffier, told me that she was well known for seducing young locals, just for a laugh. "She's known as the camp bicycle," said the disgusting Ballie, on hearing that I had not had my way with her; "everybody rides her!"

The little silver dot was making off towards the open country behind Watford and one by one the searchlights gave up the chase. In a way I felt glad, just as I did when the fox got away from the hounds or the rabbits escaped unharmed from the shooting men who flocked to the farm as the cornfields shrank before the combine harvester and the terrified rabbits, hares and partridges broke cover. Jackie was trembling and I started to get up, thinking she was cold and would want to hurry home.

"Hold me, please hold me," she pleaded.

I bent over her and lifted her against my chest. She breathed heavily in great long intakes and sibilant outbreaths which excited me enormously. "Love me, Terry, love me here, now."

The boy in me – for I was still only a boy – hesitated. I had only had one fumbled and very basic tumble in Bedfordshire the previous year... I had not known what the girl needed to make it a pleasant experience for her too; and I had been puzzled and mortified when she expressed dissatisfaction. There had been no foreplay, and an element of force in my approach which I regretted and for which I felt shame for months afterwards, especially as my gleeful confidences to the farm men had been betrayed and the poor girl ragged about our brief encounter. Still, we had parted friends. I never knew if she had been a virgin and I hoped not.

"What's the matter?" said Jackie. "Don't you want me?"

I stroked her hair and kissed her as passionately as I dared. She responded with low moans and sighs, pushing against me with the sort of vigour I had thought only randy men would use. "Hold me close, closer, closer," she said; and I felt her legs close around me as she rolled me onto my back and was now sitting over me pressing hard on my chest with flat open palms, at the same time working her pelvis against my now feverish loins. I was aware of the total impossibility of fulfilling the act. I was in a boiler suit and she was in a bib and brace overall beneath a stout sweater. There was no way we could get at each other's bodies without awkward and humiliating contortions and horrific exposures which would destroy the romance of our passion. Jackie was moving and breathing faster and faster; her sighing and groaning were almost frightening me. I was terrified I would be finished too soon again.

Quite suddenly, she gave a huge groan and clamped me with her legs as she fell forward onto my chest. "I am sorry," she said. "What must you think of me?" I felt great, I felt superb. I was still in control of my urges and felt very manly. "I think you are marvellous," I said and gently crushed her to me. I did not feel frustrated; rather, I felt as though I had put off a treat for another day.

We lay there for a long time before walking the rest of the way to her home. Jackie stopped in a telephone box to repair her face and comb her hair in front of the tiny mirror before walking past the last few houses to her gate. As I was about to say goodnight, her mother called us in. I was terrified, expecting an inquest and tearful rebukes for my tardiness in bringing her daughter home from the dangers of the night, quite apart from any suspicions that her parents might have had about our doings on the way home. "We missed the bus and walked," I began.

"Don't blame you, old chap," said Jackie's dad with the suspicion of a wink. "Its a lovely night, in spite of Jerry." Mrs Henderson brought in a large tray with steaming cocoa and a delicious apple sponge with hot custard. "Got to keep your strength up, young man. You are probably still growing too."

Mr Henderson snorted as he filled his pipe. Jackie appeared to be choking and looked away from me as I flushed and choked. "He can't grow much more, he's big enough already!" Mrs Henderson heaped my plate with the delicious sweet. Jackie sat on the arm of her father's chair and beamed at me: "I made that. It's called Eve's Pudding."

I walked, tired but happy, back to my father's house on the little crescent off the Watford Way. "Had a good day, boy?" asked my dad.

"Yes, Dad, we've had a great day. We got the thirty acre harvested and a start on the wheat below Belmont. It was Jackie's last day at work but I expect she will come back on her weekends off." I found that I was finding it a pleasure just to mention Jackie's name. My sister Daphne put her head round the door. "Are you hungry?" she asked. "I'll cook you something. " "No, thank you," I said with manly pride. "Jackie's mum gave us some supper." I paused and said proudly, "I've just had my first helping of Eve's pudding."

Jackie went back to her teaching at Hendon Tech and I settled back into the grind of autumn work. The harvest tailed off into a damp struggle to claw in the last of the grain. One Sunday, when the gang were busy carting off sheaves of malting barley, a seemingly endless stream of Halifax and Stirling bombers mixed with Dakota transports passed overhead. Most of the bombers towed ungainly Horsa gliders, some of which followed steadily on their long tow lines; others weaved drunkenly as they attempted to keep some sort of formation. The noise was deafening as the great machines wallowed overhead with their charges. The gang's work came to a standstill as we marvelled at the sight of so many aircraft. As they roared off into the east, I imagined all the fully armed airborne soldiers sitting cramped in the gliders and fervently wished the poor buggers luck.

The military war seemed suddenly closer. The endless successes which had followed the breakout from Normandy had made the daily flying bombs and rockets a bearable if terrifying experience. This great armada of low-flying and very vulnerable-looking aircraft was somehow much more real than the high-flying disciplined squadrons of Flying Fortresses and Liberators, which we had become used to seeing as they set out on their daily bombing missions.

That night, on the BBC news, we heard that an airborne landing had been made to seize the bridges over the river Rhine at Arnhem in Holland. The general opinion was that the war in Europe would soon be over in spite of the stubborn fight the Wermacht was putting up along the north bank of the Scheldt River and on the islands commanding the approach to Antwerp. The denial of this port as a supply base for the Allied advance towards the North German plain was a severe problem to the Allies who were also coming to a halt on the central front as General Patton's 6th army ran short of fuel and shells.

I thought a lot about Jackie and even went with her one Saturday to a dance at the Technical College. However I felt rough, prickly and out of place amongst the sleek, self-satisfied students and staff, many of whom paid a great deal of attention to Jackie. I didn't like being one of a crowd of admirers and an interloper at that. Over the next few months, as the golden harvest turned into the backbreaking, grey mud of potato-lifting and then the frosty rawness of mangold-pulling, the romance cooled and faded. The farm men told me that I had been a fool not to make the most of my chances. "Tha should ha' bulled her, mate! Once she'd had that great thing o'thine inside 'er she'd ha' never left yer!" I agreed in some ways. I would certainly have liked a stable sexual relationship but I did not love Jackie and feared the possible social and practical consequences.

I did not regard my present situation as a real one. One day I had to be better off with prospects but I could not see how. My father's romantic vision of having our own farm one day seemed a fast-fading prospect. I certainly did not want to be like so many of my mates on the farms who all seemed to get girls into trouble and have to marry them. The resulting poverty and squalor of life with a family to support on a pitiful wage appalled me. I was not sure if it was wisdom or cowardice which emasculated me. It was certainly not a regard for conventional morals.

The war dragged on. The optimism of the Arnhem landings faded as a sad and shocked public realised once more that the enemy's strength and will to resist had not been broken by our overwhelming air superiority. The 88mm guns which had decimated the 8th army tanks in the desert three years earlier were still capable of holding up the armoured divisions trying to move up the causeway like roads linking Neimhagen, Eindhoven and the beleaguered handful of airborne survivors holding out at Arnhem.

The bold stroke to end the war had failed.

Some of my age group in Mill Hill started to receive their call-up papers. The unlucky ones were sent to work in the coal mines as Bevin Boys. The lucky ones went off, fairly sure the war would be over by the time they were trained; and they confidently expected a cushy billet in the occupying army. My boss told me that I was unlikely to be called up as the government was giving agriculture absolute priority due to the resurgence of submarine attacks on shipping which together with the demands of liberated areas were causing severe food shortages. I had mixed feelings about this. I had always wanted to get into the RAF and was bored with the farming scene, having learned all I could and having no prospects for promotion in the presence of two farmer's sons.

The war in the Pacific hardly entered our minds as the Americans seemed to be rolling up the Japanese front, "island hopping" towards the mainland. The colossal cost in men, ships and materials was not reflected in the jubilant press reports. Even the "forgotten" 14th Army was on the move in Burma. As Christmas 1944 drew near, the flying bombs and rockets petered out as the Allied troops overran the launching sites in the Low Countries. Squadrons of

RAF bombers were now passing over in daylight to join the American bombers in devastating Germany. The Arnhem disaster was being treated as an epic rearguard action and there had been a mini-Dunkirk evacuation thanks to heroic efforts by Polish troops, who somehow improvised ferries to bring survivors back across the Rhine.

Just before Christmas, von Runstedt counter-attacked the American army through the Ardennes using almost the same routes and tactics as for the breakthrough in May 1940, but under cover of fog and low cloud instead of the clouds of Stuka bombers and air supremacy. The vastly superior tanks of the German Panzers, together with bold deceptions and dashing thrusts, completely demoralized the American troops; and one whole army group, finding themselves cut off in the high country in severe winter conditions, surrendered with little resistance. The road to Liege, Namur and Antwerp seemed open. However, speed and an early success were vital to the German attack. Heroic American resistance at vital road junctions and at besieged Bastogne delayed the lightning advance sufficiently for reinforcements to be brought into action. Shortage of fuel slowed the Panzer spearheads which had bypassed Bastogne and threatened to "motor" unopposed into the American rear with devastating results. As the weather cleared, the allied air superiority helped stabilize the front but not before the Luftwaffe, in a last despairing throw, caused havoc by staging a massive offensive against allied aircraft on the ground and in the air where the new German jets were proving vastly superior to both RAF and American fighters. Fortunately, Hitler's personal interference had hindered quantity production of these new fighters.

General Montgomery took partial command of the "Battle of the Bulge". The British Sixth Airborne were recalled from Christmas leave and the desperate position was gradually reversed. It was Hitler's last fling in the West.

The freezing weather, which was now making movement possible through the waterlogged fronts, was not equally appreciated on the farm. Tractors refused to start. Frozen water troughs were surrounded by bellowing thirsty cattle and hours were wasted thawing out and carting water which slopped and froze solid on the men's clothes. I had no doubt it was worse for the soldiers at the fronts, especially the Russian fronts, but every morning seemed to bring fresh problems and hardships. I was beginning to appreciate that farming was largely a war against the forces of nature. There were tides and seasons when one could harness these forces; but basically, farming was a struggle to conquer nature. A struggle which was never more than partially successful.

One of my jobs was to collect swill from the RAF cookhouse at Hendon aerodrome. This was a welcome break from the cold and I envied the cheerful "erks" in their warm cookhouse. I looked with awe at the officers' mess which had taken a direct hit from a flying bomb with terrible carnage. I envied the smart young airmen chatting up the pretty WAAF girls who never even glanced at the overalled farm boy collecting the pigswill. My mind went back to the bright morning in March when the boss had come into the yard with some pink papers. "Do you want to go in the army straight away?" "I don't mind the army," I had said jokingly, "but I don't want to go down the mines as a Bevin Boy." "Well, it won't be either for a bit," said my boss; "I am getting you deferred." As a seventeen-year-old boy, I had been flattered at this suggestion of my importance to the farm and its all-out drive for food production. It did not occur to me that this bright morning's decision, taken instantly and without consideration, would be irrevocable and would deeply affect the rest of my life.

The New Year brought endless Russian victories as Marshall Zuchov's troops and artillery swept the German rearguards out of Poland and crossed the rivers of Eastern Europe with startling ease. Why they had been held up for so long outside Warsaw was a mystery to me. I still had faith in our Russian allies. I could not believe it had been a deliberate act to let the Germans wipe out the premature Polish rising.

Churchill had been to the front line watching the successful crossing of the Rhine; and as President Roosevelt's death hit the headlines, General Paton's columns had reached the great industrial regions of the Rhur which were quickly encircled and taken.

The end was in sight.

One night, returning from some light-hearted fun with my friends, I found my brother George had unexpectedly returned from Italy. This was not the smart, pink-faced young officer who had visited me in Cumberland prior to sailing for Egypt. This was a tough-looking, bronzed warrior in an extraordinary mixture of civilian and military garb. A black Tank Corps beret and red-spotted neckerchief topped off a battered and in places charred battledress blouse worn over sand-yellow corduroy trousers and suede desert boots.

George was now an acting Major and had escorted two senior German officers to London as part of the negotiation for a German surrender in Italy. George was now very posh, with a clipped officers' mess accent. It took some time for him to adjust to the family's reduced circumstances and he was also suffering from severe emotional shock. On returning to his young wife's flat in Finchley, for the expected joyous reunion, he had found a Canadian officer's uniform in the wardrobe and the news that his wife was away for the weekend with an American flyer. George was cheerfully aggressive about this and although deeply hurt, he threw himself into meeting his old friends and enjoying his brief leave in a wild round of nightclubs and flirtations with the many girls he had courted before the war and who were delighted to have a young beribboned English officer to escort them.

I basked in my brother's reflected glory. I was even quite pleased when Jackie asked George to squire her to a College dance. George asked me if I minded. I said no, but I could not suppress a pang of jealousy, partly of George's smart uniform. George had abandoned his "Desert Rat" outfit after being stopped by military policemen at Victoria station for being improperly dressed. "Christ, look at this one!" I had heard one say as we approached. The provost officer, wearing a perfect but almost ribbonless uniform, told George officiously that his dress was only acceptable if travelling to or from leave; otherwise, he must conform to King's regulations.

For his date with Jackie, George had raked up a tunic and Sam Browne belt from somewhere and with much polishing he now looked the perfect young cavalry officer, as befitting a 13th/18th Hussar. All the girls and women of Mill Hill loved him and he seemed determined to prove to all of them that his wife's infidelity was in no way going to spoil his leave.

I was clearly an enigma to George. When he had left for the war in the desert, I had just left a posh school as Head Boy; but now I was a particularly rough-looking farm worker. So much so that one day a police car, passing the family home as I went in, had come racing back and the occupants had jumped out and surrounded the premises. My father had opened the door to an excited policeman who told him that they had seen a rough gypsy-looking fellow go into the garden and disappear. The bewildered officer was greeted with howls of laughter from the family as the scruffy Terence, begrimed with farm dirt, was produced. For me, it was just one of many explanations I had to try and make. My workmates wanted to know why I was a workman when I had a "swell" officer for a brother and lived in a big

117

house in the posh end of Mill Hill. It was not helped by my famous family name, which connected the family with power and therefore, everyone assumed, with money. I even had an uncle in Churchill's war cabinet and a cousin, Angela, who was a rising Hollywood film star. Equally my ex-schoolfriends regarded me as something of an embarrassment while the young people of Mill Hill, with whom I now mixed, simply assumed I had no brains and it must be the work I was most suited to.

George, probably with some relief, went back to the army HQ in Italy and from his letters was having a super time being feted by the faded Roman aristocracy.

Early in May the Germans surrendered to Monty on Luneburg Heath and on May 8th the farm shut down so that the men could join in the celebrations. I went with a chum to Piccadilly to join in the fun but we felt out of it as most of the crowds were a year or two older and all seemed to have plenty of cash to eat and drink in the well-lit bars and cafes. In any case, all the girls had paired off with young men in uniform.

It was no time to be a civilian.

We walked down the Mall to Buckingham Palace in time to see Winston Churchill and the Royal Family come out and wave to the huge crowd massed in the great avenues. My companion Fred and I cheered ourselves hoarse. We felt we were witnessing history. Later, tired and hungry, we slept on the floor of a Charing Cross Station waiting room with hundreds of others. During the night someone was sick over my legs and I got up feeling depressed and filthy. I managed to clean up and refresh myself in the Gents', after which we walked to Whitehall where already the crowds were gathering to see Churchill and the Royal Family drive past.

Outside Whitehall Court I looked up at the balcony of my school's old boys club, which was packed with "good chaps". Churchill went by, his two fingers raised in a V sign. Soon after, the Royal Family drove by and several staff cars with red-tabbed generals. It was all very chaotic and disorganized but very jubilant.

I spotted some girls from the Mill Hill youth fellowship, one of whom seemed to be fainting. I pushed through the crowds and picked her up. I carried her through the crowd shouting for a gangway and was gratified by the way people stood aside and made a passage through the impenetrable mass of bodies. I strode proudly with my burden into Old Scotland Yard where she was hugely sick in a dustbin.

I half expected angry policemen to move us on but the "Yard" was deserted that day. I knew the girl vaguely as Jenny, one of the Girl Guide leaders. She soon recovered and I told her not to be embarrassed. We made our way back to the others.

At that moment, a battered lorry festooned with bunting and carrying students and young servicemen went by. Sitting on the roof of the cab were two young fellows, both with their arms round a girl who was radiant with excitement and happiness as she waved to the crowd.

It was Jackie. She did not see me; and in any case I did not want her to see me as just another face in the civilian crowd.

I felt a little pressure on my hand. Jenny looked steadily into my eyes with sympathy and kindness. "Good God," thought I, "this little girl feels sorry for me." I smiled and laughed: "Good old Jackie, always in the midst of the fun." Later we all made our way into Green Park and in the shade of the monstrous fort by Horseguards Parade Jenny and I made love: very, very gentle love. I did not know how it happened, why she let me do it or why we did it; but it was an infinitely gentle and friendly thing to do. All around us couples lay caressing in the warm May sun. Nobody seemed in the least interested or disturbed.

All day, a constant stream of Liberator and Fortress bombers flew recklessly low over the rejoicing capital. Somehow the news got round that they were flying back newly released prisoners of war. My young friends and I made our way back to Mill Hill in excellent spirits. Jenny and I talked brightly together with no lingering on what had happened between us. I did not want to start anything serious with her although it had been my first experience of willingly completed sex. I knew too that she had a boyfriend of sorts and I did not want to complicate things. I wished I had used a contraceptive but I had, I thought, used admirable control to protect her.

Funny, I thought, I never actually made it with Jackie.

When I got home I found the house in darkness. My sister Daphne, whose husband had been called up late in the war, was in bed. I heard a sound in the front room and went in. The curtains were drawn and the light was on. It was as if my father had forgotten that the war in Europe was over and the blackout lifted.

My brother Bill's picture was propped against a bottle of whisky in front of my father, who was quietly crying.

He had not forgotten anything or anyone.

Chapter 6

False Dawn

Next day the farm gang was back at work and, like the rest of the country, we now addressed ourselves to the war in the Pacific. There was no let-up in the campaign to increase food production which had become an obsession with me since I had heard horrifying stories of starvation in Europe and even worse ones about a famine in Bengal during 1944 when two million Indians had died. One day, in my dusty farm overalls, I paused at the Rising Sun pub at the top of Highwood Hill to slake the thirst brought on by hours of dusty work threshing damp mouldy barley sheaves. Standing in the sunshine outside the lovely old pub, resplendent in his blue Flying Officer's uniform and medal ribbons, was Ken, my dead brother Billy's best friend, who I remembered as a youth helping Billy pull me up into the tree at Hendon air display six years earlier. Ken had survived two full tours of bombing operations over Germany in Lancaster bombers and had won the DFC and bar with a Pathfinder squadron. We talked about our families and the past, especially about Billy and his exploits before going to sea. I mentioned my doubts about being stuck on the farm instead of being in uniform. Ken was in no doubt that I could best serve my country by staying on the farm. I felt better; not that I had any choice in view of the Essential Works Order which now locked me into my job as a "key worker". Ken even quoted a garbled passage of philosophy to me which I never forgot. The simple words were to influence my actions for the rest of my life. It went something like:

"If a man can make two blades of grass grow where one grew before, he will have accomplished more than all your philosophers, politicians, generals and Kings."

* * * * * * * * * * * * * * * * * *

Harvest came round quickly and a new man called Alex joined the gang. He, unlike me, had completed his school education and was openly derisive of my lack of education and the expected School Certificate. It soon became evident to me, however, that this rather arrogant young man was no brighter than me when it came to solving farm problems. Furthermore, the new man's grasp of politics, farm economics and the war situation was no better than my own. When

Alex disclosed that one of his brothers was a doctor, another a barrister and that he himself was destined for a senior post in his father's business, I began to lose my respect for and fear of more educated people. This seemed to take a great load off my mind. I started to enjoy a few wartime pleasures with my workmates: a night at the dog track or a visit to a dance hall.

One night I went with some of my other friends to a Jazz club in a cellar on Oxford Street. This trip into London's West End, as a near adult, was a great adventure. Number 100 Oxford Street was known as Max's Café, but on Sunday night it became the Feldman Club. The club was managed by a Jewish textile merchant's family. There were three gifted sons who included an infant prodigy drummer called Victor Feldman who was later, like many of the musicians who dropped in there for a relaxed "jam session", to become world famous, as were the premises themselves.

This outing was a rare treat for me and I could barely afford the five shilling (25p) entry fee. The instrumentalists from many American swing bands dropped in while serving in Britain and a sixteen-year-old schoolboy called Johnny Dankworth struggled to keep up on a reedy clarinet. A blind cockney pianist called George Shearing played strange ethereal chords and rhythms with locked hands. It was all very stimulating as I learned to distinguish between "jazz", "swing" and "commercial" hot music. There was mention of a new music called "bebop" being played in America by Dizzie Gillespie. Although some ship's bandsmen in Geraldo's navy spoke of the weird high tempo rhythms and demonstrated snatches, it had barely reached England.

Back on the farm, the men regarded my interest in this music as some sort of madness. The "new man", Alex, spoke contemptuously of "that rubbish" but knew nothing about it; nor did he seem familiar with the few classical pieces or operas which I knew of from my own schooldays and from my elder sister Esme. His combination of arrogance and conceit while exposing considerable ignorance made me much less intimidated or excessively respectful of other people's apparent superiority and their tendency to be automatically dismissive of my views. As time passed, the new man mellowed and became less defensively aggressive. Eventually, quite a warm friendship grew between us and we enjoyed exploring each other's ideas. I started to realise that my general knowledge and ability to grasp and argue a case were equal to that of many of my "educated" friends.

Deciding that I must make a move to progress from the rut into which I seemed to have fallen, I went to see the Principal of the Hertfordshire Farm Institute. The Principal, a kindly old man who had won the Military Cross in the First World War, told me that the Institute would reopen once the war was over. He said that I might be able to get in, despite my lack of schooling. I would have to pass the entry exam and have good references from my employers. The old gentleman said that he saw no reason why I should have any difficulty with this. I went back to my work overjoyed that all doors were not after all closed to me.

Winston Churchill, to everyone's amazement, called a General Election soon after this and I, although too young to vote, worked enthusiastically to return a Labour candidate in Tory Mill Hill. To my surprise, most of the returning ex-servicemen were enthusiastically supporting Labour. On the farm, however, the boss, and most of the men, despite their abysmal wages, were staunch Tories. I could not understand this and frequently said so. Some of them were swayed by my arguments, which were purely concerned with social justice and a historically-based distrust of the Tories. I was not union-minded and was deeply hurt when the boss said I was a trouble-maker. I had never obstructed the flow of work or production at any time. It would have been against my country's war effort and the needs of the hungry world, which weighed large in my socialism. Labour won the election with a landslide victory in spite of Churchill's speeches predicting a Gestapo state if Labour won. The mild-mannered Clem Attlee became Prime Minister and Britain worked and waited expectantly for victory in the Pacific and the chance to build a new Utopia.

I introduced the "new man", as he had become known on the farm, to Jackie at a dance in Mill Hill. After a whirlwind courtship they were married and I was honoured to be asked to make a short speech at the reception. I was shy and embarrassed, forgetting the humorous bits and floundering at other parts. To my surprise everyone clapped, including the New Man's doctor and barrister brothers.

Jackie thanked me later and looked into my eyes, holding my hand just a little longer than necessary. "That was a nice speech; I always said you were wasted on the farm. I wish you luck when you get to college." I was pleased; but there seemed no chance of me getting to a real college. Even the Farm Institute presented a difficult goal. However the main thing was that I had been treated as an equal by a "posh" family and not as some kind of oddity. I had even been praised for something other than my labours!

On the bus going to work next day, I saw a headline on a newspaper being read by a man opposite. SUPERBOMB DROPPED ON JAPAN. I wondered what this could be and what damage it had done. The men at work were speculating wildly about it and Alex, the new man, was pontificating about atomic physics. It was all science fiction stuff to me; but clearly something new and terrible had been released. Apparently clouds of dust over the bombed city of Hiroshima were preventing an assessment of the bomb's effect but news was released about tests in New Mexico showing a vast crater and a vaporized test tower. Almost before the dust had settled a second bomb was dropped on Nagasaki and the Emperor of Japan was said to be asking for peace. A few nights later, as I was going wearily to bed after a particularly hard day's work, I heard Clement Attlee's voice on my father's radio, announcing in his flat unemotional tones that Japan had surrendered.

It was almost six years since as a small boy on my uncle's farm in Dorset, I had heard Neville Chamberlain declare war on Germany. I felt strangely flat and unexcited.

Peace brought few changes. We had already got used to bomb-free nights. Every day more servicemen returned from Europe. Some had been preparing to be sent to the Far East; but the preoccupation with the war had lessened. South East Asia seemed a long way away. Food rationing got tighter as the problems of feeding a devastated Europe became apparent. I found myself at odds with many people who advocated letting the "bloody Germans" starve so that we could have improved food rations. The Labour government diverted resources from Britain's recovery in order to succour Europe, including Germany; and an unpopular austerity was imposed on the long-suffering people. Food production remained a number one priority and I realised that my entry to Farm Institute was going to be considerably delayed. I was not going to be released from my key job until all the servicemen had been demobilized and given first chance for vocational training or college places.

Most young men of my age group had now been called up and were going off to maintain the status quo in many strange places where the newly liberated peoples were demanding too rapid advances towards democracy and self-rule. Greece, Indonesia, Malaya and

Palestine were all in ferment and needed policing by British forces.

Feeling very frustrated, I attempted to join my mates in one or other of the services... A relatively short spell in the Forces, prior to getting into college, seemed preferable to standing still, working on and on as a penniless agricultural worker. I was ready for change and new horizons, whatever the dangers. My frustration was such that I even tried to join the Palestine Police, who were advertising for volunteers, despite the fact that it was well known that this force would be targets to be shot at by both Jews and Arabs. However, even this escape route was closed to me by a surfeit of trained soldiers who had tried civvy street and found the grey austerity too much after the blue Mediterranean theatres of war. The Forces proper, although still calling up men for service in world troublespots, were not interested in a volunteer enmeshed by the all-powerful Essential Works Order.

I decided that I must have a change, whatever the consequences. Once more my employers threatened me with instant call-up, either to the Forces or to be sent down the mines as a Bevin Boy. After a week spent looking for jobs, I went to work on another farm in Hertfordshire. The change, I thought, might bring new opportunities for learning or promotion. In fact it took me to the true nadir of my life and career.

I had only been working at the new farm for a week before I realised it was staffed by an incredible collection of social misfits and part-timers. Perhaps this was due to the proximity of the less reputable parts of North West London; but a more shady lot of workmates would have been hard to imagine.

One of the female workers was Irish Mary, a retired prostitute who had seen God and was trying to reform between bouts of drunkenness and a lechery unusual in one of her trade. Most of the young boys on the farm had been introduced to the biology of sex by her. One day, I – who found her repulsive – discovered her in a stackyard with her breeches down, trying to get her legs far enough apart for a very young lad to inspect her secret parts. The young lad almost had his eye touching them in his eagerness to satisfy his curiosity about nature's decision to make men and women differently. Later he told me that he had no sisters and Mary had only charged him a shilling for a look. Mary when sober was a grand worker and could handle sheaves and straw bales as well as any of the men; but when drunk, she was a fighting fury. More than once I separated her from adversaries she seemed determined to scalp. On one occasion when the farmer's son annoyed her, she seized a pitchfork and attempted to impale him. I managed to tear the fork away from her but sustained a badly punctured hand in the process. To my surprise I was severely told off by the intended victim for interfering.

They were a hard gang. Several had criminal records and I suspected several of the men were deserters. There was certainly one escaped German POW who was being sheltered by another Irish girl on one of the farms which formed part of the estate.

One of the oddballs was an interesting conscientious objector. I had met "conchies" before and had usually got on fairly well with them. Most had deep religious convictions, which I as an agnostic did not share. The strange and diverse backgrounds of these conscientious objectors made them interesting to talk to and, on the whole, they were an agreeable lot even though I did not share their views. Some of the older men had proved themselves to be extraordinarily courageous under fire by serving as medical corps orderlies and stretcher bearers. Others had been ambulance men and rescue workers in the Blitz. One had even been a bomb disposal soldier until his refusal to accept orders which infringed his noncombatant duties, resulting in court martial and reclassification.

The young "conchie" Adam, who I befriended, was totally different. He was an atheist anarchist, but a devotee of the works of William Blake. I could not see the connection and our long discussions, when work allowed, irritated the other men who could not follow our complicated and at times heated political arguments. Adam argued that a socialist state would stifle individualism and that man was capable of policing himself as an individual without regulation. I saw this as a return to barbarism and an opportunity for the strong to grab everything at the expense of the weak. In spite of my own frustration with the Essential Works Order, I believed state regulations were essential for the preservation of order and fair play. I saw nothing wrong with rationing or reasonable direction of resources, if it was in the national or –better still, world – interest. I did not like the phrase "national interest". It was too easy to abuse; but I was prepared to judge activities in its context.

Adam had been educated at Harrow Public School and was an accomplished artist. He was contemptuous of my plans to go to Farm Institute and said that I should set my sights higher. He recommended a novel called *The Corn is Green* by Emlyn Williams, in which a young man studies his way from insignificance and poverty to achievement and respectability. When I read the book, I thought it a little over-sentimental; but it revealed possibilities which I had previously overlooked, and I became determined to reeducate myself. Adam had equally anarchistic views on free love. He was living with a beautiful young teacher who had been married to a master at Harrow School. Adam said that he had no responsibilities towards her as they were both adult free agents. I attempted to justify my view that marriage was desirable to provide security for women who might become dependent through pregnancy or advancing years. Both Adam and his girl derided me and she expounded the view that a woman's body was hers to do what she liked with. If she got herself pregnant, that was her choice and she would bear the consequences, whether it be a baby to support or an abortion. I was shocked. I had a high regard for the sanctity of human life and the need for women to be looked after by men. I did not want to understand either anarchism or feminism; and judging by these two people, neither creed was very attractive. However, I soon realised that these two rather weak physical specimens, in terms of farm work, were a pair of tough nuts ideologically, who regarded me as a sentimental dimwit.

I quite liked the new job, in spite of the weird gang I now worked with. Perhaps this was a good measure of how low I had sunk. It was clear that these farms were not as well-run or as well-equipped as the farms I had left. The farmer's son was an ignoramus and most of the bailiffs of the scattered farmsteads were equally backward. Few of them seemed to be *bona fide* farm men, but were there to serve other purposes or hide from various consequences. How the business managed to prosper in such a haphazard way puzzled me. I eventually discovered that a black market racket was being operated from dilapidated sheds near Elstree. I did not want to be associated with the midnight slaughtering of sheep, pigs and cattle which the men whispered about, or the loads of wheat and barley which were being sold illicitly to pig and poultry producers. Some of the men were hiding sacks of wheat in fieldside ditches, and coming back to collect them at night for sale to backyard poultry keepers. The whole operation seemed to reek of petty criminality.

Apart from my confusion with events at the farm, I was disturbed by Adam and his girlfriend's sexuality. She walked about their little house naked in front of Adam and me and laughed at my discomfiture. As if to tease me, Adam would sit her half-dressed on

127

his knee and talk openly about the positions they had attempted and the intensity of their lovemaking. My own sexual frustration led to an appallingly squalid groping session with Mary one rain-sodden afternoon when, bored and idle, we were sheltering in a smelly cattle shed.

Realising that the time had come for a much more radical redirection of my career, I went once more to see the Principal of the Farm Institute. The Principal advised me that I would probably gain admittance the following autumn, if I passed the simple entrance exam; but he went on to ask me if my parents could afford the fees and provide me with spending monies. This shook me. I had not considered the cost of fees and had little in the way of savings. There was no way I could ask my father for more than token help. No war damage had been paid for my father's bombed factory and he was still living on diminishing capital. My sister's husband Alex had a poorly paid job and my brother George, now demobbed and unable to land a job suitable for an officer and a gentleman, was also at home trying to find his feet. It was no time for me to rock the boat.

The Labour government had judged the time right for a slight relaxation of austerity and allowed a small ration of petrol for pleasure motoring. My friend, Tom Cochrane, used part of his precious allowance to visit me on his second-hand Calthorpe motor bike. As I admired the red and chrome machine with its smell of hot oil and rubber and the promise of open roads, fresh wind in one's hair and a girl on the pillion, Tom revealed that he had been accepted to read medicine at Oxford, provided he could pass the Latin exam. I was extremely jealous of both the gleaming Calthorpe motorbike and of Tom's good fortune to have a rich dad who was well-connected at the University. I was also very envious of Tom in having an attractive Latin tutor, a youngish lady graduate who coached Tom for pocket money and had, Tom confided, already allowed him a feel of raw breast and hinted at more delights to come. I could never understand Tom's success with women. He was certainly no Adonis with his bulging forehead, small chin and innocent babyface topped off with thin, forward-sprouting hair. Neither was he physically impressive or athletic, since he suffered from a weak heart and migraines. He could, however, play the guitar and piano reasonably well and was in demand in the pub as a singsong accompanist. His nickname at school had been "Bottle" due to the remarkable appendage which he sometimes managed to keep in his trousers.

During Tom's visit, he told me that he was leaving his temporary job of driving a tractor for a Barnet agricultural and landscape contractor. This relatively unskilled job paid almost double what I was getting as a skilled worker on the farm. He suggested that I should apply for the job. This sounded like the answer to my financial problems. Perhaps I would now be able to save some money for my future days as a student.

I landed Tom's job with the contracting firm and it was a real eye-opener. Almost all the workers were ex-servicemen of the most easy-going, happy-go-lucky kind. None of them seemed to resent the fact that I had not worn uniform and I got on well with the boss. Both the boss's sons worked with the men and both had been Warrant Officers in the Royal Army Service Corps. I soon found that my wide experience of agricultural machines was of great value to the firm. Apart from my ability to plough decently, I could maintain the tractors, mowing machines and loaders with ease. I soon came to be regarded as an expert. Most of the men seemed to have picked up no skills at all in the army; only one of them, Bucko, an urbanised gypsy, had actually seen any extensive action. Bucko and the boss's two sons had been caught in France when the Belgium army collapsed leaving the outflanked British Expeditionary Force to find its way out to its eventual evacuation from Dunkirk. Both the sons had escaped from France but my best pal in the gang, Bucko, had been captured.

Bucko had been a promising centre forward for Barnet Town football team before the war; but his career had been interrupted when he was called up on his twenty-first birthday at the outbreak of war. In France, his platoon had been ordered back time and time again from what seemed like good defensive positions along the Belgian canals. In all this time Bucko had barely seen an officer. Back in France, at Calais, he had manned a hastily erected roadblock before being marched down to the harbour to await the ship which was to evacuate them. A local squire from South Mimms, near Barnet, was the officer now in charge of them and he inspected the tired and grimy men on the dockside. An air raid had sent them scrambling into cellars which, to their surprise, they found were full of French stragglers. This had mystified Bucko for up till then, he had hardly seen a French soldier amongst the defenders. After the raid they were reassembled and the officer told them there would be no evacuation. They were to hold the town, which commanded the approaches to Dunkirk, where the main evacuation by sea was taking place.

With only a few Bren guns, some anti-tank rifles, and their personal ancient Enfield 303 rifles, they had somehow held the line. Bucko kept locating snipers above and behind him on the roofs of buildings. As he could not see how they were getting into the town past all the defences, he concluded that they were fifth columnists and German soldiers who had got in by mixing with the refugees who streamed in every day. While firing his rifle from a prone position behind a sandbagged corner, with the buildings of Calais burning round him, he had felt a thud on his backside. Looking over his shoulder he saw the handle of a German hand grenade between his feet. His next memory had been of an Austrian doctor bending over him and saying, "For you the war is over."

Bucko had been a prisoner for six long years in Germany and Poland. He had seen terrible deeds and experienced terrible hardships culminating in the last forced march in front of the advancing Red Army. The panicky SS guards had killed anyone who fell out of the marching columns and Bucko had been forced to bury some of them at the roadside. Some were barely dead and the SS men would finish them off with a blow from Bucko's shovel. After a while they no longer bothered. Too many were dying. Bucko was eventually liberated, by advancing American infantrymen. The SS men had all vanished.

Although Bucko had had a very different war from me, and was eight or nine years older, we became good friends. It was some time before I realised that Bucko could neither read nor write. He was, despite this handicap, a brilliant raconteur. His fund of impossibly funny dirty stories was endless. He was a gambling addict who had at times won huge sums at the greyhound racetracks only to lose it all. Every week he "subbed" all his wages to place bets which occasionally came up to be followed by acts of great folly and generosity. I helped get him home in states of gross intoxication on several occasions. Once we boarded a tram with bundles of notes bulging out of Bucko's pockets. Bucko had refused change from £5 notes, any one of which represented half a week's wage to him or me. He wanted to share his good fortune and believing he was still in a pub, he would shout up drinks for everyone, much to the confusion of the tram conductor; and it was a relief to get him home without being robbed.

I taught Bucko to operate a tractor and how to set a grass mower. In return Bucko showed me the finer points of turf cutting, a skill which subsequently enabled me to earn a great deal of money when during the next winter I was recovering from the shock of a year's postponement of my entry to Farm Institute. The Principal had been very sympathetic but there were ex-servicemen wanting to do the course and I, as a civilian, would have to wait.

Turf cutting was a mindless task requiring vast reserves of stamina. For several weeks I could hardly get up the stairs to bed after a full day's cutting. My speed increased as I acquired the various knacks of marking out, keeping the blade of my turfing iron sharp, and using my whole bodyweight rather than my arms to thrust the gleaming iron through the soil. In time I was earning almost three times my farm wage and was saving hard for my college fees. I even bought an old 1926 Triumph motorbike which Tom Cochrane christened Big Tim. This flat-tanked monster I lovingly rebuilt and sold in order to buy a better machine. I repeated this process several times until I was able to acquire an ex-US Army Indian Twin. This must have been one of the ugliest motorbikes ever built but it was great fun and much admired as a "heap of machinery" whenever I met up with fellow bikers. Somehow, the great clumsy machine was a good match for the big rough youth that I had become.

The work, although hard, involved fewer hours than the farm job; and I felt some guilt during harvest time when, unlike the farm workers, we knocked off for the weekend. It felt great to lead a normal life with some time off for recreation. One Saturday morning I was working next to the old Mill Hill rugby club ground on the spur road at Stanmore, when I was seized by an impulse to play the game. I had not had the time or opportunity to pursue any sort of sport since leaving prep school. Spotting one of the club members leaving the pavilion, I pushed through the hedge, much to the man's astonishment, and asked if there was any chance of a game. The man – taken aback by my appearance, muddy, bedraggled and having pushed through a hedge, albeit forwards – demanded, "Have you played before?" "Yes, at Mill Hill School," was my reply. It was only a white lie, for I had not actually been at Mill Hill Public School but at the Junior School. The club member looked disbelievingly at the rough youth before him. I was lucky, for I had fortunately confronted Jack Sillar, the club secretary. Jack later recalled that he had thought it was some villainous gypsy springing from the hedge to rob him. However, as there was something slightly polite about my manner, he invited me to the club trials the following Saturday.

131

What I lacked in skill and knowledge of the game, I made up for in sheer animal strength and stamina. I also initially lacked the athletic training to run for long periods. The years of labouring and, more latterly, turf cutting had given me enormous power in my upper body. I found that I could maul the ball away from anyone but having won possession, I did not always know the best thing to do with it. I enjoyed my first practice match against a strong Finchley side and especially the fellowship in the bar afterwards.

Much to my surprise, a few days later, I received a card telling me that I had been selected to play for the first fifteen the following week. I had been wondering if I would get another game at all as I feared that I had contributed little apart from some good catches in the line out. I had admired the fleet-footed wingers and twinkle-toed halfbacks; mentally contrasting their finesse with my own red-faced grunting and heaving in the mauls and scrums...

Back at work the men thought I was completely mad to give up a rest day to such a demandingly energetic game which they did not understand. "It's a bloody nob's game," said one of the boss's sons. "You've no business playing it." Undeterred, I went off with my battered case of kit consisting of ex-army shorts, an old rugby shirt begged from Tom Cochrane, short grey army socks and a pair of old football boots loaned to me by Bucko. I was later able to scratch together some clothing coupons and bought a club shirt and decent boots. Saturdays became a source of great pleasure as I got on Christian name terms with the other players and felt myself accepted by them.

No one had blown the whistle on me yet.

Chapter 7

Dawn Breaks

I was disappointed that my mates at work did not appreciate my new-found enthusiasm for rugby. It was the first time since leaving school six years earlier that I had found time for any recreational activity outside of my work. I still felt a little guilty about enjoying my Saturday afternoons off when I knew the farm men would all be working. I could not understand the attitude of those who could not see that the nation's interests were the same as their own. I was shocked by the class war attitudes of my workmates, who hated all "toffs"; and I was equally horrified by the contempt with which my public school friends regarded the lower orders.

I found it difficult to argue about politics, as inevitably it brought in military matters about which I was loath to comment in view of my own lack of military service. In some ways it was a blacker time for me than the desperate years of the war. The Labour government, of which I had such high hopes, had run into severe difficulties. Food was still strictly rationed. There were shortages of almost everything and our Russian allies, who I had admired so much, were proving to be as despotic and uncooperative as my Conservative friends had always predicted.

I enjoyed the good fellowship of the rugby club enormously. My agricultural occupation was a subject of good-natured banter amongst my clubmates who were mostly in well-paid office jobs. I was regarded as an amiable son of the soil and something of a curiosity. When beer removed my self-doubts and inhibitions I would burst into song with the best; and one or two of my more Rabelaisian efforts brought me much acclaim. Once or twice, when the older players had plied me with beer, I would flirt with their ladies, quoting Shakespeare's love sonnets, dimly remembered from my days at Belmont School. When Jack Sillar, now the club president, told me that I was a bit of a character, my cup of happiness was full. By contrast, life at home was rather bleak. Neither my brother George nor my brother-in-law Alex had managed to find properly paid jobs in civvy street. My sister was grossly overworked, looking after her twin children and four adult men, none of whom were any more domestically inclined than she, who was by nature an artist and was never cut out for a housekeeping role. Circumstances had changed a gay young girl into something of a scold, whom my father and I feared in spite of our love and respect for her.

That winter the rugby season was interrupted by the coldest weather and heaviest snowfall ever recorded. This freak weather brought transport and many industries grinding to a halt. Power stations, the rail system and the coal mines, all badly maintained and almost worn out by the demands and shortages of the war, could not cope with demand. As coal supplies dried up and electrical power was cut off, the nation, so recently euphoric in the afterglow of victory, shivered in a bitter mood of resentment. Workers, including myself, were laid off from work. For the first time since 1939 large numbers of men were unemployed. Painted slogans appeared on walls and bridges attacking the Labour government. The Communists were first with "1945, we put them in. 1947, they put us out."

Winston Churchill, the former war leader, seized the opportunity to stir the discontent. "Where are the fruits of victory?" he rumbled, knowing full well that many of his Conservative cronies were relieved not to have to face the problems of post-war recovery. I boiled at the unfairness of it all. The Young Conservatives were even more delighted by being able to make the most of Labour's problems. A shortage of barley combined with regular power cuts resulted in the breweries not being able to supply all our pubs with the normal quota of beer. At once the Young Conservatives were out with jingles which in turn were quickly taken up by my formerly solidly Labour workmates: "No ale, no stout. You put them in: now get the buggers out!"

Trains froze to the tracks, potatoes and vegetables froze in the ground and the people, no longer united in the classless wartime spirit of defiance against danger and a common foe, became sullen and resentful of each other. Press photos and stories of wealthy industrialists, film stars and MPs including Labour MPs enjoying warmth and sunshine in the Canary Islands and other suntraps elsewhere, did little to help. A new and nasty element of envy had entered politics and class consciousness.

Finding myself jobless, I filled my time earning a few quid renovating old motorbikes, which I dug out of Bentley's scrapyard below Highwood Hill. This scrapyard was a vast pyramid of rusting motor cars and bikes in which desperate men, young and old, burrowed for spare parts unobtainable elsewhere. It was owned by a piratical figure resembling Popeye. Old Bentley, or Ben as he was better known, wore a battered flat cap sideways on his head and a well-chewed pipe projected sideways from his prominent jaw, emitting an incredibly strong smell of plug tobacco. In spite of these ghastly fumes, his lungs seemed in no way affected by the noxious effluvium. Indeed, his bellows of rage or impatience could be heard at the Rising Sun pub at the top of Highwood Hill whenever he caught some miscreant attempting to sneak spares without paying. Old Ben was reputed to be a wicked old twister but I always found him to be kind and helpful when in a good temper. It was a point of honour for the local lads to try to defraud Old Ben, but little escaped his eagle eye.

Once, when I was in search of a Binks carburettor for an ancient Ariel motorbike, Ben directed me to a corner of the yard inhabited by a goat and some ducks. Delving into the straw and duck slime I found what I sought but inadvertently smashed some half-buried duck eggs. "Bloody young vooil!" roared Old Ben, sending clouds of smoke up from the ever-present pipe which almost overcame the foul sulphurous stench of the rotten eggs. "You'll have to pay vor them eggs!" I gladly paid a few pence for the damage and carried off the mucky object of my search, which, after a thorough dismantling, cleaning of numerous jets, chambers and mysterious holes, polished up into an impressive-looking component. I was delighted with my acquisition and fitted it to the now complete bike which I sold later that day. The capital resulting from this sale financed further old bikes which I worked on for the rest of that frozen winter in the icy garage outside my father's house.

Somehow my enthusiasm for the task, and the rude health and strength which my hard life had built up over the years, made the extreme cold of that desperate winter insignificant. I hammered at bent levers, oiled seized and rusted parts and "persuaded" the more stubborn parts to function with a combination of penetrating oil and brute strength. "Nothing wrong with a bit of brute strength and bloody ignorance wisely applied," said my dad with his usual enigmatic chuckle. Judicious use of "brute and bloody" was to become a useful tool to me in my future life on the farm!

The spring of 1947, when it came at last, was a leap from winter into summer. In the north and west of Britain it was a time when the smell of death from rotting sheep carcasses on the hills was pervasive for many weeks. Thousands of animals had frozen to death or been suffocated in deep snowdrifts as they sought shelter from the bitter winds beside the stone walls of the bleak hillsides. In the luckier south and east, the bright sunshine allowed work to catch up quickly, on the farms if not in the factories. I found that in spite of my temporary unemployment and my proud unwillingness to collect the dole, I was better off than if I had been working. My brief spell repairing motorbikes had brought in more than my lost wages.

Back at work after the thaw, the back-breaking but well-paid turf cutting was now in full swing and I was accumulating a bit of cash for my impending year at farm institute. In June I heard at last that I had a place at Oaklands, the Hertfordshire Institute. My dreams were coming true. The rest of the summer passed very happily. I collected and was put in charge of a new Chaseside Mechanical Shovel. This was a crude forerunner of the front loaders and diggers now commonplace on farms and building sites. It consisted of a huge steel bucket, raised and lowered by a system of cables and pulleys attached to a friction drum bolted to the rear of a Fordson tractor. Huge boxes of pig iron ballast built onto the back of the tractor counterbalanced the bucket. The huge orange machine was in great demand and apart from loading soil for sale from the stripped turf fields, it was contracted out to wherever materials were to be moved, on building sites, farms and even in film studios. At Boreham Wood Film Studios, while loading up a discarded garden set, I found myself in close proximity to Stewart Granger, Michael Wilding and once, to my delight, Marlene Dietrich, who smiled pleasantly at my gawping.

It was not all work that summer. I had a week off when I returned to my beloved Lake District, revisiting Joyce and her family. Joyce and I went for a quiet walk together and I kissed her for the first time since the puppy-love days at school. It was a friendly and reassuring embrace which I enjoyed; but I sensed its innocence and we parted good friends, and that was all. Later I met her brother for a few beers and enjoyed a wild night's dancing in Cockermouth Public Hall. I saw some of my old workmates from Pardshaw. "See'est thou, it's Terry lad!" "Is 'e onny better?" "Nay lad, 'e's wus!" I was amazed to find them all as shy and oafish with the lasses as ever. I would probably have had several romantic adventures that night if all my old flames had not been present at the same time. In the event I fell between too many stools and dropped myself in the ordure with all of them but one, a vaguely-remembered face from my earlier years in Cockermouth. I walked the young woman home via the old footbridge over the river Cocker. Although not really interested in her, I kissed her roughly. Quite unexpectedly, she responded to my heated clutching and made violent love with me, suspended as we were over the cold darkness of the river below. It was an incongruous situation and, I reflected, a hurried and wasteful experience. She was after all a pretty, young, Women's Auxiliary Air Force corporal and deserved better treatment. Quite rightly she lectured me afterwards on the wrongfulness of passion without love. Feeling the effects of the beer I had recklessly consumed to impress Joyce's brother, I was inclined to agree. My bed was calling and I felt cold, sticky and uncomfortable. Furthermore, my conscience was troubling me and I was not at all pleased with my own behaviour. We walked the rest of the way to her home and I kissed her goodnight with a little more gentleness, but I wanted to get away as quickly as possible. I had been a rotter.

Late next day I returned to London, having spent the morning on Skiddaw mountain. I had walked up under a blue sky with late lingering snow under my feet and incomparable lake and mountain scenery all around me. Despite the beauty and fine weather, I felt lonely and unfulfilled as I made my way down to Keswick station. I needed a proper relationship, a girlfriend or a wife; but there was no way my present situation in life would justify the latter. Once back in the South, I felt strangely disembodied and thoroughly disorientated. I could not relate to the urban surroundings of the North London suburbs; I did not know where I belonged. Certainly it was not in Cumberland, equally not with my former posh schoolmates or the roughnecks with whom I worked in Barnet. Even a jolly dance that night at Hendon County School did nothing to restore my equilibrium. By chance a very young film starlet was at the dance. I had danced with her twice before: once at a Wembley church hall dance and once at a similar function at Golders Green. Now the young Jean Simmons, her hair grown long down her back and glamorously highlighted for her part as Estelle in the film of Dickens' *Great Expectations*, was dancing with me. It was a "flirtation waltz" and at the end of each brief spin together, the couples kiss and change partners. I mumbled something about it being a privilege and kissed her lightly; our teeth clashed and she laughed. I noticed she had slightly buck teeth and imperfect legs but she was lovely nonetheless and much of her sparkle came from within. But like Estelle, in Dickens' novel, she had an ice maiden presence. None of the Hendon boys dared bother her. I had not thought to tell her that I had a cousin, Bridget Angela Lansbury, who was on the way to becoming a famous film star in America. It would not have made any difference, for although reserved, she was

137

friendly with everyone whatever their background but she was far, far out of my reach.

September arrived and it was time to pack for my departure to the farm institute. I had not saved enough to live on for a whole year off work but I had managed to get my fees reduced and discovered that I was eligible for a Ministry of Agriculture grant while I was on the course. This grant was for two pounds a week and although small, it removed all my financial worries and my dependence upon my father for the help which I knew the old man could no longer afford, willing though he had always been.

The year at Oaklands, the Hertfordshire Farm Institute, was to be one of the happiest of my life. I was avid for knowledge about farming; and the smattering of practical knowledge which I had gained on the farms in Cumberland, Bedfordshire and Hertfordshire proved fertile soil for the daily lectures and demonstrations to seed themselves in and grow into a proper understanding. I learned to listen effectively and to discard much folklore. I learned to read selectively and above all I learned how to learn from other people's experience and knowledge. Having left Prep School with only a smattering of English, Latin, Maths and French but no science of any kind, I was fascinated by the new worlds of Chemistry and Biology. So good were the lectures that I was soon reading background textbooks as if I had been a student with normal education. After a shaky start I was comparing well with my contemporaries in both theory and practice. Old Mr Hunter Smith, the Principal, was very encouraging and one day told me that it was a pity I had not qualified to go to university. I was flattered but put the thought aside. I loved the Institute farm and the daily routine, petty and restrictive though the Institute rules were. Male and female students were strictly separated. Pubs were out of bounds and church attendance was compulsory. "Lights out" was at ten o'clock and conversation forbidden after this time. As I was now nearly twenty-one years old, I found the rules irksome and reminiscent of Prep School. However, I was too grateful for my place at the college to rock the boat; but there was no way I could live within these rules after my many years of self-responsibility. Several of the older students, some of whom were ex-servicemen, felt the same way; but none wanted to upset old Mr Hunter Smith who belonged to a previous half century and was a fine, if out of touch, old gentleman.

It was not long before we found means of entering and leaving the old manor house undetected. One of the cooperative lady students would unlock a window in their ground floor common room, which, unlike the male common room, was not overlooked by the resident warden "Sergeant Major" Lugg, a stickler for discipline, who constantly threatened instant expulsion to any student transgressing. (He turned out to be a charming man when we met again in later years.) As both "Luggie's" room and the Matron's room guarded the main stairs, the students found a way through the forbidden kitchens to the old manor tower where an ancient stone stairway bypassed danger of detection but posed a severe hazard to unwary or tipsy life and limb. There was a vertiginous drop over its unguarded edge. I, who had no head for heights, preferred to risk a stealthy ascent of the main stars, past Luggie's room, then a panic-stricken stampede up the last flight into the dormitory. Luggie did pursue us on more than one occasion but failed to catch anyone out of bed. Had he pulled any bedcovers back he would have found men fully clothed and reeking of beer. I suppose as an ex-army man, he felt we had survived an exercise and deserved to be let off.

One day I received a message to be ready for collection outside the Comet pub at Hatfield. The local Mill Hill rugby club needed me for a match against Jesus College, Cambridge. Three of my classmates decided to come along for the ride, to have a look at the university and to see how the other half lived. The coach arrived on time but I wanted to make my excuses for not playing due to a severe attack of post-alchoholic remorse or a severe tummy upset. At any rate I felt awful, with blurred vision, a headache and nausea. Jack Sillar insisted I got on the coach and expressed his relief that the other lads had come; the team was three players short! Arriving at Cambridge, the coach parked down Hobson's Lane. I was fascinated by this as I remembered my Headmaster telling me that the expression "Hobson's choice" came from a livery stableman called Hobson who kept horses down the lane and always seemed to have only one horse available. I felt I was seeing a legend become reality. This feeling persisted as the other lads and I went under the ancient gilded crest at Jesus College porter's lodge and across the college courtyard. We peered into the dim studies and hoary old passages. It all seemed very fusty and battered after the bright clean rooms of Oaklands, the Hertfordshire Farm Institute we had come to love.

The rugby game was quite extraordinary. The Jesus College team was beautifully turned out, as one would expect from such a noble institution. Moreover, they all looked superb athletes and called to each other in fine commanding tones. The lads felt overawed. As they changed, some gear was found for "Slim" Rayner, a portly but strong young farmer who had never played rugby before. "Just push in the scrums and keep out of everyone's way," were the captain's instructions. There was no hooker available so another student, a seven stone semi-invalid reputed to have a tubercular testicle, was drafted in to hook. I, as usual, was to power the "engine rooms" in the second row. The team was not entirely makeshift as we had an excellent scrum half and stand-off and a fast if short-sighted winger who had the disconcerting habits of tackling his own fullback or running over the dead ball line to touch down instead of scoring tries. The match started badly. Slim Rayner was penalised for throwing the ball forward, torpedo fashion, to anyone who was far enough offside to be in the clear. This was usually the tubercular testicle limping back towards wherever play was taking place. By the time we were about 15 penalty points down, Slim had got the idea and kept as far away from the ball as possible. It was a distinct improvement and Jesus's scoring rate dropped. By one of those strange freaks arising from total ignorance of the foot-up laws, together with some strange kicking by the Jesus hooker and some lucky bounces, our own hooker, the reputed bearer of the tubercular testicle, was taking ball after ball against the head in the tight scrums and was receiving much applause and encouragement from the crowd. Being quite unused to such approval he became inspired to greater effort and started to trot about the field as if he was enjoying the game. I, who was still feeling dizzy and queasy, broke from a scrum and found myself alone and unmarked when a lucky ricochet from one of the tubercular testicle's fly hacks sent the ball skittering in front of me. I attempted to dribble and tripped forward in a series of flailing lurches. The ball seemed to stick to my feet and even when skilfully dropped on and picked up by one of the super athletes of Jesus College, my arms, flailing blindly for balance, knocked the ball back down to my foot for an almost perfect grubber kick. I stumbled after the wildly bouncing ball, which somehow popped up into my hands. A blurred shape outside me called for the ball and I, anxious to free my hands to grasp my agonisedly aching belly which was by now on the point of eruption, gave a pass which should have led to a try under the posts. However it was Bagnold the Blind, the demon deadball specialist, who flashed by. Hoarse and desperate shouts of warning from the touchline alerted the short-sighted winger and he missed running into touch in goal by a whisker, pirouetting skilfully to set off back up the field in totally the wrong direction. By now I was on my knees just over the try line, vomiting heartily, when Bagnold fell over me to touch down an excellent try. The Jesus players and referee looked on in stunned disbelief. This was hardly playing the game.

"Well done, Terry!" cried Jack Sillar from the touch line. "You made that try!"

The incident, which did not prevent Jesus College from winning handsomely, made my name in the club; and I basked in the glory for many years afterwards.

Aftermatch tea was taken in Dorothy's Tea Rooms on the High. By now the Jesus men were getting used to the strange assortment from Mill Hill and both teams repaired to the Bath public house in Downing Street. A few pints of Bass soon calmed my heaving stomach and even the bearer of the tubercular testicle forgot his aches and pains.

By eleven o'clock the lads were ready for the town, but the Jesus men were unable to join in due to the university curfew. Some of us made our way to the Mill where we had been told punts were tied up. It was a simple enough job to untie a punt and push off. Slim Rayner knew how to propel a punt standing in the bottom but I had been told that at Cambridge one had to stand up on the polished wood deck at the back. My efforts with the pole resulted in erratic curves and bumps which had Toby the tubercular testicle gibbering with fear and laughter. With a crash my pole hit Queen's Bridge, an angular wooden structure said to have been designed by Isaac Newton. As my pole stuck in the woodwork I felt the punt slip away from beneath my never too steady feet. For a moment I was suspended and reached up to grab the wooden beams above me. Alas! Newton's bridges, together with his laws of gravity, were too much for a clumsy youth and I dropped into the black river Cam fearing an unwanted second bath. To my surprise, the river barely reached my knees although the muddy bed sucked horribly at my only pair of decent shoes. Tubercular Testicle had by now reached the bank opposite Kings and was making his way back towards the Mill when I heard a despairing shout and splash as he fell into one of the waterways cutting across the Backs. Eventually we made our way, wet, cold and muddy, back towards the coach parked near Jesus College.

As we passed the end of Downing Street we saw a group of gowned students lurking in the shadows along by Emmanuel. The cause of their skulking in the shadows was what seemed to me a most unusual procession. Two large men wearing top hats and bearing large flashlights were preceding a figure in long gown and mortar-board cap who in turn was followed by a further pair of betoppered figures. They had clearly seen the students and were about to challenge them when they spotted me and my bedraggled companion. Slim Rayner said, "Christ, it's the Proctor and Bulldogs!" I had heard of neither and was startled when a stern voice called, "Sir! Are you a member of this University?" One of the top-hatted bulldogs shone a flashlight in my face which dazzled and angered me. "Bloody hell, what do you want?" I thought; but before I could answer, a plummy voice from the cap-and-gowned Proctor observed, "I think not," in a thoroughly disdainful tone; and the procession walked on in pursuit of more suitable quarry. We continued to squelch uncomfortably back to the coach and the trip home. We had had a mixed day and concluded that Cambridge was another world, which was not yet ready for us!

There was some rearrangement of the seating on the return journey. Harry Poole, the scrum half, who had brought a smashing young lady with him, was laid out on the back seat nursing a painful broken nose, incurred when Slim Rayner, endeavouring to avoid the action, had run into him just as he was making a spectacular diving pass. The ball had been deflected to Slim's feet via his unfeeling hands and somehow the ball had reared up and over the posts for a magnificent dropped goal. This triumph was somewhat marred for Harry, for in the collision, his nose was deflected almost as effectively as the ball without scoring any points. Harry's discomfort was compounded by the fact that his beautiful young lady friend was now snogging with Doug Rickard the vice captain, and making most unladylike noises as he explored her very shapely breasts through an extremely skimpy blouse. Two young waitresses from Dorothy's Tea Rooms, wanting a lift to Hatfield, had joined the coach after spending the evening with two crafty lads who had got themselves fixed up with crumpet while my mates and I were drinking, a lesson which I was quick to take on board for future reference. By the time the coach reached Royston the crafty lads had hung two discarded bras and one pair of very brief pants from the luggage rack and unbelieving players were crowded round the seats occupied by the abandoned foursome shouting ribald encouragement. I was too tired to feel anything but disbelieving envy and fell asleep dreaming of the ancient colleges and traditions of a university life I could never hope for.

I was woken by the need for a pee. The bus driver stopped and a row of men were soon lined up at the hedgeside, shifting their feet as they peed and farted with grunts of relief and satisfaction. Their breath and hot urine made clouds of steam in the frosty night air. Doug Rickard was still with Harry Poole's girl. She appeared to be asleep, or at least her eyes were closed... I could no longer see Doug's hands on her breasts; indeed I could not see Doug's hands at all, nor, for that matter, his head. In fact it was difficult to see whose legs and arms were which. The girl was smiling in her "sleep" and seemed to be sighing or snoring. The snorts were growing louder and rose to a loud sobbing groan. "Is anything wrong?" I asked innocently. "Fuck off," came Doug Rickard's muffled reply...

At Hatfield the two girls from Dorothy's Tea Rooms got out, stuffing various garments into their handbags. With their make-up rubbed or licked off, they looked pale, scratched and spotty. I was glad I had not been one of the lucky ones. At the Farm Institute gates I got my kit together; the bearer of the tubercular testicle was asleep naked in the luggage rack and two players were being sick at the roadside, much to the relief of the coach driver. It had been an altogether grand day out. I was only sorry that I was on early morning milking shift next day; but at least the rugby had cured my stomach ache!

Round about half term I met Pat Powell, a young actress. I had known her for years as a teenage cousin of my friend Peter Flood. Peter had got himself engaged to a stunning redhead and it was at the party celebrating the event that I was bowled over by the vivacious young lady who wafted up to me in a cloud of expensive perfume. "Hello, Terry," she said, to my bewilderment. I had no idea who this glorious creature was, but dawning recognition on my big red face made the girl flash her perfect teeth in laughter at my surprise. Little Pat, Peter's pest of an adolescent niece, had turned into a beautiful swan. Almost at once, she was surrounded by admirers who threatened to separate her from me. She grabbed my hand and whispered, "Stay with me. I am lost in this lot." I danced with her to tunes from *Oklahoma* and *Annie get your gun*. We laughed a lot about my surprise at finding her grown up. She was now a drama student and full of the theatre and her new life. I was quiet about this. There were too many actresses and stories of actresses in my family already. I did not take kindly to theatrical folk, who I found pretentious, ruthless and insincere. Pat had to leave the party early as she had an audition next morning. She asked me to see her to the bus and we walked down the road after a last dance to Frank Sinatra singing "Time after Time". I went straight home instead of returning to the party. My father was, as usual, carefully studying the day's newspapers. "You look excited, boy." He was right. I was very excited.

My status at the Farm Institute and at the rugby club rocketed when I arrived with Pat on my arm. She sensed my pride and played up to it. Her stylish make-up and clothes were all groomed to impress at auditions and interviews. Her diction, body language and facial expressions were exquisitely projected and always, there was this mischievous look of intimacy which I suspected was not solely for me. Nonetheless, I was proud of her and the effect she had on my friends. She talked a lot about her theatrical colleagues, their sexual freedom and the trouble she had rebuffing their advances, particularly it seemed the lesbian advances of older actresses and producers. It sounded as if her life was one long resisted seduction. I adored her for a time. I particularly loved the way she could change her personality. One minute I could be walking with a Hampstead flapper, the next with a broad Irish colleen or the coarsest of Brooklyn tarts. She loved necking but would only sometimes let me move "below the shoulders" as she called it. I found it frustrating; and one night after a long necking session in St James Park, I missed the last bus from Edgware to Mill Hill and had to walk the two miles home in an agony of "lover's nuts". It could not go on.

At Christmas I received a formal invitation from Vikkie, one of Pat's friends, to a bottle party in Bloomsbury. Pat firmly instructed me on the correct mode of reply and I was a little niggled by her bossiness. The party was quite unlike any party I had seen before. Although the girl's parents were there in the early stages, they soon retired, looking pale and shaken as the theatrical types quickly became tipsy and free with both their outrageous conversation and groping hands. Girls sat or lay about with scant attention to how much leg or bosom they were showing or whose hands were where. I found myself on the stairs between two couples who, when not exploring each other's tonsils with much gasping and sucking, were swigging gin from the bottle which they invited me to share. One of the girls, who I mentally called "Garters", put a generous thigh across mine. She wore a garter-like Alice band round bright red hair and two similar bands held up black silk stockings on her very white thighs. I could not quite tell whether she had on very fine black lace panties or no pants at all. I

144

was at that moment aware that the other girl, in spite of her companion's attentions, was feeling under my shirt and pressing my free hand hard against her inner thigh. My country boy system was working hard to absorb the shocks of city life; my head was reeling from the noise, smoke and neat gin and I felt as if I was not really there.

Pat came up the stairs in a swish of silk. "Ah, there you are! I have been looking for you everywhere." I had not seen her in the room for some time and I noticed that her lipstick was smudged and her chin looked roughened. I knew the signs. Pat took my hand and led me up to the bathroom where she repaired her face, looking at me in the mirror as she did so. I preserved my well-practised inscrutability. "Love me?" said Pat. "In my fashion," I replied, moving forward and holding her close.

Pat sighed, obviously relieved that I was not going to make a fuss. Freeing her arms she lifted her full skirt and hooking her thumbs in her pants she sat down on the WC and peed, smiling up at my astonished face with the innocent expression of a young child. She shook herself and pulled up her pants, flushing the loo as she did so. I suddenly felt terribly roused. I slammed the toilet lid, sat down and pulled Pat roughly onto my knee. I kissed her violently, pushing hard with my tongue. She pressed against me, breathing deeply through her nose. Her dress was only just holding up. I noticed that someone else must have undone the many hooks and eyes at the back. Her front-fastening bra was also undone. I was suddenly aware that she smelled of gin and someone else's aftershave. I was too far gone in lust to pull back and I slid my searching hand up her thighs, feeling the warm wetness of her as I forced her legs apart on either side of mine. I had never had a girl like this, sitting facing me across my thighs. The randy pair on the farm, Adam and his mistress, had teased me with descriptions of how they did it like this. "Make you piss blood!" Adam had said.

At this moment, riding high in the clouds of ecstatic expectation, I believed him. Every nerve end was tingling and I was trembling uncontrollably. Pat was wriggling towards me, hitching her bottom along my thighs till I felt her softness burning against my straining rod. I forced my hand between us to undo the metallic zip which was all that now lay between me and the act of love with someone I desperately wanted.

The action broke the spell and with a convulsive heave, Pat was standing up, flushed and straightening her dress. She kissed me softly and shook her head. "You know I can't. It wouldn't be fair!"

I was desperate; I could have raged and cried, I could have punched and kicked the fittings in that now hateful, stinking bathroom. I ran some cold water and splashed my hot red face. Pat had left the room. I dried quickly; mentally I cursed her for a prick teaser, though in my heart I knew she had never even half-promised me anything.

I turned to find Pat's friend Vikkie looking at me thoughtfully. She too had smudged lipstick and her dress was partly off her shoulders, revealing a much bigger swell of bosom than Pat's. Wordlessly she went on her knees in front of me, her eyes staring fixedly at my middle as she grasped me behind my knees, almost causing me to topple forward. Looking down, I realised I was still undone and that my only partly subsiding staff was still out. "Do you like it French?" she mumbled. Already she was running her tongue up and down the under-ridge of my staff. I groaned; my anger with Pat had not yet subsided, but neither had my lust. I pushed the girl to the rubber floor, noticing the rusty tap connections and huge flakes of grubby paint on the wall under the hand basin and the ammoniacal smell of urine round the pedestal of the WC. I parted her legs and almost roughly thrust my hand for the shadowy wetness.

Vikkie groaned and sighed a thousand tiny sighs at my rhythmic kneading. I became impatient as my ministrations brought on an ache across the tendons at the back of my busy hand. I lifted myself and slid up her body as if to enter her. "Do you want to?" I said. "Oh yes! Now, now!" sobbed Vikkie. I hesitated and the girl, sensing my hesitation, spoke but made a big mistake as she said, "Don't worry about Pat. She has gone back to her boyfriend from the theatre."

A pang of jealous rage overwhelmed me. Pushing the gasping girl aside I jumped up, doing up my trousers as I ran downstairs. I passed Pat who was sprawling on a sofa with an affectionate arm round a young actor.

"Goodbye, Pat," I said coldly.

"Goodbye?" she questioned in a deep trembling voice, achieving a very good imitation of Sarah Bernhardt at her most tragic.

"Yes! Good bloody bye!" I shouted, going out of the front door without looking back.

146

Vikkie's father was loitering in the garden, enjoying a calming cigarette. He was clearly shaken by the behaviour of his offspring and the new Bloomsbury set to which she aspired. His distressed wife was being calmed and comforted next door. Nonetheless, he spoke politely to me. "Goodnight, young man. I hope you've had a pleasant evening. It looks like rain." I was in no mood for pleasantries. "Piss off!" I shouted, and walked off miserably into the cold night.

It seemed sophistication was not yet for me.

Somewhere a horn was blowing. Again, it was not mine!

The traumatic experience with Pat at Vikkie's party was followed by more disturbing events. George, my elder brother, had run off with Peter Flood's beautiful red-headed fiancée.

Mill Hill was buzzing with rumour, shocked outrage and suburban viciousness. I got a fair bit of earbashing from Peter's female relatives but found the menfolk fairly philosophical about it. Life was suddenly a series of dramas. Pat wrote passionate letters, proclaiming her love for me alone and expressing her horror at Madge and George's affair. I did not want her back. The magic had gone. George and Madge asked for my support and approval for their wedding plans. I was not sure about this. I had enjoyed some interesting encounters with Madge myself at dances and parties before she met my brother, even after her engagement to Peter Flood. Nonetheless, I went to their quiet wedding where Madge wore a "New Look" outfit. This was the first real post-war fashion and consisted of an Empire Line jacket with a tight waist, flaring out just above the hips. This was worn with a long skirt and looked very elegant on a slim redhead wearing a matching mini bowler hat and veil. I thought she looked a bit like Rita Hayworth and wished them both the best of luck. Madge was very glamorous; but I could not see it lasting.

Towards the end of the Christmas break, I was in a somewhat bitter and worried frame of mind when I met an old friend, Peggy, at a party. Emboldened by beer I boasted to my friend, Tom Cochrane, that I would have her that night. Peggy had come to the party with a boy I did not like and I had no compunction in setting out to charm her. Feeling disrespectful towards all women in general, I asked her outright to make love. To my amazement she said yes.

There was nowhere private in the large flat which was teeming with Temple Fortune Tennis Club types. We went out onto the carpeted stairs between floors where I, cool-headed even in drink, realised I did not have a contraceptive. I went back into the party and asked Tom for a johnny with a triumphant leer. "Lucky bugger," said Tom.

I was a brute to Peggy, uncaring for her needs as I roughly satisfied myself out on the staircase. Afterwards she told me I had been a rotter, so I cuddled her gently and affectionately. Some time later I made love to her again. It was better and I really felt both grateful and affectionate. She had made me forget Pat and I wondered about asking her to be my girl. Soon afterwards the boy who had brought her to the party found us and said he was going home. He added that she could come with him now or find her own way. She looked at me but I did not respond and she got up and left. I let her go. Perhaps I was a rotter. Peggy was a nice friendly girl, and the first who had really satisfied my sexual longings.

Next day Pat's mother rang and invited me to stay for a few days at their home at Southend on Sea. I weakened and agreed. Her parents were very kind and Mr Powell, a regular army major at the Shoeburyness garrison, was particularly friendly and quite won me over. He asked about farming and land values. I was pleased to show off some of my knowledge.

That night, Pat and I were tactfully left alone to talk. Pat gave me a copy of Fitzgerald's translation of the *Rubaiyat of Omar Khayyam*. She read me a passage:

"Ah love, could thou and I with fate conspire
To grasp this sorry scheme of things entire.
Would we not shatter it to bits, and then
Remould it nearer to the heart's desire."

Her huge grey eyes appealed to me and I was lost. Perhaps I loved her; perhaps I could forgive her after all.

The rest of the stay was romantic. We walked, we talked, and we listened to Chopin. I did not even think of doing more than kissing her affectionately. I went back to my studies reconciled with Pat and feeling very proud and grown up after all the dramatic events of the vacation.

The visit to the old university at Cambridge and its ancient colleges had awakened an interest in new horizons. I wondered what university students learned about in addition to what I was learning at Oaklands. I was intrigued by the student gowns, their confident accents, the top-hatted bulldogs and the flowing gowns of the Proctor, whose little party reminded me of the naval shore pickets I had seen in Portsmouth or the red-capped Military Police prowling the West End of London during the war. However, Cambridge was not a world to which I ever expected to belong.

At Easter, Pat was to make her first public appearance at a small West London theatre. I sent her a good luck telegram but I was not invited to the occasion. Afterwards I was surprised to hear that several of my friends had been there. A young army captain, who had known Pat from childhood, had escorted her and the usual admirers to a pub in Harrow. I was angry rather than hurt. Apparently Peter Flood had organised the party and had clearly not forgiven me for my brother's sins.

I was too proud to contact Pat again after this and surprisingly quickly she was forgotten as I was once more swept up into the busy Farm Institute life. That summer, academic work gave way to outside visits. The students toured research institutes, allied trade factories and leading farmers. We felt flattered by the attention we were given and drank in new knowledge thirstily. We met famous cattle breeders, the great names of Friesian, Shorthorn and Ayrshire cattle, Moffat, Vigus and Mackay, as well as great scientists, Sir John Russell of Rothamstead and Sir John Hammond of Cambridge. There were also aristocratic landowners including Tim Abel-Smith, who, with well-bred courtesy, seemed to treat me with respect as a knowledgeable equal.

It was a heady time and I felt I was riding the crest of the wave, small though the pond may have been!

Chapter 8

Those Two Imposters, Triumph and Disaster

All too soon the course at Oaklands, the Hertfordshire Farm Institute, was over. I passed all the examinations easily and found that I was the second highest placed student in theory and top in practical work. I celebrated success by taking Sally, a staff nurse from the nearby outpost of Bartholomew's Hospital at Hill End, to the end-of-year dance. Inevitably I got more than a little merry. She was a nice kind girl who had been in the Woman's Auxiliary Air Force. I took her back to Hill End on the handlebars of my pushbike. All attempts at riding with her on the crossbar had failed. The presence of an old-fashioned Sturmey/Archer three-speed gear change had threatened to damage those parts which I, emboldened but not incapacitated by beer, was hoping to reach. We both sang and shrieked in mock panic during the hilarious and perilous ride through the Hertfordshire lanes. We nearly came to grief on a level crossing and twice collapsed in helpless laughter as we ran into bushes while crossing the dark hospital grounds. There was much flashing of torchlights as the watchman, charged with the sanctity of the nurses' quarters and armed with a wicked bamboo cane, sought to intercept us.

Ignoring the nurses' quarters, we made our way to the ward block where patients needing special diets were quartered. The ward kitchen was fairly safe from interfering guardians, apart from the regular ward sister's rounds, which were indeed regular and well-heralded. Sally's pal, who was on duty, offered to cook us supper of bacon and eggs to be washed down with stout from the special diets cupboard. Sally, in view of my condition, opted for black coffee for us both. This was just as well. A banging of doors and heavy footsteps indicated the Duty Sister's approach. The girls bundled me into the communal bathroom. Here it was the practice to lie on the floor between two baths, safely out of sight, in case Sister put her head round the door. I, bursting for a pee, was groping along the wall for the handbasin undoing my zip as I went... I staggered sideways and spun with flailing arms into one of the vast cast iron baths. Here I lay in the classical crucifixion posture, arms outstretched, eyes closed and head to one side. I continued to belch, fart and giggle foolishly in the darkness, my bursting bladder temporarily forgotten.

With a thump the door opened and the room was flooded with bright light. Sister towered over me like an avenging Amazon. At first she scowled speechlessly; then her face twitched and she too started to giggle, then laugh uncontrollably. "Get rid of him!" she choked, pointing at the flaccid object which was drooping from my unfastened zip. "Get rid of him, he won't do any harm to anyone tonight!"

Sally pushed me out into the darkness. "You have got me into trouble, you idiot!" she hissed. I, who could remember no such pleasure, mounted my bike and wobbled off with a final burp. Somehow I managed to control the machine and pee sideways without spraying myself, an achievement of great skill, even when sober. At the same time I kept a wary eye open for the watchman with his notorious stick. Back at Oaklands, I wearily crept up the stairs past Luggie's room. Even in my befuddled state I knew something was up.

Luggie's door was open and there were sounds of revelry upstairs. Entering the larger dormitory, I found my fellow students singing heartily round Sergeant Major Lugg, who was sitting in a chair smiling broadly and nursing a half empty bottle of my beer which had been hidden so carefully up the chimney of the unused fireplace. Luggie chuckled. "I believe you know a verse or two of 'Abdul the Bullbull', Lansbury! Let's hear them, lad!"

And so I learned that even discipline was a flexible commodity, at the end of the day, of course!

* * * * * * * * * * * * * * * * * * *

Mr Hope, the farmer in Bedfordshire for whom I had worked some years before, had asked me to come back and help with the harvest. It was not the sort of job Mr Hunter Smith wanted me to take. My training and experience merited a bailiff or manager's job on leaving the Institute. However, I thought it would be a good way to get back into the swing of farm work. It would only be a temporary job as my father, having now been paid a modest amount of war damage compensation for the loss of his bombed factory, was again talking of buying a farm for the family to work and live at.

I found the Bedfordshire farm much changed. The American bombers and all the colourful airmen had gone. There was now little or no competition for the landgirls and country lasses but I did not find them attractive. I was more interested in showing off all the skills and knowledge I had acquired since leaving the farm as a callow youth. I sought responsibility and was soon relief milking. When the corn was ready, I was able to show the farmer's sons all that I had learned about combines and modern farm machinery. The farm had prospered in the war and there was quite a lot of new tackle but it was not on the scale of the big Hertfordshire units where I had worked before my spell at college. Nonetheless, I had a most enjoyable time and was able to go into Bedford with my fat wage packets and kit myself out with gear to match my new status. Some tweed knickerbockers, long woollen stockings, brown market boots and shiny leather gaiters. These were the togs of the boss class and went well with the hairy Harris Tweed jacket, fawn waistcoat and flat cap which I had already bought as part of the farmery clothes beloved by agricultural students. I thought back to my first meeting with Mr Young at Greenlands farm near Cockermouth. Then I had first realised the class distinction between boots and wellies! The brown leather boots I had bought in Bedford were certainly as good as those Mrs Young had been so proud of; and my shiny brown leather leggings would have got admiring glances at Cockermouth market. Clothes may not make the man, I thought, but they certainly made me feel like a farmer!

Immediately after the 1948 harvest, I left the farm to help plan and execute my own family's move into farming. My first shock was to discover that not only my father, who I loved and respected, was to be involved, but also my brother-in-law Alex and sister, Daphne. I was even more shaken to find that my elder brother George was expecting to join the enterprise. Alex did not want George in; but I knew that George could do hard manual labour. George had sometimes come to work at the Barnet turf contractors and had surprised me with his strength and stamina. On the other hand, I doubted Alex's suitability for the unrelenting hard work of farming. My sister, Daphne, was also a towny and hardly cut out for the simple and sometimes isolated life in the country.

In spite of these reservations, I set off in high spirits to find a suitable holding for the family. I had advised them that a dairy farm was most likely to succeed because the hard work was balanced by the certainty of a monthly milk cheque. Consequently I directed my search to the grass country of the west of England. Most of the farms I inspected were quite unlike the estate agents' descriptions. Many farms had been bought by speculators, who hoped to resell them at huge profit to gullible ex-servicemen or businessmen, anxious to invest their demobilisation gratuities or war profits respectively. I soon learned to read between the lines of estate agents' guff but I still made some wasted journeys. To my annoyance, Alex gave up his job in anticipation of an early purchase and start to farming operations. Worse still, he insisted on accompanying me on my inspections of properties. I felt this was a waste of money and it somehow implied that the family was keeping an eye on me. My pride was hurt. Furthermore, as a non-smoker, I was impatient with Alex's constant need to break or delay journeys while he went in search of cigarettes.

One day after an abortive visit to a bleak stony farm on Bodmin Moor – which had been described by the estate agent as a "useful, productive dairy farm with substantial buildings", whereas the farm was clearly derelict and the "substantial buildings" were in fact, stone and corrugated iron shacks – Alex and I stayed the night in the Old Ship Hotel in Exeter. The bedroom had very uneven sloping floors making one feel dizzy and unsteady, however sober. There were two beds but no handbasin. The bathroom and loo were down the creaking corridor.

Once more, Alex needed cigarettes; and the pair of us set off to find a pub with supplies. Both of us fancied a pint and we were about to order when the Devonian landlord, sensing foreigners and a chance for fun, suggested that we should try the local "scrumpy". "It may be too strong for you," challenged the Devonian. I, quick to rise, downed my pint of the sour grey rough cider equally rapidly and banged down my pot for a second. Alex ordered a small whisky and stuck to shorts for the rest of the evening. I was warming to the foaming scrumpy and also to the landlord's daughter who was enjoying the spectacle of my obvious intoxication and fast-growing unsteadiness. "You'm bedder take your pal home zoon," she advised Alex. He and I, now befuddled and songful, wove our way back to our room at the Ship Hotel. Alex seemed to occupy the bathroom for ages. I guessed that he was having a last drag at a fag as smoking was not allowed in the bedrooms. I found a huge old china utensil under my bed and emptied my distended bladder with gurgles and sighs of relief. "Almost as good as a bonk, having a good piss when you want one!" I muttered to myself. The half-filled chamber pot tilted dangerously on the uneven floor. The frothing contents were nearly up to the rim on one side but well down on the other.

Both of us slept well and we were awakened by the chambermaid who told us that breakfast was ready and that we had better hurry. Alex bagged the bathroom first and I knew I was in for a long wait. Alex always sat on the loo for ages, smoking a fag and waiting for action. I was desperate for a pee. I knelt down and got out the half-full pot. I sighed with relief as the contents swirled round, driven by my blissful discharge. An old nursery jingle drifted dreamily through my mind: "Little boy kneels at the foot of the bed." My train of thought was interrupted when I realised with horror that the pot was almost full and I could hardly stop. With an enormous effort, I cut off the flow.

The pot was now so full I could not put it down on the sloping floor. With infinite care, I carried the almost level vessel to Alex's side of the room. By a wonderful communication of eye, coordination of movement and great strength of wrist, I managed to place the pot on a level area of floorboard. I dressed rapidly and went down to breakfast. Alex was still in the bathroom where a small queue of impatient guests was forming.

I had just started to fork beautifully crisped bacon into my young mouth when a crash and scream of despair came from immediately above my head. I looked up and my full mouth fell open as long damp streaks appeared on the ceiling plaster above my head. It was as if I had been transported back to the dreadful day at my father's house when I had missed the pot after a rugby club dinner. The poor chambermaid had reached for the potty under Alex's bed and not realising its weight of contents, she had dropped it with the frightful flood that ensued. The landlord, on hearing the scream, rushed upstairs to find the maid, hand to mouth, pointing at the sodden floor and staring pop-eyed at the unfortunate Alex, who having just arrived back from the bathroom, unaware of the damp drama, was calmly picking up my belongings prior to coming down to breakfast.

Downstairs in the dining room, I was still frozen to my seat in spite of the odd drips which were now forming and falling among the seated guests as they tucked innocently into their fine Devonshire marmalade and toast. One or two ladies patted their hair aware of something falling and one woman leaned over to wipe what she took to be a drop of perspiration from her husband's balding forehead. "Good God!" a voice said. "There's been a burst or an overflow!" I smiled weakly and started to make for the door. A commotion on the stairs materialized in a flurry of figures as Alex clattered down

154

followed by my case and jacket which had been hurled after him by the irate landlord. "Filthy bloody Scot!" he shouted. "Coming in drunk and pissing the bed! Get out of my hotel!" The bewildered Alex looked accusingly at me but I managed to maintain an air of shocked innocence. Fortunately we had paid our bill in advance the night before and we were able to make our escape without further recriminations or explanations. I considered the loss of my uncollected pyjamas and spongebag a cheap price for an easy getaway!

Thankfully, Alex was not so keen to accompany me on my next trip which was to a farm in South Wales. This proved to be a useful dairy farm near Swansea. The pastures were good, being made up of good modern varieties of grasses and clovers. The buildings were of very solid stone and slate and the house was dry and sizeable. I was quite taken with the farm. It was no more isolated than the Pardshaw farm I had first worked on in Cumberland and the hilly pastures within the stone walls and hedges gave the place a feeling of familiarity. However, the family after the long journey down from London saw it through different eyes. "How could the children get to school down that precipitous road? Was that outside toilet the only one there was?" There were silverfish running about in the fireplace and worst of all, my sister had seen a frog or a toad in the spring-fed water cistern from which the domestic water was drawn. No: the family would not move to Wales

Undismayed though a little impatient I set off; this time accompanied once more by Alex, to look at a small farm in Lincolnshire. The train journey took us to Gainsborough, a depressed-looking place which seemed, from the train, to consist of one huge redbrick factory and rows of terraced brick and slate houses. I shuddered at the thought of living and working in such a place. We got off the train at Kirton Lindsey and set off on foot past the old RAF fighter station towards the village of Redbourne. We passed fertile fields of sugar beet and dense stubbles of what had obviously been a successful harvest of heavy wheat crops. Things looked hopeful and my spirits rose. We trudged through the prosperous-looking village and down the lane to the farm.

From a distance the buildings looked sound. There was a newish steel dutch barn and a cluster of traditional red brick and claytile buildings round a small farmhouse. To our disappointment, the fertile land ended almost upon entering the farm gate. The soils in most of the fields were a thin grey sand or shallow black peat. There were some half-used clamps of skinny-looking carrots and a puny stack of rye straw. A biting wind swept up the valley from the river. My heart fell. The agent's runner was waiting for us and we were shown into the house. Up in the bedroom, even with the windows closed, the tatty curtains were being blown almost parallel to the cracked ceiling. "Last fellow shot 'is wife then 'ung issen," commented the agent's runner. Alex and I, now cold and weary, looked at each other in dismay. I gave Alex a nod and we left the house in disgust, the agent still extolling the virtues of the bleak little holding. We made our way along the road marvelling at the estate agent's misleading description: "A nicely laid out farm in a much sought after district of fertile arable land, having the advantage of fine river frontage." I thought of the black canal-like ditch at the bottom of one of the swampy fields and grimaced. That charming race of rogues dressed as country gentlemen who professed to be estate agents had not risen in my estimation. "Doubt if they ever got out of their car to open the farm gate when they surveyed that one," I said. "What a bloody waste of time!"

By now it was getting dark and in the absence of transport we hurried on foot into Waddingham village and tried the pub. We were cold, disappointed and hungry. It was not yet open but the landlord's wife opened the door, carrying a young baby. She informed us that she did not take guests as it was just a pub and not an inn. As we turned away, she called after us: "Are you from the Catering?" We said no. "Are you from the Ministry?" Once again we said no, this time with a laugh. The woman then asked us back in. "I have got a room," she said, "but we are not supposed to let it. Rationing regulations and all that. We are not s'posed to cater and I thowt you might be inspectors! My husband don't like me to take anyone till he's checked 'em but you look all right."

At this Alex turned on the charm. "We just want a bed for the night and a few beers. We are hungry if you can manage something." "Something" turned out to be a fine meal of Lincolnshire "hacelet", cheese and pickles, washed down with beer from the barrel. The landlord proved to be a truck driver from the steel works at Scunthorpe. In the beet season he drove a lorry from the sugar factory at Brigg. He had an extensive knowledge of the local farms and laughed when he heard that we had been to the "murder farm". "Nowt theer but trooble, sand and wet! Lucky if tha gets tha seed back."

There was, however, a small farm he knew of for sale near Welton, just outside Lincoln. "Aye, it's on Cliff land, rare good soil and drainage theer!" I perked up. I had heard of the grand land along the Lincoln cliff and this sounded very promising. Perhaps the morrow would bring the homestead which my father and I dreamed of.

We slept but fitfully that night. The sign depicting the Marquis of Granby, swinging outside our window, gave out occasional eerie squeals and creaks. My dreams were a mixture of inspecting good "Cliff" land and the horrors of the "murder farm" at Redbourne, as I now knew it.

When I awoke, feeling far from well rested, the landlord and his wife were already up and had breakfast ready. I was a bit put off by the un-nappied baby crawling about the kitchen but after my disturbed breakfast in Exeter, I supposed I could not grumble if minor accidents occurred. I had finished my scrambled eggs by the time Alex started on his. Like most smokers, he was more interested in having a fag than getting any nutrition. I was more than amused when Alex turned pale at the sight of the inevitable accident performed across the floor by the smiling baby. I could not resist an old joke.

"What's the difference between a seagull and a baby, Alex?"

"Search me," said Alex, trying to swallow a mouthful of scrambled egg.

"A seagull flits across the shore..." I whispered.

Alex's eyes turned to the innocent baby and he pushed his plate away. "Rotten pig!" I, who had an unfailing appetite, polished off his unwanted breakfast with a contented grunt. Perhaps I was a bit of a pig!

After breakfast we said goodbye to the friendly landlord and his buxom wife. We caught a local bus towards Lincoln, alighting at Scampton RAF station, which was the nearest we could get to the Welton farm. It was from Scampton that Guy Gibson had set off with his brave force of Lancaster bomber crews to drop Barnes Wallis' bouncing bombs on the Mohne and Eder dams. There were Boeing Superfortresses there now and I compared these to the old B17 Flying Fortresses which I had been so familiar with in Bedfordshire. The Superfortresses were nothing like as graceful but had awe-inspiring size and power. From the Welton turn-off, I looked along the perfectly straight Roman road of Ermine Street and I could see the splendid cathedral towering above Lincoln a few miles away. How bloody sad,

I thought. All those poor bloody night bomber crews who took off over that beautiful building but were never to see it again.

Down Rylands Lane, we found the farm. It was a nice honey-coloured farmhouse and yard of Lincolnshire limestone with a red tiled roof, right on the roadside at the edge of Welton village. We had passed a neat, modern-looking school, which must please my sister; and the tidiness of the village was almost suburban. With the city of Lincoln so close, I thought the situation ideal. A threshing gang was at work in the stackyard and I inspected the fine big wheat grains admiringly. Behind the yard was a field of huge mangolds and from the buildings I could hear the grunt of contented pigs. Alex was lighting his cigarette and nodding. The foreman broke off from his work and showed us round the land. It was a nice friable loam, obviously well drained and in excellent condition. It did indeed seem perfect for our needs and we might even be able to farm it without the drudgery of dairy cattle! On the journey back to Mill Hill, we discussed our ideas for the farm. The land was good enough for corn growing and the house was excellent apart from an outside loo and no mains water. There was, however, a good well supply and the mains were not far away; and I reckoned it would cost very little to have water laid on. The price of the farm was £6,000 for 140 acres. Less than £50 an acre! I knew that it was more than my father wanted to spend but with a two-thirds mortgage available at four percent, it seemed too good to miss. I calculated that to buy, stock and equip the farm, we would only have to find a total of £6,000. I was excited and keen to get on with it.

Disaster, the end of a dream !

Back at Mill Hill, the family were less enthusiastic. Lincolnshire they had heard was cold and bleak. It was a long way away. After hearing Alex's views, my father agreed to go and look at the little farm. Next morning, however, my sister greeted me with the words, "We can't go on with this. Look at the state Dad has got into, worrying about it all." My dad was indeed looking grey and shaky.

"I am sorry, Tel, but we cannot face the risks and upheaval. We cannot go farming."

My world crashed about me. Everything I had endured for the last six years, the brutalising company I had kept, the long hours on low pay, the ostracism by my suburban peers, the years of trying to

158

learn from wise but uncommunicative yokels, the loneliness of not being "one of them" wherever I had worked or played. The only really happy time had been at Oaklands, the Hertfordshire Farm Institute; and now even that had been for nothing! It was all too much!

Angrily, I demanded the right to go my own way in future and not to be included in any of the family plans. Alex went back to his job in a Cricklewood aircraft factory. George and Madge went off to join the groundnut scheme in Africa.

My father sold the family home on Watford Way and went to live with Alex and my sister Daphne in a small house on the wrong side of the tracks in Mill Hill. It was only a few days since I had been full of happiness and confidence, telling them of the good fertile farm I had found in Lincolnshire. Now the cold grey autumn streets of Mill Hill seemed to mock me. It was to be a further twelve eventful years before I could fulfill my dreams, when together with my lovely young wife and family, we would have our own first farm in that county.

I spent a few miserable autumn weeks relieved only by Saturday afternoons at the rugby club where I worked off my frustrations and aggression. Apparently my robust performances had been noted and one day I was approached to go and play for Old Millhillians in spite of only having been at the Prep School. I was flattered and went for a trial. My old friends at the local club took it badly and I was very unpopular.

Short of an occupation, I began to make a few quid dealing in old cars and hanging about with some shady characters who rented sheds under the railway arches at the bottom of Mill Hill Broadway. One day I found a huge heap of pinkened garden lime behind the sheds. This had been dumped by one of my shady mates who was filtering unrationed commercial vehicle fuel through chalk and charcoal to remove the pink dye which distinguished it and betrayed its illegal use to inquisitive traffic police. The clear petrol was fetching a fortune on the black market. I had been buying the odd gallon from my "friend" not realising the risk I was running. I was horrified at the situation and decided to distance myself from the whole shady scene.

1948 was a sad Christmas. All the Mill Hill girls seemed to be bagged by flash young men in sports cars. My sister Daphne did her best, with the meagre rations we were allowed, to make a cheerful Christmas dinner. This brought back memories of the great pre-war times at the old family home when the whole family had been together and old Grandad, George Lansbury, would raise his glass and toast the cook. I remembered the dancing shadows of the great roaring fire, the crack of walnut shells, the smell of port and the exciting snap of crackers and the rustle of paper hats. Above all, I remembered my mother's warm bosom when I snuggled up contentedly at the end of Christmas day.

I needed a clean break from Mill Hill; and after reading another friend's glowing account of life as an agricultural exchange student on a farm in Denmark, I took the necessary steps to join him. I could not face looking for a job in British agriculture after all my disappointments. I was determined to make a bright fresh start and Denmark, with its much vaunted agriculture, sounded just the place to do it.

Early in the New Year of 1949, I set off for Harwich dock on the motorcycle and sidecar combination which I had just purchased from Tom Cochrane with my last savings. It was a tricky journey. I had not driven a combination before and was nearly taken by surprise when the sidecar rose into the air every time I turned to the left. At a roundabout near Colchester I nearly lost control; but by the time I reached Harwich I had not only mastered the beast but was amusing myself by driving along with the sidecar wheel up in the air. After a long delay, satisfying the obstructive and surly officials that I had all the necessary documents, I boarded the Danish ferry *Kronprinz Frederik* and set sail for Denmark. The family and all its ramifications were behind me. I was free!

Chapter 9

Danish Pastry

The big ferry did not plough through the waves; rather it slithered and yawed over and round them. The motion soon had me as sick as a pig and wishing that I was still cutting turf, shovelling shit, anything to escape this terrible dizzy sickness. After a stiff brandy, I had recovered enough to watch the Dogger Bank trawlers bobbing wildly in the huge seas. I pondered on the wild panic, which had made the gunners of the Czar of Russia's Imperial Fleet open fire on these tiny boats, when leaving Kronstad for Vladivostoc on the other side of the world. How could they have imagined they were Japanese destroyers? Perhaps the Russian gunners had felt as ill as I did. I had another stiff brandy and went to my cabin. An equally sick cotton salesman was already hunched over his vomit pan. Both of us had a terrible night, tossing and groaning in our bunks between bouts of sickness. In the morning we apologised to each other for the appalling and embarrassing noises each had made, and then went on deck.

We were passing the area where Admiral Jellicoe had "crossed the T" but had failed to win a decisive victory in the Battle of Jutland during the First World War. Soon Jutland itself was in sight and the low coast of Denmark began to change from a grey blur to a detailed shoreline. The approach to Esbjerg harbour was dull and uninteresting, unlike the port itself, which was bustling and seemed delightfully foreign to me, who had not been out of England since before the war. I was off the boat and through the formalities in a flash. The Danish officials were friendly and polite. Most seemed to speak English and, as they cleared my bike and luggage, told me where to find a petrol pump and indicated the main road to Copenhagen. The peaked-capped pump attendant smiled at my attempt to speak Danish and said in perfect cockney, "You want her filled up, mate?" It transpired that the attendant had served in the Royal Engineers during the war having escaped to England just before the Nazi invasion of Denmark. He could not understand why a man from North London was going to work on a farm in Denmark. He was still shaking his head as I drove off on the N1 road for Copenhagen...

It was a bright, crisp day as the trusty old Ariel swept me out of the town and into the countryside. The 600cc side valve engine had the throaty roar worthy of a far more sporty machine, but it was the

161

ideal companion to the large sidecar, weighed down with spare petrol and my luggage. I studied the fields and small groups of farm buildings in the flat hedgeless fields. There was not a grazing animal to be seen at that time of the year and apart from the odd patch of lucerne, I saw very little grassland as I crossed Jutland towards Fyn Island. This, I had heard, was where the Danes grew tobacco for their pungent little cigars. I had already been shocked to see women smoking these in Esbjerg.

I was soon crossing the huge bridge which spans the middle straits between the mainland of Jutland and the islands. Once over, I headed for Nyborg where Hans Christian Andersen was born. The plain countryside could not have inspired his fantastic stories, unless it was by inspiring a desire to escape, I thought. In Nyborg I forgot to drive on the right and nearly took a tram head on. "Bloody foreigners," I thought. "Why can't they drive on the left like us?" A policeman, dressed in what looked like an SS uniform, blew his whistle and waved me down. Seeing the GB plates he smiled and waved me on, shouting an unintelligible but obviously friendly rebuke. The tram continued to clank along its tracks, leaving me ruefully considering my own stupidity.

It was by now late afternoon and I was absolutely frozen. I was more than glad to reach the ferry which would take me on from Fyn to Zealand, the main island on which Copenhagen was situated. The passenger saloon of the ferry was warm and welcoming. I feared a return of seasickness during the twenty mile crossing but it was as still as a millpond. A friendly lorry driver teased me about my old motor bike. "Ve vant new maskines in Danmark! Vy you bring this old heap?" I did not want to go into explanations as to why I could afford no better. The driver bought me hot coffee and a pastry. It was a flat oval of shiny brown flakey twirl with flaked almonds lying on a bed of thin sugar icing. I bit into the delicious fatty texture, feeling the fresh currants and tasting the exquisite richness of my first post-war Danish pastry. "You can like Wiena Bread," said the driver. "Yah," said I using my smattering of Danish successfully for the first time. "Tusind tak! Det er got!" It was good indeed!

By the time the ship docked, it was getting dark and I was worried about finding the way to Copenhagen. I need not have worried. The lorry driver offered to lead me across Zealand to the outer suburbs. It was desperately cold and for mile after mile I squirmed and shook in an effort to keep from freezing. The signposts for Copenhagen flashed by but the distances shown to the capital seemed to diminish agonisingly slowly. The cold affected my bladder and I was glad that amongst the accomplishments I had picked up at Oaklands, I had learned the trick of urinating without stopping on my bicycle. It was far easier on a stable motorbike and sidecar; but in this case I had to take care not to spray pedestrians or passing cars and above all, avoid getting a frostbitten willy. Not that I had had much chance to use the damn thing for any more pleasurable purposes lately, I thought bitterly.

The bright lights of Copenhagen showed up over the horizon and eventually the lorry in front slowed down and peeled off the main road, leaving me to find my way into the city. My first impression was of brilliantly lit streets and shop windows. Important buildings were floodlit and the bright standard lights along the sides of the many bridges shone back brightly from the water below. It was all a great contrast to the bleak streets I had left behind in London where, due to continuing fuel shortages, austerity still ruled and there was little illumination other than that which was absolutely necessary. The Danish men all seemed to wear coats of coarse tweed, not unlike elongated Norfolk jackets, together with small fur hats worn at jaunty angles. Many wore leather jackboots and all seemed very smart.

The first two hotels I tried were either full or did not like the look of the strange apparition I presented at the reception desks. I was wearing an ex-WD waterproof tank suit. It had kept me from freezing on the motorbike but was obviously not the kind of apparel they were accustomed to see in Copenhagen. At length I was directed to a small sort of motel where I crawled gratefully between icy sheets. I had never felt so cold and even with my head beneath the covers it was some time before I stopped shivering and was able to sleep. Even then my night was disturbed by the couple in the next room, who seemed to be making love all night. I could hear almost every word as an American girl and a male voice of indeterminate accent giggled and gasped their gratification. I had seldom come nearer to thumping on the wall. From the name on the sheets and towels I divined that the motel was called the "Thor". I wished the couple next door were, "tho that I could get thum proper bloody sleep!"

Next day I almost slept too late to order breakfast. I had pictured Denmark as a land flowing with cream, butter, bacon and eggs and expected a fine breakfast of these accordingly. As I was to discover, these were rarely on the Danish breakfast table of the 1940s!

Breakfast consisted of coffee served with black bread topped with various slices of beetroot, pickled cucumber, cold hard boiled egg, brawn jelly (which I detested), cheese and raw pickled herring. I could not face this and asked for toasted white bread and butter with jam. The tall blonde waiter looked at me with some disdain. After a long wait, a dish of what appeared to be sliced rolls, irregularly toasted and of all shapes and sizes, was placed before me. A moment later a young girl brought me a dish of butter and some curious "mermelathe" which was more like redcurrant sauce. Later I found out that I could have ordered eggs and bacon; the waiter probably wondered why I preferred toast.

After breakfast I made my way to the main railway station where I had arranged to meet Sutty, the friend who had written to me about the delights of farming in Denmark. Sutty arrived punctually and showed me round the city. We saw the Radhusplatz and Kronberg Castle, where toytown soldiers marched in close order outside the royal apartments. The Tivoli gardens were shut so we made our way down through Newhaven, the red light district, to the harbour, where we shivered as we viewed the famous Little Mermaid. Seeking warmth, we went into a smoky bar hoping to meet some Danish girls. There were none about and we left Newhaven believing that Danish women must curl up indoors and hibernate for the winter.

That evening we went into a small plain-looking restaurant for a meal. Clearly we had misjudged the place. Beautifully dressed waiters, in black tie and tails, hovered round the two "Englanders". Globular glasses of foaming lager were placed in front of us as we tucked into lamb chops and beautifully cooked vegetables. Sutty recommended the local "aeble kage", a delightful confection of cream, caramelised brown sugar, crumbed nuts and stewed apple in layers. We rounded off our meal with very bitter black coffee and I was persuaded to try the local schnapps. The schnapps was brought to our table in tapering glasses with no feet, the custom being that the glass was always emptied in one swallow and could not be set down unless empty.

"It tastes like a mixture of caraway seed and paraffin," warned Sutty. "Get it down in one and the second won't taste so bad!"

"The third should be quite good," I added with a grin. I gulped the small glassful down and found myself gasping for air as the burning liquor scorched my throat. The hovering waiter said "Skaal!" and refilled my glass before I could protest. Already I felt warm and well disposed to Denmark. The second glass went down very easily. This time I observed the local custom and tilting my head, I caught Sutty's eye and uttered a guttural "Skaal!" Neither of us refused a third glass, lingering over it and accepting a small pointed cigar from another hovering waiter who leaned forward and clipped the wet end which in my ignorance of smoker's ritual, I had placed in my mouth before being offered a light. I leaned back in my chair. "If only Bucko and the Barnet turf cutters could see me now, or better still, Farmer Eddie from Pardshaw!"

Pride, as always with me, came before a fall.

The bill was presented with a flourish and a clicking of heels. The total shattered me. It was for far more than I had ever been paid for a week's work and my share of the total ate badly into the meagre wad of Kroners which were to supplement my tiny allowance as an exchange student... I had forgotten Sutty came from a Rolls Royce-owning family and probably had a liberal allowance and therefore different ideas of value for money!

During the afternoon, as we had been walking the apparently all male streets of Copenhagen, it had soon become clear that Sutty no longer held the views of Danish agriculture which he had expressed in his earlier letter to me. This had painted a golden picture. By now, he was fed up with the food, with his accommodation and with the arrogance of his Danish boss. I began to wonder if I had made a bad mistake in coming to Denmark.

I saw Sutty back onto his train to the southern town of Valloe and walked back to my room. I went to bed early, undisturbed by the lovers next door. They had either moved out or exhausted themselves. It was just as well. I was suffering from enough mixed emotions without sexual jealousy rearing its ugly head. Not, I mused, that anything else was likely to rear up in this bloody freezing climate!

Next day I set off northwards for Fredrikssund. As I drove out of Copenhagen it was a glorious winter's day. The sun shone from a cloudless blue sky and the countryside looked clean and inviting. My spirits rose and I made up my mind to make the most of Denmark whatever I found. As I neared the town at the head of the fjord which ran down to Roskilde, I saw white storks nesting on the roof of a red-tiled farmhouse. It was pure Hans Christian Andersen. The streets of the villages I passed through were spotless, as indeed were the farmyards and gardens along the road. Everything seemed so clean and tidy that it could have been an illustration from a children's book.

It was a great contrast to the scruffy, cowshit-spattered villages of West Cumberland.

After crossing the swing bridge over the fjord at Frederikssund, I saw the first signs of the comparatively recent German occupation: the remains of a roadblock and swing barrier with a striped sentry box, such as I had seen in many war films. I wondered what my reception would have been four years earlier. Reaching Krostrup, I enquired for Brohojgaard where I was to work and live. A most attractive blonde girl in the telegraph office directed me. She told me that the farm name meant "High Bread Farm". She too could not understand why an Englishman was burying himself in the wilds of Denmark having come from "vonderful London". Had I met the King and Queen? Did I love Winston Churchill? I avoided explanations of my antipathy to Churchill's fervid anti-socialist politics, which I believed had partially created the iron curtain and the cold war. Somewhat regretfully I left the pretty girl and her warm office to go out into the freezing afternoon air. Following her directions, I rode up the hill past the milk factory and turned down the long farm drive.

The drive led to a square of wooden buildings and passed through a gated archway beneath a barn. I brought my machine to a stop outside the house. A small grizzled man appeared from a shed. "Herr Jepsen?" I said politely. The man stared at me, then, without a smile, he started to shout frenziedly, "Kama, Kama! Den Englander har komme! Han er lige om stor bjorn!" which, I gathered later, meant that he was telling his daughter Kama that I looked like a big bear! Herr Jepsen was in too much of a hurry to welcome me himself, a characteristic I was to get used to in time. Indeed, Herr Jepsen's most frequent words were "Hurtig, hurtig, farlig tempo!" and "Tide er penge!" which meant "Get a move on!" and "Time is money!" Kama was a large-boned, broad-faced blonde with a wonderful big-busted, wide-hipped figure. Her mother was dark and bore all the marks of a hard life and overwork. Her shoulders were pulled down from carrying heavy loads and the exposed skin below her neck was raw from sun and freezing air. I was surprised to hear that she only had two children, both girls. She looked burned out. Ilse, the elder daughter, was a music teacher in Hillerod.

There were two other men on the farm. Karl, the horseman, was a saturnine figure, unwashed, unshaven, bleary-eyed and slow of speech. He spoke no English but I found I was able to communicate quite easily by signs and the few Danish words I had learned before

166

leaving England. When Karl spoke slowly I found I could follow the gist as many of the words were similar to the Cumbrian dialect. The other man or boy, for he was only nineteen, was Bent the cowman. Bent was a highly intelligent farmer's son from Jutland. I found him to be very well educated and good at his job. I, in my turn, could not understand why Bent was wasting his abilities working for Herr Jepsen. Apparently it was the practice in Denmark for farmers' sons to work away from home for a few years before returning to work on the family farm. I thought of the many arrogant farmers' sons I had met in England who had never taken an order in their lives. "Would do some of them good," I decided. Jepsen exploited Bent's keenness and good nature but the boy did not complain. In no time he and I were the best of friends.

I soon found that Sutty had been right. The much-vaunted Danish agriculture had been left behind by the huge strides in mechanisation, in the use of fertiliser and the high-yielding crop varieties made by British farmers during the war years. There were no tractors or up-to-date machinery on the farm and any Danish advance on British land use and animal husbandry could be put down solely to the availability of very cheap labour. The twenty-odd Danish Red cows and their calves were tied up, groomed and cosseted like cattle being prepared for an agricultural show, by all the men and the farm women. This work was done every evening and on Sunday, much to my irritation as Jepsen himself always managed to avoid this chore by going off to chapel, where he was a lay preacher. "He must go to pray forgiveness frequently," said Karl, "because he has so many sins to be forgiven!" I was also irritated to find that I was expected to sweep and rake the yard and garden paths every Sunday after the stock had been groomed. Jepsen liked the sandy paths to be raked to form fan-shaped patterns. I fumed at such a fetish! I soon realised that I was not going to learn much. However I enjoyed the challenge of hard work; and there were few jobs I could not do as well or better than the Danish farm workers.

At my request the family did not attempt to speak English and in no time I was fluent enough in Danish to be mistaken for a Schleswig Holsteiner. I made an exception for Frau Jepsen and Kama who wanted to improve their English... Fortunately for me, Frau Jepsen was too shy to try English except at her tutor's lessons. Kama, however, was keen to learn and I began to look forward to the evenings by the huge peat-burning stove with the big blonde girl asking me questions as she ironed and folded the family wash. She was not bad looking; she had nice tits, a bit on the large side for my taste; and what's more, she often made me coffee and cakes when her parents were out. I began to fancy my chances. Kama was engaged to a heel-clicking young man from Jaegerspris, a neighbouring village. The young man must have been some sort of a part-time soldier because he often turned up in uniform, but Bent said he was working in the local council offices.

One afternoon the skies blackened and the first flurries of snow danced along the stable roof tiles. It seemed less cold as the snow started to settle. I had got used to the intense cold and pitied the Frederiksborg horses, which stood patiently by the root clamps while I shovelled loads of turnips or potatoes into the long plank wagons. Sometimes the horses had icicles a foot long hanging from their nose whiskers. By morning the world was white all over. Herr Jepsen hurried me into a small shed. Here there was a fairytale sledge. The harness and links were similar to those I had used in Cumberland and even Herr Jepsen was impressed by the workmanlike way I was able to yoke up Piers, the great Fredriksborg stallion, into the traces. We manoeuvered the outfit round to the milkshed, and loaded up the churns from the primitive dairy. Joyfully I drove the sled up the drive to the roadside. It was quite a long way and I gloried in the blue skies and golden light of the winter sunshine on the snow. I had been to see Howard Keel in *Oklahoma* just before I left London and I found myself singing loudly, emitting great clouds of vapour as my warm breath mingled with the icy air.

> "Oh what a beautiful morning, Oh what a beautiful day,
> I've got a wonderful feeling; Kama might give me a lay!"

I unyoked the sledge at the roadside where the milk lorry could pick up the churns. Backing the great stallion beside the sled, I clambered up and cantered the willing beast down the snowy track back to the yard. As I passed under the barn and onto the swept surface of the yard, the stallion's shod hooves set up a clatter. Kama came smiling to the door . "Saa du kan ride?" "If I get half a chance," I thought wickedly to myself. By now I quite fancied her.

The snow went as fast as it had come and work started in the fields. I found myself harrowing behind a team of five horses and had to admit that on the light sandy soil, I could not have covered any more ground with the Ferguson tractor I had been extolling to Jepsen. The huge sweep of harrows was difficult to turn at the ends, as the vast straight stretcher bar was inclined to dig in, causing the eight light harrows to rear up and tangle. Once Kama saw me untangling the interlocked harrows and came over to help me before a frantic and gesticulating Herr Jepsen arrived, bewailing the loss of time and money! As she bent over the harrows her breasts danced and bobbed beneath my nose. I was beginning to scent possibilities. Sometimes when Karl and I were working together we would see the scampering figure of Jepson coming towards us. "Farlig lille mand," said Karl. "Han har ikke tid at lade vandet!" At this he imitated a man attempting to plough with one hand while holding his widdler with the other. ("Nasty little man; he hasn't got time for a piss!") I understood Karl only too well, remembering my frozen motorbike ride.

An extraordinarily dull country dance at Jaegerspris made me feel like a night on the town. Bent and I decided to ask Jepsen for two days off to visit Copenhagen. Jepsen protested but as neither of us had had a full day off for a month, we carried the day. Bent had relatives who put us up for the night and we went into Copenhagen. The Tivoli gardens were still closed and Bent was not prepared to go after girls in Newhaven despite my urgent pleas for a bit of adventure. We went instead for a meal and a show in the National Scala nightclub. The meal and floor show were excellent value but finished quite early. Not yet ready to go home, we went on to the Scandia club where we watched the dancing and I had a short dance with a tiny blonde to the tune "Slow boat to China". She said something to Bent and he laughed.

"You are a big bear again!"

Next day we visited the Rosenberg Slot, a fairytale castle straight from Hans Andersen. I loved the extravagant paintings of horse riders lining the staircases. There were charming rooms with fine views from the tiny windows. Best of all were the wonderful ceramics and jewels of the royal collection. All too soon the excursion ended and we came back to Brodhojgaard by way of Helsingor Slot, the Elsinore castle of Shakespeare's *Hamlet*.

When we arrived back at the farm, Kama was still up and made me some coffee. Her elder sister, Ilse, who had arrived on a visit home, joined us. She spoke good English and we were soon discussing classical music. I mentioned that I liked Chopin and out of politeness to the great Scandinavian composer, I expressed an interest in Sibelius. The girls went on to quiz me about my family. I did not reveal my family's financial problems and I deduced from some of the comments I overheard that they seemed to think I was a suitable catch for Ilse. I did not fancy her at all but Ilse was shameless. She would play one or the other composer's music whenever I was in the house and I was forced out of politeness to leave the cosy kitchen, which I normally shared with the other men, to go and sit in the much colder room where the piano was kept. While Ilse played and beamed her toothy smile at me, Kama sat mending a large cupped bra which could only have been hers; and my eyes were drawn to it. I looked up to find Kama looking sternly into my eyes. Ilse was playing on and throwing languishing looks in my direction but Kama had transfixed me with her blue-eyed stare. Despite my best efforts, my lips began to twitch. I looked again at the bra she was holding and back to her unblinking eyes. I smiled and then grinned with a wink. Kama showed the tip of her pink tongue. "You have wicked eyes," she said quietly.

Once more, I settled down to the daily routine of the farm. I had got used to Danish breakfasts and tucked into the hard sour bread. I suffered agonies of wind, which I could not contain at all times.

"Hvem fisa?" ("Who's farted?") Herr Jepsen had demanded.

"Den Englander," said Karl, "han altid fisa!"

"Englander! Fisa du?" said Herr Jepsen.

"Undskylde meg," said I. "Den Danske mad er for strang!" ("Forgive me, Danish food is too strong!") Jepsen roared with laughter. "Good Lord," I thought, "he is human after all."

It was not long before Kama and I got together. She had invited me in for coffee in the afternoon and later she showed me her bedroom which was next to mine. I had been too sleepy from the cold and heavy work to have been curious up to now. Ostensibly she was showing me the many samplers she had made and other examples of her needlework. I was surprised to see an illustrated copy of the *Rubaiyat of Omar Khayyam* beside her bed and I quoted a few lines to her. It brought back memories of Pat Powell but no regrets. We read some of the pages together and she leaned close as I puzzled over the quirky translation. I kissed her lightly as I left the room and was surprised at the fervour with which she returned my tentative peck. Her arms were strong and I was pinned close to her. I noticed the slight smell of sweaty wool which I had come to associate with farm women. It did not put me off; indeed her womanly scent was turning me on fast when we heard footsteps ascending the wooden stairway.

Kama pushed me away in a panic. I moved out into the passage and went towards my room. "Got nacht, Kama, sovi got!" ("Good night and sleep well!") I called innocently as Ilse came into view. "Good night, Tehra!" the two girls called in unison. It had been a near thing.

Bent and I went off to Roskilde on my trusty old motorbike the following Saturday night. Here we met Sutty; he too had driven sixty miles in the intense cold and we were all hungry. We ate and drank at the Hotel Prinzen where I loved the enormous, beautifully cooked pork chops served with rich gravy and sweet red cabbage with sauté potatoes. This was followed by *aebleskiver*, a delightful dumpling of which I could not eat enough. By now I had developed a taste for the sharp Pilsner lager which we alternated with schnapps. The local dance hall beckoned and we three tipsy young men stumbled about happily. We were soon chatting with the locals who took me for a German or South Jutlander. One fisherman, on realising I was from London, peered suspiciously at me. He could not believe that I was working for Jepsen as a "Landarbeidersmand". Eventually and none too soon, we went out into the Scandinavian cold. As we walked back to the car park beside Roskilde Domkirk, happily singing Danny Kaye's latest hit "Bongo, bongo, bongo, I don't want to leave the Congo", we noticed the fisherman following us. Approaching Bent, he whispered something to him and dashed off towards the police station. Bent laughed. "Get on your bike and let's go! He thinks you are a spy or something. Let's get off or we will be here for hours!" We said goodbye to Sutty and set off. As we left the Domkirk (cathedral) square, we saw the unfortunate Sutty explaining himself to the police and the excited fisherman.

Next day Kama hung round me as I worked busily chopping firewood for the house. I had backache through bending to use the low chopping block and had dug myself a pit to stand in. Kama praised my intelligence! Jepsen would have grumbled at the few minutes wasted in digging it. That evening she was all warmth and friendliness, brushing close to me on every pretext. Bent winked at me and Karl made a revolting gesture, pushing his thumb between two fingers.

I went to bed as usual and though flattered, I was not too pleased when Kama came into my room with another coffee. I was already worried about lasting the night without getting up for a pee. The combination of cold and Kama's coffee was bound to drive me downstairs and out into the freezing night. I did not feel randy enough or confident enough to make any move towards her and she went off demurely to her room.

At daybreak, I was busy chopping wood when Herr Jepsen called me to come and ladle out the sewage settling chamber outside the kitchen. It was only when I saw the Jepsen family turds abounding in it that I realised what I was being asked to do. I was furious. I reacted as I had often done in response to frustrated rage. I burst into song. However, the song was an insulting parody of "The good ship Venus". My strong voice rang out:

> "That nasty little Jepsen,
> A greedy Danish farmer,
> He isn't fit
> To shovel shit
> From one pit to another!"

Herr Jepsen stood smiling toothily in the kitchen: "The Englander is singing; he must be happy!" Kama, blushing scarlet to her splendid bosom, turned her face away. Her command of English was quite enough for her to understand all the verses I made up to follow in ever-increasing volume and obscenity.

That night, possibly because Jepson had some feelings of guilt about the tasks he was allocating his British student, I was allowed the luxury of a bath in the family bathroom. I was happily scrubbing myself when a tiny voice said, "Do you want some cake?" Kama, pretending to avert her eyes, was standing by the bath. "I heard what you were singing about father. You are very rude!" I rolled in the water. "You had better smack my bottom then!" Later on, in bed and warm for once, I pondered her behaviour. Sometimes I thought she wanted me. At other times she talked endlessly of her fiancé.

I woke up hearing female voices and much coming and going on the stairs and in the passage outside my room. I went back to sleep but was woken by the sound of my door opening. I could see a glint of blonde hair. A warm hand touched me and quickly pushed my duvet to one side. I said nothing. The warm girl slipped in beside me and I hugged her joyfully. This was better than the quart bottle of hot water which I had been bringing up from the dairy to warm my bed. However, despite the closeness of her body and clasping legs, the girl was not moving sexily. I was enjoying the warmth, feel and smell of her body too much to worry about this. I thought of the pink bra and

172

felt for her breasts. They were not as big as I had imagined and I also noticed her teeth seemed to be catching my lips more than I would have expected. Suddenly she started to move against me with the quick violent movements of an athlete. I was surprised and delighted. "She's a goer," I thought; but deep down I sensed something was not quite right in her behaviour. I could wait no longer. I pulled her to me and started to push myself between her thighs. "Ah, Kama, how I have waited for this!"

"Kama!" A violent blow brought bright lights of pain, which redoubled as a hard athletic knee found my softest parts. "Svine! Englander svine!" The girl bounded out of my room, screaming hysterically. It did not take my pain-scrambled brain long to realise my mistake. The voices I had heard had been the family welcoming Ilse home. The girl in my bed had been the appalling Ilse. Raised voices downstairs promised further problems.

I threw on my outdoor clothes. Years of practice of quick dressing at the sound of air raid sirens stood me in good stead. I lowered myself out of the window and dropped into the farmyard. My old Ariel motorbike was standing under the archway below the barn. By now I could hear terrible shouts and screams in the house. No doubt she would say I had tried to rape her. As I started to kick my machine to life, Bent came out of his little room, his friendly face contorted with questioning concern. The saturnine Karl stood framed in light at the farmhouse door from where the clatter of feet ascending the stairs could be heard. As I kicked the trusty machine into life, Karl closed his eyes to slits, stuck out his revolting tongue and once more gestured with his thumb and fingers. Bent shouted something but I was in gear and away. I did not stop flogging the poor old bike until I was well on the road to the Storbjaelt ferry. I knew old Jepsen could not catch me in the family car but I wondered if he would phone ahead to have me stopped at the ferry.

I reached the docks just as the last cars were being loaded. I ran to the ticket office which was just closing. Breathlessly, I implored the official to take my money for the fare and allow me to board. The official was suspicious of my urgency but seeing the GB plates on the motorbike, he relented and I was able to load up my machine and climb the companionway to the passenger deck. To my surprise my lorry driver friend from the journey out was on board. He greeted me and expressed his surprise at seeing me on the way back to England so soon. I said that things had not worked out and that I had

had "woman trouble". Immediately the lorry driver was full of sympathy; he could now understand why I was on the way home. I had left my warm tank overall at Jepsen's farm and I was very, very cold. The lorry driver saw this and suggested that when we reached Fyn Island, we should load up the motorbike into the back of his now empty lorry. I could then ride in the warm cab. This warming news allowed me to settle down a bit. I bought the lorry driver coffee and told him a bit more about what had happened to me. The lorry driver was highly amused. "Saa they are all alike in the dark after all!" I kept looking anxiously about me. Some of the ship's officers seemed to be staring at me and I wondered if Jepsen had managed to contact the ship by radio? My imagination was running wild. I kept remembering the lines of a poem: "Oh to be in England, now that April is here!" Indeed, if only!

We reached Fyn harbourside safely and loaded up the machine. The driver had a call to make in Nyborg and I took the opportunity to look at Hans Christian Andersen's house. I was too agitated to enjoy the experience and was relieved when the lorry driver returned and we were once more on the road. After we reached the mainland, the lorry driver, much to my dismay, insisted that we stop for some sleep. It was midday but the driver pointed out that I had driven from Copenhagen during the night and was very tired. I had to accede. We slept in a small guest house in a tiny village alongside the main N1 road to Esbjerg. I could not sleep for long and sat shivering by the window looking for signs of pursuit.

Late in the afternoon, we set off again and reached Esbjerg in the early evening. I went straight to the shipping office and enquired for the next sailing. There was one that evening at nine o'clock. I offered my last remaining traveller's cheques but the clerk refused them. "Only cash," he said. I was in despair.

One of the other clerks was discussing the matter in urgent whispers. I was ready to run. Perhaps they had had a message about me? The clerk approached the counter.

"Are these sterling traveller's cheques?" he asked.

"Yes," I said, and showed them to him.

"I will give you cash for them," said the clerk. "I can use them to buy goods which are for export only."

Much relieved, I paid for my ticket and went out to my motorbike. I remembered that the petrol tank was empty and that I would not be able to buy any petrol in England where petrol was still strictly rationed. I had given Tom Cochrane all my petrol coupons when I left, thinking I would not be coming back for six or seven months. Fortunately the petrol kiosk was still open and I had enough Kroners to fill my tank together with a five gallon drum which I stowed in the sidecar. "Hope no one spots it at Harwich," I thought. "Miserable buggers are sure to confiscate it." I bought some cheese and bacon with my remaining Kroners. I thought they might soften the blow of my unexpected return to the Mill Hill family.

At eight o'clock I went through customs without a hitch. I boarded the small steamer and watched them winch a couple of cars, some big wooden crates and lastly, my trusty motorcycle on board. There was a lot of shouting as the Danish seamen put the hatch covers in place, and then they pulled over a green tarpaulin and lashed it securely. It looked like they were expecting dirty weather. At nine o'clock sharp, the lines were cast off and the little steamer *SS Aarhus* set off slowly down the channel towards the North Sea.

At last I could relax. I was safe!

Chapter 10

Toffee Balls

The voyage back to England across the North Sea was much smoother and more enjoyable than the outward journey. I found I was in an empty cabin and I slept well. Next day I ate a hearty breakfast in company with three English girl tourists and a cotton yarn salesman from Yorkshire. The girls evidently took me for a Scandinavian for they asked me to pass various items of food in Danish. It amused me to let them think I was not English. The Yorkshire salesman was shooting quite a line to the prettiest of the girls. The eldest girl was not impressed. "It's all a bit of a yarn," she said, obviously delighted with her pun. I sat quietly listening to the banter. I was already wondering how I would deal with the family when I arrived back unannounced and jobless.

The good ship *Aarhus* steamed slowly up the Stour estuary. The port of Felixstowe was on the north side of the river and I could see an old seaplane tender and a few small steamers unloading. Nearer to Harwich, we passed a cruiser and some rusty destroyers looking neglected and forlorn. I wondered what sort of a war they had had and if they had been mothballed ready for the next one. As we docked, I heard the welcome sound of English workmen's voices. It was music to my ears. I had not realised how much I had missed my native tongue. I recalled a schooldays' poem of Sir Walter Scott's which went something like:

> "Breathes there a man with soul so dead
> Who never in his heart has said
> This is my own, my native land
> Whene'er returning from some foreign strand."

The tussle with customs and immigration proved much easier than I expected. They seemed mainly interested in any books I might have brought back with me. The petrol can was not noticed and I set off for London in good spirits. The hedges were in leaf and the glorious scent of spring flowers filled my nostrils. "Oh, to be in England now that April's here!" I rejoiced as I sped along the country lanes.

The family was pleased to see me and I asked if I could stay for a while to get myself organised. This was not too easy as I had to get a

176

new identity card, ration books and fit myself back into the bureaucratic system of the time. I met several of my posh friends walking on Mill Hill Broadway who hailed me across the street: "Hello, Terry! Flown back for Easter then?" I scowled and simmered. "How the bloody hell do they think I'd get the money for that?" Later that day I walked down to watch the preliminary rounds of the Middlesex rugby seven-a-side at the Met Police ground at Colindale. Many of my rugby friends from various clubs were there. It was a fine sunny day and I enjoyed the games. Blind Bagnal distinguished himself for the Mill Hill local club by once more outpacing the opposite wing easily, only to touch down over the deadball line.

My chum Cobbo was particularly pleased to see me. We enjoyed a pint or two after the games and I talked about my future. Another lad, Roy Mathews, who I had not seen since my infant school days, joined us. Later Roy invited us back to his house and talked about his life as an agricultural student at Cambridge University. Cobbo and I told him about our adventures in Cambridge; but Roy was of a more serious bent and wanted to talk about his studies in Agriculture rather than boast about his nocturnal activities. I perked up. I had always wanted to know a bit more about university learning. To my surprise, Roy said that he wished he had gone to Wye College rather than Cambridge. "It is much more self-contained with its own farm and experimental areas all round the college buildings; they have all their sports facilities right in the middle of it all and the rugger sides seem to have a wonderful set-up." By the end of the evening I wanted nothing more than to get myself to University. Cobbo, who had opted for an apprenticeship with de Havilland's Aircraft Engines, poured cold water on my enthusiasm. "Waste of bloody time, matey, get yourself a job!" I knew I could never explain my thirst for real scientific knowledge; and in any case Cobbo had never read *The Corn is Green.*

Walking in Mill Hill Park with my dad, I explained my ideas which started with the need to get into University. If I could somehow swot up for Matriculation, I might be eligible for a grant. I had had a small "dot" of £750 promised to me by my father. It was the residue of my share of the War Damage Compensation which was to have been invested in a family farm. We sat down on a bench overlooking Hendon aerodrome, the same bench from which we had watched pre-war air displays and on which I had wrestled with more than one local filly. We discussed the risk of going without wages for a year while I studied for Matric. It would make a big hole in the £750 "dot" even if I managed to pass. If I failed, all would be lost. My dad pursed his lips. "It seems to me that you will be trying to do in a year what most people have three years at school to do. Your uncle Edgar Lansbury did it in a year; perhaps you too can surprise us all." We sat in silence for a few minutes, each deep in thought. I remembered the toffs who had said I worked on a farm because it was all I had brains for. I also thought of the lecture rooms, laboratories and field experiments I had glimpsed at Cambridge and the promise of new and accessible knowledge which university entrance would make available. "We've made the decision then," I said. "I'll have a go!" Dad shook hands with a smile and said, "Good luck, boy!"

Al and Daphne very kindly agreed to give me lodgings for a small rent. I was delighted. I loved my sister and brother-in-law, in spite of frequent friction and disagreements caused by too many strong characters living under one roof. I also loved their twin children, Billy and Patsy, who I played with and tormented and was tormented by in turn. Like the old family home, it was a house of happy confusion.

I did not reveal to my friends my decision to go back to studying but went back to work at Barnet, cutting turf and driving the machines. My evenings were spent writing to technical colleges offering one year courses for university entrance. Only Battersea Polytechnic on the other side of London could offer Chemistry and Biology in addition to the compulsory English, French and Mathematics. I accepted the polytechnic's offer of a place on the introductory course the following autumn after an interview with a charming Dr Waring. This kindly and scholastic gentleman told me that my lack of previous schooling would be a great handicap; but being more mature, and assuming that I applied myself and worked hard, there was no reason why I should not succeed.

This interview was a turning point because I had actually spoken to a real academic who was interested and encouraging. After it, I felt reinspired, and really felt I could do it.

The spring and summer passed quickly. The weather was splendid and I worked as hard as I could to accumulate money. I did not tell my mates what I was going to do. Most of them would have thought me slightly mad. Indeed, the odd friend and relative who found out about my plans shared this view. Some thought it was far too late, others simply thought I wanted to skive off work for a year.

178

Cobbo's brand new fiancée, a Lancashire businessman's daughter, told me I was a "lazy waster"!

Meantime, it was not all work. My mate Cobbo and I took to visiting the Red Lion at High Barnet every Saturday night. This kept us out of circulation in Mill Hill but we felt free to let our hair down without social censure. A few pints of Bass proved a great reliever of worry and tension. Each weekend we would drive over on three wheels and drive back on two as I became more and more proficient at driving the combination with the sidecar wheel off the ground. One night, well-uplifted by Bass bitter, I managed to drive from Barnet to Arkely without the sidecar wheel touching the ground once. "Good on you, matey!" cried Cobbo, who always lapsed into Australian when excited or drunk. This was strange, as he had never been outside England.

One Saturday evening, Cobbo and I had come to Barnet after playing an out-of-season rugby game at de Havillands aircraft company at Hatfield. We had been at the bar since five o'clock and were quite merry, having entertained the top deck of the bus to songs and repartee all the way from Hatfield. We both enjoyed a few more pints and wandered into the well-ordered dance which was held every Saturday at the Red Lion. Cobbo struck first with a big bonny Scottish nurse called Duffy. Pretending to be Scandinavian, I chatted up a smart-looking blonde who was sitting aloof from the rest of the popsies. She spoke a little Norwegian and we were soon talking animatedly, I in simulated broken English to which she responded in a mixture of Finchley and Norwegian.

It was some time before Cobbo interrupted our animated conversation with a rumble, "Who is this Sheila you've picked up, Bluey?"

It turned out that she was Maggie, a staff nurse at Barnet General Hospital, then known as the Wellhouse and famous for Dr Alexander Fleming, who had discovered penicillin there just before the war.

Cobbo looked at her and said, "You have got eyes like bumble bees' bottoms."

I was impressed with this tribute. Her eyes were indeed large, brown and full of challenging mischief. Some time and several pints later, I tried to introduce her to my boss, who had come in for a quiet pint.

"Thish ish Maggie! She'sh got a fluffy bottom!"

179

Maggie struck me a sharp blow to the solar plexus causing me to fart! Nonetheless, she laughed, pulling her top lip over her teeth, and snorted. Her brown eyes danced and she shook her blonde hair. "Come on, you fake! Come and dance!"

We danced as romantically as possible, considering my inebriation. "My God," she said, with another of her laughs and a snort, "You really are high." I could not see her home as another fellow had brought her to the dance. I did however arrange to meet her again; and it was the beginning of a golden summer.

Maggie had been blown up during the Blitz and had lost several teeth, resulting in an endearing habit of laughing with her top lip over her teeth. This coupled with the snort which invariably followed laughter made her quite a character. She had been a sort of juvenile sweetheart of the exiled Norwegian forces and had really believed I was a Dane. It was obvious that we were mutually attracted. She was not only very presentable but very jolly company. We exchanged jokes and light-hearted kisses. She reminded me of a playful kitten. I explained that I didn't want anything more than a fun relationship. I had neither the time nor the resources for a serious romance. Besides, I was not yet smitten and just found her great fun to be with.

Cobbo and I double-dated the girls several times; but Cobbo found Duffy's insatiable appetite for Kunzle cakes too much for his meagre pay. Maggie liked the gin and tonics and I could not bring myself to ask her to go dutch on her nurse's pay. It was not, I reasoned, her fault that I had no proper income. Cobbo's problems came to a head one night on Hadley Wood Common where, after a few pints in the pub, we were lying on the grass cuddling the girls. It was a bit of a mystery to me as to why we were doing this. Both girls had made it plain that there was nothing doing in the sex line. The subject of sex had come up with the third gin and tonic or so, as it usually does. Both girls were sure they would enjoy it but said they "were saving themselves for a secure relationship with their future husbands." I had shrugged but Cobbo said, "Christ!" Now here we were, snogging with the girls on wet grass!

I was not surprised to find that Maggie was a very experienced petter. She snuggled very close and used her tongue deliciously. Her breasts were not large but were almost perfect. Her legs were long, very pliant and embraced me strongly. I was getting more surprised every minute. She clearly loved passionate snogging and she seemed to be warming up nicely. I risked an exploratory knee and her legs parted. Somehow I was disappointed; I had not expected an early conquest or indeed a conquest at all.

At that moment Duffy gave a great howl from where she and Cobbo were lying: "I'm hungry!" There was silence for a few minutes and I visualised Cobbo wrestling with a dilemma: his desire for more carnal knowledge and the desire to keep her happy. "I'm hungry!" came the wailing voice of Duffy once more. "It's no use, matey," boomed Cobbo's deep brown voice. "The greedy cow won't settle till she's eaten."

We all went back to the Copper Kettle in High Barnet where Cobbo fed Duffy more Kunzle cakes. Maggie had a welsh rarebit. I did not eat; I was spent up and could only just pay for Maggie's tidbit. Cobbo did not take Duffy out again but I was mad keen to see more of Maggie. Her conversation was of sophisticated places and doings. She seemed to have been everywhere and done everything. I was besotted, in spite of my resolution not to get involved.

I managed to keep up a manly front of callous disregard for chivalry and respect for women when with my mates at work. "Come on lads, let's get finished," I bragged, "I've got a nice little heifer to bull tonight!" The older countrymen thought I was a dirty young devil. They little knew what a chaste life I was being forced to lead. Maggie was a great smooch and said she loved me in a way; but there was no way she was going to let me into her knickers.

In August I got a card to attend training with the Old Millhillians Rugby Club. I was thrilled. This was a first class club who, at that time, played against the best sides in the country. Cobbo seemed even more excited about this chance for glory than I, although it meant we would no longer play together for the local Mill Hill club. Training was hard but I was fitter than I had ever been. I was delighted when I heard the OM's Captain, Ian Garioch, saying that I was not only big but fast. I was surprised they thought so as it was only by colossal, heart-pounding effort that I could keep up with the others. I had overlooked that the other men training were all backs or back row men. One night, at the end of training, the skipper shouted that there was a pint for the first man to the pavillion. I anticipated his words and got a good start. To my surprise no one accused me of cheating and the Captain of the Old Millhillians bought me a pint. Once more, my cup of joy was full!

Soon it was time to start the course at Battersea. The journey by bus and underground railway took an hour and a half each way. The Battersea Poly Introductory Department was not in the main building but was housed in a primary school next door. The old Victorian school was grimy and forbidding. The students had to struggle through a horde of shrieking kids in the playground and ascend endless stairs to reach the top floor where the course was held. Most of the students were sixteen and seventeen-year-old school leavers who had failed School Certificate. I felt a bit like Gulliver among the Lilliputians. I soon felt as hopeless. Most of the students were years ahead of me in every subject and were quick to realise my academic limitations which together with my farming background formed the basis of huge amusement amongst the streetwise kids. Inevitably, they nicknamed me "Farmer Giles"! I bore it stoically. There was no way I could explain my late entry to education without long rigmaroles and there were few opportunities for me to display my wide knowledge and experience of subjects outside their ken. Occasionally I thought of my lost wages and diminishing savings when some idiot was deliberately disrupting classes. More than once I verbally chastised them roundly in yeoman language, which left them shocked and speechless. "Why don't you fucking well shut up or piss off home!" I had shouted on one occasion. The kindly Dr Waring had thanked me for my concern but suggested that I be less robust in my strictures in future!

There was also a sprinkling of interesting characters on the course and even one or two others approaching my age: some Poles who had fled from the Russian communists, some Pakistanis fresh from the partition massacres in India and some Greeks who had fled the civil war. In addition there were one or two ex-servicemen cramming for university entrance. With the exception of me, they had all covered most of the subjects before. However, their experience of hardship and life's tragedies had made them less arrogant than the young school leavers and they proved to be good company as we overcame national and racial prejudices.

By chance, my name had been spotted in the sports reports of a Sunday National and suddenly I, despite being one of the flotsam in the introductory department, was in demand. The Polytechnic wanted me to play on Wednesdays but it would have meant missing classes and this I would not do. I had too much at stake.

Travel is said to broaden the mind. Saturday Rugby with the Old Millhillians took me all over England and I was soon playing with confidence and some success, especially at poker on the long train journeys back to London. On one occasion the opposition, Northampton, fielded thirteen current and ex-internationals. Undaunted by – or ignorant of – the stature of the opposition, I broke from a set scrum and somehow tackled Lewis Cannel, the England centre in possession. Don White, an England flanker, congratulated me. Later in the same game, I out-shoved Mike Berridge, an England prop, and fell on a loose ball just over the line. My first try in a first class match.

I was now living life at two levels and somehow fitting Maggie in on a third. She was undemanding but her obvious sophistication, apart from winning me respect from the wealthy barons at the Old Millhillians club, was bothering me. She always told me who she had been out with during the week and the catalogue of rich surgeons, doctors and service officers rankled. She was still keeping me at bay sexually but I could not believe these other men would be so easily fobbed off, especially when she spoke of gin-laced trips to theatres, nightclubs and – worse still – to Brighton.

My particular pal at Battersea was the serious son of a plumber. He was remarkably wise for his tender years and in addition, he was prepared to help me with the mysteries of Mathematics instead of mocking my ignorance. In return I could do little to help him until the last few months of the course, when my easy grasp of language and Biology enabled me to explain things my pal did not understand. The grind of learning was relieved each day by a walk through Battersea Park. The calm deer and the wonderful flowers and shrubs backed by the river were a great soothing influence. We used to treat ourselves to a cup of tea and a fairy cake in the park cafe where we would chat and listen to the latest tunes on the radio. Currently it was Theresa Brewer, singing "Put another nickel in, in the nickelodeon!" Life was almost good, only shadowed at all times by the potential consequences of failure. My essays were attracting favourable comments and my French was coming on well. I was surprised how much I remembered from Prep School. Biology presented no problems; but Chemistry and Maths were a real headache. I solved this by paying the Chemistry lecturer fifteen shillings an hour for extra tuition. This involved an extra three-hour journey every day during the holidays which I paid for by cutting turf on Sundays.

Maggie complained that I was always tired and less fun than I used to be. An Old Millhillian friend, Brian Livsey, seemed to be always with us when we went out; and Maggie seemed reproachful when I tried to shake him off to be alone with her. We had words several times at Christmas parties when she seemed to go out of her way to embarrass me by flirting with older and richer men. I was not surprised to hear from Cobbo that Brian and Maggie had been seen out together when I was busy elsewhere.

I was upset and my pride was hurt. The fun and laughter had gone out of our friendship. I did not contact her again and she did not contact me. It was over. Maggie had not been the happy, fulfilling interlude I had expected, but she had set standards of sophistication and ambition which I was all the more determined to achieve.

Soon after Christmas 1949, I was travelling home on the underground when I felt severe abdominal pains. The pains grew worse during the night and I was vomiting violently with each fresh wave of agony. The doctor, when he arrived, took one look and called an ambulance. On arrival at Edgware General Hospital, I was given a pre-med and operated on almost at once. I had an abdominal obstruction arising from my illness ten years earlier in Cumberland and probably aggravated by a rugby strain.

Meantime a card arrived at my sister's house, inviting me to attend a Middlesex County rugby trial. This was a long-awaited honour and a big step up the rugby ladder.

"You can forget that," said the doctor. "You will not be playing rugby again."

The loss of both Maggie and my rugby in the course of a few days should have broken my heart. Instead, I saw it as clearing the decks for my assault on the academic bastions which stood between me and my goal. I swotted in my hospital bed and at home during convalescence. The long, boring journey to and from Battersea was taken up with revision. I could revise standing in a bus queue. Mathematics suddenly became a pleasure. I could not understand why it had caused such a mental block at school. I loved each new facet as I progressed. Logarithms, factorials, simultaneous and differential equations, geometry, trigonometry: all yielded to me as I progressed onwards and upwards. Money was an ever-present worry. My little notebook listed every withdrawal and expenditure from my meagre funds. My sister laughed at the weekly amount of three pounds which I allowed myself for "heavenly pleasures". This was my Saturday night trip to the Red Lion at Barnet where my singing and good-natured drunkenness made many more friends than enemies; though more than one angry swain threatened to knock my block off if I came near his girl again!

In June I travelled to the London University Examination Hall off Exhibition Road in South Kensington to take the special university entrance exam for mature students. It was a watered-down Matriculation exam and one only needed four passes to get in. I marvelled at the great edifice and the huge showy buildings surrounding it. Inside I queued with a large number of older men who were now seeking university education. As we trickled past a marble statue of Queen Victoria, I realised that they were all as nervous as I was. I thought I had done quite well in the written papers. A week later I went up again for the oral examination. A peppery little man questioned me on a botanical experiment and on digestive enzymes. The examiner seemed very hostile and appeared to be deliberately confusing me. I felt hot and uncomfortable under this aggressive cross-examination. Eventually the man told me that I had failed the oral, as well as the written Biology and French.

I came out of the great building and down the steps to where my father was waiting. He must have seen from my unconscious body language that I had failed. He spoke kindly: "Ploughed, lad?"

"Yes," I replied. "But I'll show the buggers yet!"

At South Kensington station my father watched me carefully. He said I looked absent. In fact, I was already planning my renewed attack. Later my father told me that my preoccupied look had frightened him and that he had been afraid that I might jump under a train. I laughed. Nothing had been farther from my mind.

Next day I took the biological question papers round to a girl friend at Mill Hill who had just passed her finals at Bedford College. She explained what she thought I had answered wrongly; but after asking me a few more questions, she said she thought I knew enough to pass if I tried again. As for the French paper, it remained a mystery to me as to how I had failed. I had consistently been one of the highest marked students of my year. Even Dr Waring seemed puzzled by my failure.

Another month soon passed as I swotted and polished up my subjects from six in the morning to near midnight every day, except for Saturday nights when I still allowed myself the indulgence of letting off steam at the Red Lion. Soon it was time to sit the full

Matriculation examination. Although it was a far harder examination than the special entrance exam I had just failed, I felt confident.

On the Saturday night before the examination week, I met an old flame, Ginger Lee. She seemed very pleased to see me and we had a riotous evening, drinking, dancing, laughing and cuddling. On the way back to her home in Whetstone we had gone into a workman's hut and had great fun playing with each other's parts as we snogged and giggled drunkenly. Ginger was a tiny thing and I had to stoop down to her upturned little face. In the streetlights I could see her vivacious shining eyes and pert little turned-up nose. She was so sweet and she let me do almost anything I wanted. Finally, as neither wanted to take foolish risks, we manually stimulated each other to a last thunderous climax. Thus relieved, I went home feeling far less tense and awoke on Sunday morning eager for a few last hours of swotting. The next day, I returned once more to the great examination hall. Many of my classmates were already there and they laughed at my last minute reference to my notebooks. "No use doing that now! If you don't know it now you never will!"

We trooped into the hall and settled at our desks. The question papers lay turned over on each desk and the invigilator solemnly told us it was now time and we should write our numbers clearly on the answer books and could then look at the questions. A young foreign-looking student next to me read his paper and began to blub. After a few minutes of this, he suddenly and noisily threw up over his papers and the desk. Fortunately the vile-smelling vomit did not reach me and the boy was helped out and did not return. I felt sorry for all his wasted study but felt the lad was probably young enough to try again. Two attendants quickly cleared up the mess and I, only marginally distracted, got on with my writing. The English papers suited me admirably and I was equally satisfied with the French and Biology. Even the Chemistry paper contained subjects which I had studied and understood well. The Mathematics proved a tougher nut. I had managed the arithmetic problems fairly easily but some of the algebraic problems had gone wrong and I had wasted too much time on them. Short of time, I turned to the geometry section. My luck was in. The very theorems I had been studying on the underground train on the way to the exam had come up.

Who said last-minute cramming did not pay?

I could see the diagrams in Hall and Stephens' Geometry textbook as clearly as if the textbook was still in front my eyes. I completed what I believed to be near perfect answers with time to spare.

With the battle behind me, I walked up to the Albert Hall and caught a number 52 bus back to Mill Hill instead of the usual tube train from South Kensington. It was a longer journey but I wanted to relax and think about the papers. I was quietly confident. So deeply was I immersed in a replay of the exam that the conductor had to ask me twice for my fare. The bus went along the side of Hyde Park and round by Buckingham Palace. Everything was bathed in sunshine: the golden-topped railings, the bright red guardsmen's tunics and the glossy coats of horses on Rotten Row. The bus rounded Marble Arch and set off down Edgware Road. I hoped it was my last ride home from a London polytechnic. I had applied for a place at Wye College, the University Faculty of Agriculture. Subject to passing Matric, I was to have an interview.

For the rest of the summer, I went back once more to cut turf and drive machines at Barnet. I was now driving big Bedford lorries throughout North London, delivering turf, soil or materials for on-site landscape jobs which the firm was doing. I had previously met and pursued a very good-looking landgirl, Monica Hagel, who I later saw on television leading two Shire horses at the Lord Mayor's show. However I now found she had married a Barnet spiv, and I turned my attention to her younger sister, Eve. Eve had been a child actress due to a very sweet face, like a miniature Anne Todd, and had such white hair and eyebrows that many thought she was an albino. However, she had blue eyes and assured me that it was her natural hair colouring. "You'll soon find out, matey," boomed Cobbo. I did not soon find out. Eve was only seventeen and her mother guarded her virtue assiduously.

I was allowed to take her to the Feldman jazz club as she was a "bop" fan and was well known to most of the musicians. I found the club much changed. The music was less exclusively "bop" than at Club Eleven round the corner but although relatively mainstream, it was not the jazz I had heard and loved four years earlier. After brief ensemble introductions of standard melodies, the mainly saxophone solos went rambling off as if lost, throwing in a familiar phrase or chord here and there but mainly playing as if trying to find their way back to the original theme. The occasional irrelevant chords from the pianist or crash of cymbals from a bomb-dropping drummer did not satisfy my ear which was tuned to the classical polyphony of traditional jazz.

I had not come to terms with "bop" and "progressive" jazz. Even the vast orchestras, which Woody Herman and – worse still – Stan Kenton were putting together were too much for my conservative tastes. Eve thought me "square"! I could not believe it. I took her to hear Freddy Randall's jazz band at Crooks Ferry Inn but she destroyed me by saying, "That jazz appeals to the feet; our progressive jazz appeals to the mind!" I had been well and truly put down by a teenager.

Most of my friends thought I had gone slightly mad in my association with Momma Hagel and her two bop-crazy daughters. Cobbo certainly did not approve. He and his new fiancée, Pam, were back on the scene after a period in Preston where Cobbo had been working on the new English Electric Canberra bomber. Pam and I had terrible rows on almost every subject. She was a very active Young Conservative who saw the unionised working class as the "enemy within" who were bent on destroying western democracy. I at that time saw the unions as my workmates' only shield against oppression and exploitation. It was the time of Joe McCarthy's infamous attacks on liberals in the United States. His committee of investigation into "Un-American activities" had destroyed many innocent men and was blighting independent thought, literature and the film and theatre industries. Even Oppenheimer, "Father" of the atom bomb which had brought the war in the Pacific to an early end, was accused, besmirched and deprived of his career and his rightful place in American society.

However, Pam was a good drinker and loved to get singing drunk with Cobbo and me. We knew the words of every rugby song and were in demand amongst the young Saturday night boozers. David, the landlord of the Red Lion, would cry forlornly, "No singing please!" as the entire saloon bar supported my rendering of vulgar ditties. "You ought to make a record," said an onlooker. I laughed at the idea but someone else managed to make and sell a pale shadow of my, Pam and Cobbo's renderings into both records and a song book several years later. I swore I had made up many of the verses and considered I had been plagiarised!

One particularly successful night at the Red Lion, when song and sexual byplay were at their height, Pam, Cobbo and I were confronted by a police inspector, a sergeant and constable. The inspector demanded immediate silence. The sergeant, who knew me, winked and indicated to me with a nod of his head and a rapid flick of the eye that I should clear off. I slipped out of the bar; once into the foyer and emboldened by beer, I struck up a chorus of "Mrs Hall's toffee balls are the best". An immediate response from all the customers swelled into a mighty roar. I slipped out into the high street and round to the pub's back entrance. As I reentered I saw the back of the small police party going out the front. I joined the party who were following the inspector out through the doors and swaggered mightily to the continuing choruses extolling the virtues of Mrs Hall's toffee balls. The crowd gradually melted away to reclaim the drinks left standing on the saloon bar tables. The police had gone into the police station opposite. Pam, Cobbo and I found ourselves alone on the steep police station steps, still singing the easily remembered second, third and fourth verses of "Mrs Hall's toffee balls are the best". The words of every line were the same! A weary looking constable came to the doors. "Go home to Mill Hill toffee balls before I have to run you in!" I was getting ready to protest my right to sing when I recognised the man as a Met Police rugby player whom I had shared a pint and a song with at Imber Court. As we walked quietly back to the Red Lion we passed Momma Bagel and her daughters. "Good night, Toffee Balls!" cried Eve, the "albino". It was a nickname that began to stick.

On Monday I waited as long as I could for the post to arrive. The Matric results were due. I had to go to work before the post arrived and by ten o'clock I was immersed in the task of replacing a duff magneto on a Fordson tractor. A shout from the office informed me that I was wanted on the phone. It was my father saying that the letter had come; should he open it? I readily agreed and my father read out the brief contents.

DW Logan, Principal of London University, informed that Terry Lansbury had satisfied the examiners of the London University Matriculation Board in English, Mathematics, French, Chemistry and Biology.

I had matriculated!

The whole family could clearly be heard chattering round the telephone at home and everyone wanted to congratulate me. I could hear my sister's young twins singing "For he's a jolly good fellow". However the office clerk, who clearly disapproved of outside workers being in his little domain, was making sounds and signs of impatience. I thanked them all and rang off. I could not resist telling the clerk of my success. "I suppose you think that makes you an educated man?" said the clerk sarcastically. Nothing could deflate my euphoric mood. Not many shared my pleasure. Most of my mates found it amusing that I should have matriculated at twenty-four! "All set for a brilliant academic career," Harold Alston, my old form master, said when I met him while enjoying a celebratory pint in the Three Hammers pub later that night. I did not know how to take this apparent glibness, but I instantly determined that I would indeed have as brilliant an academic career as I could! At home the family were all obviously delighted. It had been partly their success, because without their tolerance and generosity I could never have done it. My father seemed to have swelled up with pride and pleasure. Cobbo's fiancée, Pam, brought me back to earth. "Bloody hell," she said. "In the last analysis, it is only what most of us do at sixteen!"

Work continued much as usual. The boss's sons made some amusing comments about employing a matriculated tractor driver. Bucko wanted to know how soon I would be in the cushy money.

At last a letter came from the college bursar inviting me to attend an interview at Wye College, the London University Faculty of Agriculture.

I was a confident young man as I travelled down to Ashford and made my way to the beautiful old college. The building around which the college had developed was over four hundred years old. It had been a seminary under Archbishop Kemp; and the Old Latin School where I was interviewed was almost unspoiled early Tudor. I thought I was being interviewed by Norma Penston, a botanist, and the bursar. I did not realise that in fact the male interviewer was Dunstan Skilbeck, the Principal himself.

My puritanical obsession with work did not go down well at the interview. I appeared before them as an older than average candidate with little to recommend me apart from a modest Matriculation and a record of labouring jobs. Miss Penston felt that a Matriculation pass in Biology was not good enough preparation for the Botany I would need at Wye. Dunstan Skilbeck questioned me about my hobbies but I maintained that work gave no time for outside interests. I did not mention my first class rugby experience with the Old Millhillians or my love of mountain walking. I did not mention my interest in and family connections with politics, art and theatre. I was still thinking in the austere way of my Essential Works Order days. Dunstan Skilbeck, having become conditioned to confronting articulate, swashbuckling ex-service officers and clever young men straight from public school, must have found me a dull candidate indeed. At any rate, he told me, kindly and politely, that I was not yet ready for Wye College and he suggested I went away and tried to get some 'A' level passes in the new exams. Chemistry, Botany, Zoology and either Geology or Physics were required.

I had plenty to think about on the way home. I did not know quite what to do after my rejection. I wondered about trying for a short service commission in one of the services. My boss at the Barnet contractors firm wanted me to stay on and run a garden shop. Finally, I decided to have a go at college again. I had about £350 left which, if I was careful, might see me through another year at Polytechnic if I could find one offering the subjects I needed. I put on a brave face at home, telling them that I had been accepted at Wye for the following year, subject to passing 'A' levels in the meantime.

My sister, Daphne, could not hide her concern that I would be studying and occupying scarce space in her house for another year. However she was a very kind person at heart and made me welcome for a nominal rent yet again. None of the polytechnics were prepared to take me as an 'A' level candidate. "We are not a grammar school," said one polytechnic lecturer, evidently affronted at the suggestion. Eventually I got into Northern Polytechnic at Holloway, on condition I sat for the considerably more difficult Intermediate Bachelor of Science exams. None of the tutors were prepared to accept candidates for the new and easier GCE 'A' levels at that time.

I finished off the summer vacation working hard at Barnet. I was able to save quite a bit of money as Momma Bagel, very wisely, would not let her daughter stray far from home with me. I did take her to a party at the American Embassy at Winfield House in Regents Park. My Old Millhillian friends were impressed; but I found the evening dull in spite of the presence of the US Navy band who were playing a lot of Artie Shaw arrangements. If I had known that this was in fact the band which Artie Shaw took to the Pacific war zone, I might have paid more attention. As it was, Eve's youth and the young company I found myself with were beginning to make me feel uncomfortable. I had grown a beard at this time and I heard an American General's daughter asking Eve, "Who is the beard?" Suddenly I felt old! Later in the evening I danced with a rather attractive older girl who turned out to have come from Preston. "I've seen you at the Red Lion," she said. I expressed surprise. I told her that I thought she was a "rich American broad. One who would keep me in the manner to which I have become accustomed!" The girl laughed and said, "That is exactly what I am looking for; but they are all kids here!"

Seeing that Eve was enjoying the company of a very young trombone player from Barnet, I went over and asked her to excuse me if I went home early. The young trombone player could take her home. My new friend Paula and I went off together in her small car. It turned out that she was working as a student nurse in London and had a small room in Highgate. I took her to the Spaniards Inn on Hampstead Heath and we enjoyed a quiet drink together. I had high hopes of a night of passion. Paula told me that she had been married and had a young daughter. Her husband had custody as she could not support the child until she was qualified. Although I liked the girl and she clearly found me amusing, I backed off. I could not risk this sort of involvement; it was far too adult for a penniless student. It was to be a year before I met her again, by a strange coincidence at Cobbo and Pam's house in Preston. That time I was less reticent and sparks were to fly between us.

On October the eighth 1950, I set off for Northern Polytechnic. I had to travel by bus to Mill Hill East and then by tube to Archway where a high bridge carried east-west traffic over Holloway Road. It was a notorious jumping place for suicides in those days before the sides were fenced securely to deter those in a hurry to meet their maker. From Archway I had to get a bus to the poly. It was a much shorter journey than the trip to Battersea.

On my first morning, I was embarrassed to meet Paul Sellers in the train at Mill Hill East. Paul was the son of a famous judge who had been a junior boy in my school dormitory when I was Head Boy. Now Paul was sitting next to me dressed in black jacket, striped trousers and a city bowler. I felt very much the poor relation; but Paul was pleased to see me and told me that he now worked on the Stock Exchange. I hardly knew what this meant but guessed it must mean loads of money. I did not let on that I was still a struggling student.

I noticed some girls sniggering across the carriage. When I reached the poly, the girls were just going in. "Who's your funny friend?" they giggled, "the one in the funny hat?"

At that moment, two tough-looking men came out of a door and nearly bumped into me. "Good Lord, it's Toffee Balls!" My acquaintance from the Met Police rugby team was doing a short course at the poly.

"Toffee Balls, Toffee Balls!" A shriek of laughter went up from the girls who I later found were pre-nursing students, the lowest form of life in the poly hierarchy. From now on I had only one possible nickname.

Chapter 11

Fulfilment

The year at Northern Polytechnic, apart from my first year on the farm in Cumberland, was to be the hardest and most disciplined of my short life. To start with, I was informed that I could only possibly attend three Intermediate Bachelor of Science courses if they required practical laboratory work. It was not possible to fit any more into the week's timetable. The course director was adamant about this. Only three subjects were required in order to obtain an Inter BSc. or First MB and that was that.

Knowing that I could be exempted from the first year at Wye College if I passed four subjects at one go, and would thus catch up on the year I had lost through my bad interview with Dunstan Skilbeck, I was determined to study four subjects whatever the authorities said.

Doctor Francis Jones, who ran the Geology course, was sympathetic. Why didn't I come to Geology night classes? I thought about it. Chemistry, Botany and Zoology could just be timetabled in if I missed the Wednesday afternoon sport. However, Chemistry practicals were on Wednesday afternoons and once more, I could not afford to miss them. Geology classes at night would mean that there were two less nights for revision of the other subjects. What a problem! Revision and writing up notes would have to be done in the meal breaks and while travelling. It would be a fearful grind.

My fellow students said it would inevitably lead to a crack-up.

I plunged into my new studies with a vengeance. Once again I found myself at a considerable disadvantage compared with the other students. Without exception, they had covered the ground before, either when attempting Higher School Certificate or at other polytechnics.

I was the only student attempting four practical science subjects and many of the students were only taking one or two. The vast majority were taking First MB in order to go on to do medicine, dentistry, veterinary or pharmacy degrees. I was the only one intending to do an agricultural degree and "Farmer Giles" once more became a nickname, albeit preferable to "Toffee Balls".

Chemistry and Botany, to my surprise, were no problem. The lecturers were polite and the subjects straightforward as long as I listened and attended properly. Zoology presented a different picture.

I had expected to do well in the light of my experience with animals and my long-expressed interest in Biology. Mr Etherington, the Zoology lecturer, was unimpressed. On the first day he quizzed the class about their previous training. He was contemptuous of my Matriculation Biology and insultingly rude to a poor girl who had only done General Science for School Certificate. He went on to inform an experienced West Indian male nurse, who was intent on becoming a doctor and had already passed his Federation examinations, that as far as he, Mr Etherington, was concerned, the man had passed nothing.

Although – as it turned out – he was an excellent teacher and got most of his students up to standard, his attitude was rude, impatient and dogmatic. He had done some sort of army service in India and would harry tardy students with cries of *"Jildi! Jildi!"* He had clearly pigeon-holed all his students on sight and was quite extraordinarily intolerant of anything which deviated from his intended purpose. Due to the clash of Geology evening classes, I was sometimes unable to write up my laboratory notes for the next day. Both Mr Etherington and his virago of an assistant, christened "Betty Grable" for her obvious dissimilarity to that sweet and beautiful lady, jumped on me for this.

My evening class was dismissed as no excuse. Both of my Zoology mentors demanded that I give the evening classes up if I wanted to pass in Zoology. I discussed this with Dr Jones at evening class that night. Francis Jones told me to ignore the threats and find some way of getting my lab work written up. I found that there was a one hour gap between the lab work, which ended at five, and the evening class which began at six. If I missed tea in the refectory (tea, after all, was essentially a social rather than a nutritional occasion), I could grab a space in the library and get the writing-up done.

At first I was exhausted by the routine of nine to nine studies and the long journey each way. However, I found that in time I developed the same sort of fitness for mental work as I had achieved by training for rugger. My stamina and ability to learn and present my work well improved rapidly. However, I was stunned into shocked disbelief when Mr Etherington marked me down to a shameful ten per cent for my Christmas Zoology exam paper. I simply did not accept this and demanded an explanation. I found that I had been marked down heavily for bad English and for producing artistic rather than accurate line drawings. This surprised me as the Botany lecturer had at first praised my plant sketches. She too however had critised some of my diagrams as being too uncritical and impressionistic. I learned a great deal from this setback and became very literal and exact in all my studies. It tended to make me much less congenial company amongst my family and friends. I insisted on scientific analysis of every casual subject raised. This halted the enjoyable and conjectural discussions of my mates and quite naturally, I was thought by common mortals to be arrogant, pedantic and boring!

Geology, a science which was quite new to me, was a revelation. I revelled in the new world opened to me by the petrological microscope. The brilliant colours of crystals hidden in the dull wafers of rock, mounted on slides, were revealed by double refraction of the polarised light passing through crossed Nichols (calcite crystals, which organise scattered light rays into parallel rays). The sparkle of plagioclase twinning, the green of serpentine and the brilliant pink of garnets entranced me. Equally fascinating and thought-provoking were the mysterious creatures petrified millions of years ago in ancient muddy estuaries, wind-blown deserts and calcareous oceans, now resting on cotton wool as fossil specimens in the dusty Geology lab. I was fascinated by these creatures, from the simplest graptolites of the late Cambrian slates, through fantastic trilobites of the Ordovician shales, the flattened fishes of the red Devonian sandstones, to the whirling ammonites of the Jurassic clays and on again to the gigantic plants and even more fantastic titans of the age of dinosaurs.

To all these wonders could be added a completely new appreciation of the countryside, the influence of geology on the landscape and soils. Even the vernacular architecture was influenced by the underlying raw materials: the flintstone walls of South Kent, the ragstones of the Weald, the yellow bricks of Essex, the red bricks of Peterborough, the golden limestone of the Cotswolds and Lincolnshire, the grey gritstone villages of Yorkshire and the green grey slate and greywacke stone of Cumberland. All fitted nicely into the coloured geological map on the wall. I felt a warm affection and respect for Dr Francis Jones who had unlocked the door of wonderland. The world about me was becoming a richer and richer source of interest; each day seemed to bring new marvels as the worlds of Chemistry, Biology and now Geology gave up their secrets.

The old loves, music, politics and even the farm, were forgotten.

My appetite for more and more scientific knowledge was growing daily. I was no longer swotting just to pass exams, but to satisfy my thirst for more and more understanding. I had to curb the breadth of my interests if I was to pass my exams, however. Gradually my marks improved until at Easter Mr Etherington turned to me with a deadpan expression and said, "Lansbury, there is a danger you may pass this exam!" From "the Mogul", as the students had nicknamed him, this was praise indeed.

Slightly relaxed or at least less intense, I made time to read Emlyn Williams' book *The Corn is Green* once more. I revelled in my own parallel but very different climb to the revelation of academic achievement.

Once again, it was not all work. My relaxation was crammed into a few hours each Saturday. Dr Morley, the family doctor, had given me a thorough examination; and contrary to the hospital doctor's view, he had pronounced me fit to play rugby once more. Getting match-fit with so many other demands on my time took some doing, but I was again making it to the OMs' first fifteen. As had happened at Battersea, I would have liked to play midweek rugby for the poly but there was lab work on Wednesday afternoons so I was unable to turn out for the polytechnic, even if I had had time. Saturday morning was reserved for study, provided the weekly Old Millhillians rugger was near home. After the matches, I would enjoy the hectic bath and shower, my only proper bath of the week. Hot water and access to the bathroom were always in short supply at my sister's overcrowded house. The clubhouse tea was an essential part of my weekly diet and I scoffed everything I could, to the amusement of my well-fed team mates. It was a great time. I rubbed shoulders as an equal with Pat Sykes and Ted Woodward of the Wasps and England, with whom we had just drawn an exciting match that afternoon. Amongst my team mates were Jim Roberts and Johnny Williams, both of whom were later to play for England.

It was very different from life on the farm or at the polytechnic where I was a nobody. After a few pints at the rugby club bar I would go on to the Red Lion at Barnet for a night of singing and an "armful of perfumed waist". Indeed I loved nothing better than singing with my arm round a pretty girl. Later I was to hear the jibe that "all rugby players do is sing about sex, they never get round to actually doing it!" In my case, at this time, it was absolutely true. I could not afford the time or money for a girlfriend until I had passed my exams.

One Saturday after a particularly hard game against United Services, Portsmouth, I heard a fine rollicking voice coming from the bar. Standing near the door was a very good-looking, well-built blonde young man, sporting a heavily bandaged head (Jean Prat, the legendary French forward had nearly taken his ear off in an England France match) and the unmistakable pink of a brand new England tie. It was Lieutenant "Squire" Wilkins. On seeing him, the visiting team of soldiers and sailors broke into choruses of "Why was he born so beautiful? Why was he born at all?" The blonde giant laughed happily. "Life's hell!" he said to me with a proud grin. I admired his style and repertoire of rugby songs enormously. "Wilkie" had no affectations or "side", unlike many young naval officers. We chatted, drank and sang heartily all evening. I wondered where he was from and what his background might be. He was too easy-going to be a varsity man. I was mystified and envious and greatly impressed. I had no idea that he would reenter my life as a potential complication.

Exam time came and I queued once more past Queen Victoria as I went into the examination hall. Everything went like clockwork and at no time did I doubt that I had answered the written examinations soundly. Apart from a wrestle with a particularly tough-skinned dogfish in the Zoology practical, all went well. The dogfish under dissection stubbornly refused to yield the respiratory nerves running to its gills intact. I was very worried as I looked at the severed and frayed white nerves running round the feathery gills; then I remembered a fellow student saying that white thread and chloral hydrate made an excellent false nerve. I hastily patched up my battered specimen and one had to admit that it looked a most competent dissection! I had learned that even pure scientists had to improvise!

At last the exams were over and I said goodbye to my classmates. We had all grown close, sharing the burden of intense study, especially those who had shared the rigours of Mr Etherington's class. Grudgingly we had to admit that he had been a first class tutor. We went our ways but did not meet up again. None of us wanted to look back on the year's grind. Our futures lay along very divergent paths.

A few days later, the phone rang while I was relaxing alone. I was playing with Frankie, the family dog, a mangy greyhound who I had soft-heartedly rescued from being put down due to her failure as a competitor on the racetrack. In spite of the family's initial horror at the

198

mangy creature, Frankie had become the much-loved pet of my father who became a familiar figure in Mill Hill walking the now sleek and well-groomed hound. On this occasion, the family were all out for the evening with Alex's father, Granpa Day, who was staying for a few days. The caller was my friend, a fellow student called Whytcher. Whytcher was one of these extraordinary people who always find out what is going on before anyone else. This time he had heard that the exam results were to be posted up outside Senate House in Russell Square that evening. Would I come up to Bloomsbury and see if we had got through? I tried to get someone to look after the dog but no one was available. I considered the occasion important enough to take a chance and went off, leaving the dog in the house alone. It was not the first time. My father had left the dog many times before.

Arriving at Russell Square we found the glass-cased notice boards were in total darkness. Neither of us had a torch or matches. I spotted a coke brazier burning by a workman's shelter across the square. I ran over and borrowed a box of matches, giving the startled night watchman two shillings (10p) for the penny box in my urgency. By now other students were milling round in the darkness. I found a space and sought my examination number. There it was:

Candidate 016657.......BCZG.

I, Terrylad the ploughboy, Terry the Mil'ill Mauler, Terry the turf cutter, I had passed! I was Terry Lansbury, an "Inter B.Sc."!

By now other students had learned of their success or failure. Many whooped and shouted their delight. None more loudly than I. Months of repressed fear and worry were released in a wild cavorting dance of unrestrained joy. I bumped into a dark stationary figure. It was a fairly mature girl sobbing into her handkerchief. She had not passed and had been set back a year. For a moment I tried to console her but she rushed off into the traffic of Southampton Row and disappeared. I soon forgot the incident and resumed my capering. Whytcher had also passed in the two subjects he needed. He also told me what I did not know or at first believe. I had been one of only two students, out of the thousands who had sat the exams, to pass in four practical Science subjects. It was possible after all!

It took Whytcher some time to persuade me not to give my last five pounds to the night watchman whose tranquil snoozing had been much disturbed by the primitive whoops and shouts of the noisy students. Whytcher and I went off as a jubilantly happy pair to Lyons Corner House on Coventry Street to celebrate with a bottle of wine and the best meal possible, under the austere food rationing still imposed by the now thoroughly unpopular Labour government. It cost us two pounds each, more than we usually spent on food in a week! A little drunk and very happy, I went home to break the news to – I hoped – a happy and excited family.

To my surprise, the lights of home were still burning brightly. There was much activity and there were long faces to mar my all-conquering return. The wretched dog had crept upstairs in the empty house and pissed on Granpa Day's bed. The poor old fellow had discovered it as he climbed in and he had summoned Alex. "I don't want you to think I am so old I wet the bed," he had said. My sister had changed all the sheets and blankets and packed newspaper over the damp mattress. "You bloody geniuses!" she said accusingly to me. "You can't even be left to watch a dog!" I started to explain my absence but realised they were all smiling too much for such a horrific occasion. "We know," said Dad. "Whytcher's dad rang to tell us. Congratulations, boy!"

The next few days were euphoric indeed. My success had brought immediate acceptance at both Wye College and Reading University. Remembering Roy Matthews' enthusiasm for the tight little community at Wye, I opted for Wye College.

I did not go to work with my mates at Barnet this time. Somehow I would manage without the money I would have earned from the work. I had too much to do and besides, I wanted to spend some time with my father and all the friends I had cut myself off from during my two years of intense study. I was, to be frank, a bit big-headed about my achievement. After all, I had done in a little over eighteen months what most of them had spent several years at school doing. I no longer felt the odd man out. I was the equal of anyone!

My old matey, Cobbo, phoned me from his new home in Preston. I had declined Cobbo's invitation to be best man at his wedding to Pam due to impending exams. Now Cobbo wanted me to come up for a party and to meet his North Country relatives and friends. "Lot of North Country bean brains!" he had boomed over the telephone.

I got out onto Preston platform; surely it must be longer than Calcutta's? I mused, remembering my first sight of it in 1938. Cobbo's party was a splendid affair. I came to the conclusion that rationing must be a lot less strict in the north of England. There was food and drink in plenty. Cobbo's new wife Pam was the daughter of a businessman who had a bus company, lorries and a farm. She was used to the best, and also to having her own way. She was very drunk and confided to me that Cobbo was too keen on his oats. "Five minutes back from the reception and he was up me like a V2!" Cobbo grumbled about not getting enough; but he was obviously very pleased with both himself and his marriage.

I was soon tired of listening to uninformed anti-Labour Government talk amongst the smart young Preston couples. Wandering into a quieter room, I found two people talking angrily. I recognised Paula, the nurse I had taken out briefly in London. She stopped shouting and turned, red-faced and tearful, to leave the room. Recognising me she said, snuffling through her tears, "Hello, Toffee Balls. This is my bloody husband, Noel!" I nodded to him. Noel, it seemed, had not expected her to be at the party and had come with a pretty but tarty young redhead. Paula, who knew that he was unfaithful even before she went off to train as a nurse in London, was furious.

I kept out of the way; and now that the other guests had stopped discussing politics, I was enjoying the party. I boasted of my exam results and was rather boring about how long I had been an enforced celibate. The young couples were neither interested nor sympathetic.

Paula's husband Noel had meantime compounded his folly by going upstairs with the tarty redhead. They were missing for about twenty minutes. Paula sat on the sofa next to me, fuming. When Noel and the redhead came down, the girl was dishevelled and blotchy-necked; no one had any doubt about what they had been doing. Noel said he was going home and shouted his goodbyes to Cobbo and Pam. On the way out he paused by Paula and me. "Be good," he said to me, with a leer and a nod of his head towards Paula.

Paula ignored him and as soon as he had gone, she went upstairs. She came down even more angry. "The crude bastard. He even had to leave his sticky handkerchief on the bloody bed."

The party was starting to drag to a close. Several couples left, despite Cobbo's booming pronouncements that it was early yet. Paula was sitting near me and had calmed down. "Are you staying the night?" I asked, to make conversation.

"If you are good, I might," she said. I remembered Noel's goodbye. A little shiver of anticipation passed down me.

She leaned over and put her finger to my lips. "We will see."

Cobbo demanded coffee for everyone and Pam jumped to obey. I motioned Paula to sit down again, this time a bit closer. "I am not a dirty old man lusting for your body," I said. By now, of course, that was exactly what I was. Paula smiled and said nothing.

The last guests left, leaving Cobbo and Pam alone with Paula and me. "Will Noel be coming back for you?" said Pam with a wink at me.

"Not bloody likely. The swine has had all he wants from a woman tonight." I was a bit shocked to hear a wife talk about her husband like this.

We drank the fresh coffee Pam had made for the four of us. Cobbo was dropping off and snoring, eyes closed and chin on chest. Pam shook him awake, then shooed him upstairs. Halfway up he turned and boomed in his best Australian accent, "Good night, Bluey. Always said I would fix you up with a Sheila!" He chortled and burped.

"Go to bed," said Paula, evidently not embarrassed in the least.

Pam soon followed Cobbo upstairs. "You know where your room is," she said. "Be good!" I came to the conclusion that "being good" was something different in Preston.

I turned to Paula; she was looking up at me through her lashes.

"You are really quite dishy, Terry, and you do have some charming ways." She got up and, holding me by one finger, led me to the stairs. I put the room light out with my free hand as we went through the door. Every detail of the décor, the banisters, the staircarpet rods seemed intensified by the rush of adrenaline. I caught a glimpse of the room, a mess of dirty plates and full ashtrays, as the light went out.

We went upstairs to my room. I kissed her but she made me wait while she put on a nightie. I noticed the stretch marks of childbearing on her rather plump belly and a more mature bush than my previous young girlfriends had. I wondered how she had come to have a nightie with her. Was I in fact victor, or chosen victim? Diffidently I undressed and put on my pyjamas. "Be gentle with me," I said as I slipped into bed. Paula snorted. "Charmer!"

Next day the four of us breakfasted quietly. There were veiled enquiries as to whether we had slept well. I said I had. Cobbo boomed, "Had a good night then, Blue?" Paula chuckled and interjected, "Had better!" I took this to be a reflection on my performance but considering my year of enforced celibacy, I did not think I had done too badly.

After breakfast, we went off to the Kardomah coffee house in Preston to meet Pam's young Preston set. They were mostly successful young executives with a sprinkling of engineers and artisans from the English Electric Aircraft Company. Cobbo, who was on secondment to that firm from de Havilland's at Hatfield in Hertfordshire, was getting a ribbing about the superiority of the Canberra bomber to the DH Venom. Cobbo defended his southern corner well against the brash northerners. "Easy enough if you poach all the best brains from de Havilland's and Gloster's!" He turned to me and rumbled, "Bloody bean brains; they think I am a great big swede!" Thankfully, the party broke up before arguments grew heated. The women went home to cook lunch. Paula went with them. The men went on to the Angel pub near the station. My train was at one thirty so I did not have time for lunch with the Cobbos. I felt a little envious of Cobbo's new status as head of a household. I guessed the house must be rented or belong to Pam's dad. I hoped nothing would go wrong for my big friend.

After saying my thanks and goodbye, I went through the ticket barrier and onto the platform for the London train. As the train came in, a figure ran towards me in a flurry of carried clothes, carrier bag, handbag and large suitcase. It was Paula. She was breathless and as I had only one small case, I took hers and helped her onto the train. It was very full so, making a quick assessment of my cash situation, I took her into the dining car where we found a table for two without difficulty.

When we had settled down and Paula had regained her breath, she told me that she had decided to go back to her training hospital a day early. "Pam told me you were taking this train so I decided to travel down with you," she told me.

I was pleased and flattered. Paula had been gentle with me and I quite liked her. I did not, however, want to start anything too serious. After all, I was still only a student, however big-headed, and she had a husband and daughter.

We enjoyed the simple meal on the train. Paula offered to pay her share of the bill but I foolhardily insisted otherwise. At Euston we went down onto the tube train together. I thought about the wartime days when all the platforms had been lined with fugitives from the bombing above ground. How good it was that all that was behind us. Paula got out at Hampstead. She had not mentioned our night together. I kissed her goodbye. She did not respond but pushed something into my hand. It was not a five pound note, as I at first hoped, but a small piece of paper with her telephone number and address.

The next few weeks before I went to take my place at Wye College were, by my standards, decadent. I slept late in the mornings and enjoyed the sunshine in my sister Daphne's tiny back garden. I did not go to earn money at Barnet or to help my friend Sutty with the harvest. I bought a smart new sports jacket and flannel trousers in which I strutted Mill Hill Broadway with my dad. Together we visited my other sister Esme in Bedfordshire. Her husband, Peter, who loved to tease me, said, "From very unpromising material, you seem to be turning out quite well." My sister Esme hastened to reassure me. She had been a mother to me for years and was still protective although we seldom saw each other.

One day I travelled down to Tolleshunt D'Arcy in Essex for a few days with brother George and his glamorous redheaded wife Madge. I was unsettled by what I found. Madge's mother and aunt were rather impatient with George's inability to find a suitable job in civvy street. Clearly they were surprised that a Lansbury did not have influential contacts in industry or government. George, Madge and I were invited to a house party at the local manor. We went first to drinks with a neighbour who was proud to have the Lansbury boys as she had revered our grandfather, George Lansbury.

The drinks party was mostly a gathering of older people. Most of the men were retired military men of high rank: a Brigadier, an Admiral and several Majors. My brother George fitted in well but I felt out of place and uncomfortable. It was difficult to explain the ramifications of my continuing civilian status, even though the war had been over for two years by now. When we moved on to the Manor House, we were greeted by a footman in yellow silk breeches, who announced each guest in stentorian tones. I was impressed; I had not realised such people or happenings still existed.

I was soon happily chatting with other young students and young ladies but it was very clear that they all came from wealthy backgrounds and we had little in common apart from their studies. One Admiral's wife took me aside and lectured me on the need for

George to find a job soon, which would restore Madge's position in local society. I was furious but hid my rage at the unfairness of her remarks. Many of Madge's previous young men were wealthy farmer landowners' sons who drove round the countryside in ex-War Department Jeeps or brand new Land Rovers. Many raced sand yachts or dinghies on the beaches and creeks of the nearby Essex coast. I hoped it was not a misconception of the Lansburys' situation which had spawned Madge's infatuation with my brother, the handsome Captain George.

Returning thoughtfully to London, George and Madge were soon out of my mind as Paula had responded enthusiastically to my invitation to a day out at the Festival of Britain. This exhibition was an attempt by the Labour government to bring a sparkle into the grey world of post-war austerity. It was intended to be a showcase for British science and industry. Staged on the cleared bomb sites of the south bank of the river Thames, contemporary art and architecture were given free rein. Alas, by and large, the deprived and long-suffering people were not ready to make the giant stride from grey austerity to this gleaming, shimmering showpiece. Nothing seemed to go right in the preparations. The huge pleasure garden in Battersea Park, intended to go hand in hand with the exhibition, was not finished in time. A Bofors gun chassis intended to power a rotating beacon on the top of the famous old shot tower landmark, which had miraculously survived the Blitz, was dropped by the humiliated Royal Engineers who were mounting it as a demonstration of the versatility of the regiment. Even the great Dome of Discovery, housing Britain's scientific achievements, was criticised for being so brightly polished that it blinded lorry drivers on the Embankment! Huge losses were forecast. "It'll be us poor buggers as has to pay for it all," said a mature student to me, a view which reflected public opinion.

I had no such sombre thoughts as I met Paula outside Charing Cross station and we walked down Villiers Street to the Embankment. I loved the riverside walk with its wonderful views of the sweep of the Thames past the Savoy Hotel, the Shell Mex building and Somerset House towards St Paul's. One of my past girlfriends, Maggie, had got me reading an anthology of poetry and I recalled Wordsworth's "Earth has not anything to show more fair." In the light of a late summer afternoon, the city certainly wore the day with great beauty.

My thoughts drifted back to the nightmare tram ride along this same embankment in September 1940. The sky, deep turquoise as dusk fell, had been pockmarked with orange flashes as anti-aircraft fire tried vainly to turn back wave after wave of bombers as they crossed South London on their way to devastate the Poplar and dockland. I relived the moment when at Blackfriars we had abandoned the tram and sheltered in a nearby subway as the whistle and crash of falling bombs grew nearer.

"Which way now?" Paula's North Country tones interrupted my reverie and I led the way up the iron stairway onto the footbridge across the river. She was full of enthusiasm as we entered the Festival site. We explored the wonders of science in the Dome of Discovery, she eager to see all the medical advances and I fascinated by the biochemistry and geology. We marvelled at a vast computer, whose complicated valves, wires and relays filled a whole room and which had a console like a cinema organ. The wonderful machine would solve mathematical problems and calculate at incredible speed. I was used to log tables and the slide rule, and I was amazed by its accuracy and speed with vast sums. It could even play a fair game of chess if suitably prompted. I was not to know that within twenty years a greatly improved version of the apparatus would fit comfortably into my pocket!

Paula soon tired of looking at great locomotives and aircraft. Even the vast green Britannia class "Golden Arrow" did not impress her and she dragged me away from a mock-up of the new DH Comet jet air liner's cabin. We settled down at one of the small bars outside. It was an imitation village pub and would have been very nice if the scaffolding supporting the facade had been hidden. There was a band playing popular music and a few couples were dancing. We sipped at the gin and tonics, which had depleted my cash reserves considerably, and we watched the world go by. I was obsessed by thoughts of sex but Paula seemed to be in a chaste mood.

Quite suddenly the band was silenced as a large blue RAF lorry pulled into the arena. It was a barrage balloon tender with a winch and wire cage to protect the winch operator from the flailing cable should it break. Behind the lorry was a trailer loaded with hydrogen gas cylinders. A squad of aircraftmen jumped down and manhandled a bulky package. With military precision they unfolded what was obviously the envelope of a large spherical balloon. In no time at all they had connected up the gas cylinders to a large manifold and the balloon began to fill. As it swayed upwards like a huge cobra, it revealed a wicker basket festooned with ropes, sandbags and grapnels.

206

Two civilians in white overalls clambered into the basket and with much shouting of muddled instructions the balloon slowly lifted its burden. The band struck up with a suitable rendering of "Up in a balloon boys, up in a balloon". As the busy helpers released the now straining ropes, the balloon lurched upwards, narrowly missing the surrounding pavilions. It rose at an ever faster rate, drifting over Waterloo Station and away, first as a diminishing globe, then as a dot, before disappearing into the haze. I wondered what it was all about but no one seemed to know. It was all part of the hastily organised exhibition.

By now the band was playing again. This time it was Jimmy Young's hit "They tried to tell us we're too young". Paula pulled me onto the dance floor as the singer crooned.

> "Too young to really be in love
> They say that love's a word
> A word we might have heard
> But can't begin to know the meaning of."

"Our song," said Paula, snuggling up to me. I, mistaking her meaning, felt warm and flattered. I did not love Paula but I was hoping for an affectionate affair; I was feeling short of affection. "Our song," repeated Paula, "Noel's and mine when we were first married." I felt cold. I had a few more dances with Paula but I had lost my enthusiasm. We decided it was time to go and I took her back to the nurses' hostel in East London.

"You seem quiet," said Paula. I did not answer at first. I was fed up. I badly needed to release all the tensions which had built up during the past year's unrelieved grind of study and worry. The night with Paula in Preston had if anything made my frustration worse. Paula put an arm round me and I kissed her, lightly at first and then fiercely. I pressed close to her and kissed her ears and neck feverishly. She pulled back. "Terry! You really should be called the snogging king! But I've been married; it isn't enough; it just unsettles me; I want so much more than just a snog in a corner."

I was nonplussed. I too wanted more, much more, but I feared her intensity. I certainly did not want to take on Paula and her child in Preston as anything more than a wild affair. "Then why the hell don't we have more?" I said in fierce desperation. "I've been bloody frustrated for a year now and I am bloody well fed up!"

Paula was quiet for a minute, and then she put her finger to my lips, the same gesture she had used at Pam and Cobbo's in Preston. Unbuttoning her coat she took my hand and while kissing me gently, she guided our hands down between my burning loins and her own. For a moment she held them there trapped in the warmth; then she gently pressed my open palm between her legs as she stroked me gently. I gasped. Why the hell hadn't I done this sooner?

Paula drew her head back and looked at me as she reached down for the hem of her skirt and pulled it upwards before taking my hand and pushing it into the moist warmth between her legs. I could feel a cooler damp on the back of my hand from the gusset of her pants. I was trying to find a way into her with my clumsy fingers but she held them. "Like this," she whispered as she stroked herself between the soft lips. I felt the movements of her fingers with growing excitement. I had not known a girl to touch herself like this before.

Gradually my own fingers took over the rhythmic stroking and I marvelled at the moist softness, so different from some of the arid fumblings of my earlier experiences. Paula was sighing and breathing heavily through her nose as I found her clitoris. She was massaging my organ which I had by now released from its prison within my trousers. I was barely able to keep from coming but Paula, sensing this, was making shushing noises. "Not yet, not yet!" To my surprise she pulled me down onto the hard concrete paving. She was still rubbing herself with one hand as she pulled me onto her and wrapped me in her stockinged legs. With a gasp she pushed me into her. It was so easy compared with the awkward posturing I had performed in order to couple in the past.

Paula bucked and pushed at me with a thousand sighs and moans. I could wait no longer; I struggled to withdraw as I felt my orgasm rising like a swarm of bees driving my seed irresistibly upwards in great jerks. Paula held me in with her legs as with three great thrusts she sent my seed spurting into her in great gouts. I died, recovered and died again.

As I slowly regained my sight and feeling I realised we had made love on the pavement only a few yards from the Mile End Road. Paula took the handkerchief from my top pocket and was mopping herself. "Feel better now I?" I nodded; I could not speak. "Me too," said Paula.

It was the start of a fantastic month when little else in the world seemed important to me. Daphne, my sister, did not like the look of

Paula when they met and Alex, my brother-in-law, told me to be careful. I was too besotted with sex to take much notice. Cobbo and Pam came down to London on a visit but I would not give up time with Paula to be alone with my old mates. "You have treated Cobbo like shit," accused Pam. I hoped Cobbo would understand.

Sex was wonderful and seemed to generate more and more appetite in both Paula and my cockstruck self. We made love in the back of cars, on wet grass and standing in shop doorways. At the Red Lion in Barnet, I noticed my old friend, the near albino Eve, and her mother Mrs Hagel. They were studying Paula. "Does she?" was the silent question Eve mouthed. I smiled and nodded proudly. Eve chuckled and winked at me; she had a charming smile. Mrs Hagel did not smile; she looked concerned for me.

One day Paula suggested a night in a hotel. Consulting her diary for "red dates", she indicated the last weekend before I went to Wye. My friend from the poly, Whytcher, who had taken an almost parental interest in my love life, booked us into the Imperial Hotel on Southampton Row. The room was booked in the name of Colonel and Mrs Astacus. Whytcher had christened me "Colonel Astacus" because he said my eyes stood out on stalks like the Astacus crayfish whenever I saw a pretty girl. At any rate I, as the very youthful "Colonel", and my lady presented ourselves at reception. The night receptionist clearly did not like the look of us as a married couple. We had no luggage and we were both very tipsy.

Things did not go well. Paula wanted cigarettes and I had to go downstairs to a machine for them. Then she had no matches and I had to buy some off a porter. I only had a ten shilling note and I handed it over grandly without waiting for change... Returning to our room, I found Paula in the corridor; she had locked herself out. I went back down to reception and explained that my "wife" had locked herself out. The receptionist snorted. A porter accompanied me upstairs with a master key. Paula was waiting impatiently. The bedroom was hot and stuffy; a machine of some sort was making a fearful hum outside the window so I could not open it. Paula got into bed grumpily. We were both hot and sticky. I kissed her and felt between her legs. She was dry. My evening's drinking was beginning to be a hangover. "Oh, get on with it," said Paula. I tried but I was only half erect and could not penetrate the arid forest. Paula reached down to my floppy, rubber-garbed penis. "That won't do," she said, and turned her back. I noticed she had a spare tyre and coarse fair hair on her buttocks. It was over.

* * * * * * * * * * * * * * * * * * *

The trip down to Wye was uneventful. At Ashford, I changed onto the little train to Wye station. Several young people, who I guessed were Wye College students, were on the platform carrying bags and squash racquets and chatting in the loud, arrogant tones of wealthy country folk who seemed to think normal reticence was not required of them. I joined a compartment of quieter young people. They were freshmen like myself. One spoke of wanting to get into the Wye rugger team. I too was hoping to do this, although I was already committed to playing for Old Millhillians against Northampton on the first Saturday of term. Another lad was talking about his father's farm and wondering if the maid had packed all his sports gear. My heart sank. Was I going to be odd man out as a pauper amongst a lot of richies? I remembered the spacious luxury of my own pre-war youth. Then I thought of my years of back-breaking labour, hardship and poverty. I had now got a major county award on the strength of my success in the Intermediate BSc. examinations. This award covered my college fees and provided reasonable pocket money. Perhaps it was not going to be too bad financially; but there could be no more Paulas for a year or two.

Chapter 12

The Pursuit of Happiness

At Wye College, I managed to get off on the wrong foot almost as soon as I arrived. I had let it be known that I could only play rugby for the college on Wednesdays. This did not go down at all well. The college team had a formidable reputation in East Kent and playing rugby for Wye College was considered a great honour. I had let it be known that the Old Millhillians were sending transport to collect me and take me to play for them against Northampton, a top class club. It did my stature and pride no good when, instead of the promised car, a young man on a motorbike arrived to collect me. The drive to London was a nightmare. My chauffeur rode the battered Enfield like a maniac. By the time we reached the Old Millhillians' club in Whitehall Court my nerves were shattered. The onward journey in Shag Morton's car was little better. There were endless traffic jams and we arrived tense and late. As we hurried to the changing rooms, the East Midland crowd booed our late arrival.

The game was a disaster both for myself and the team. I was marking two six-foot-six, eighteen-stone forwards, Hamp and Hawke. I had no chance of out-jumping the giants but managed to steal the ball in the first two lineouts. As I tried to repeat the stratagem one of them stepped on my feet, effectively pinning me to the ground; and at the same time I received a stunning blow in the stomach from a solid elbow and another across the bridge of my nose. Every time I attempted to jump, I found someone standing on my feet or bumping me out of the line with a well-practised swing of the hips. I hardly managed to touch the lineout ball again. The scrums went fairly well and the OMs scored first. Shortly afterwards our scrum half, Bogey Borrett, went off with a badly gashed head. Minutes later Shag Hanton, playing at full back, was knocked out and played the rest of the game concussed and with double vision. The mainly international stars of Northampton had no mercy and peppered the full back with high kicks into the box which he could neither see nor gather. The score mounted relentlessly and the old boys left the field 41 points adrift.

Back at Wye, I was greeted with derision. It was clear that life at Wye would be much easier if I fell into line. The professor of Agriculture was a former Captain of Scotland and Oxford University rugby teams; he was also the college side's coach. I was not going to risk jeopardising my career at Wye. I played one more game for the OMs, a fairly successful draw against a strong St Mary's Hospital side, before leaving the club. There were no recriminations and I received a nice letter of appreciation from the captain who hoped I would still be available in the vacations.

Wye College proved to be a revelation to me. To the other freshmen's surprise, I went straight into the second year on the strength of my four "Inter" passes at Northern Poly. The grind had been worthwhile! The college staff were easy-going and mixed with the students as colleagues rather than as instructors. There was an atmosphere of being part of a team. I could not get used to the way in which Professors were casually addressed as "Prof". The rugger men even called the Professor of Agriculture "Mac". The Principal, Dunstan Skilbeck, on the other hand, moved around in an invisible but recognisable wave of awe and respect. Although referred to as "the Prin", he was undoubtably the boss and at times a rather grand one at that.

The college, despite being a single or rather a twin discipline college, for Horticulture was also taught, was modelled on the Oxbridge system. Dunstan Skilbeck was determined that every student should take part fully in the same sort of university life he had himself enjoyed at Oxford. Wye was to be no narrow instructional establishment like many of the London colleges but an intellect-broadening experience. The students were certainly cosmopolitan. The ex-servicemen were a jolly fun-loving, hard-working lot, but I found the young school leavers arrogant and presumptious. I had seldom come across so many young men "putting on side" and pretending to be of the "county" set. Whether or not this was Skilbeck's fault I could not guess. It was certainly not the influence of the rest of the teaching staff, who were all down to earth and friendly.

Dunstan Skilbeck was inclined to posture in cavalry twill and country cap. He did enjoy being seen at the hunt meets and in his town club, the Atheneum, but I admired him for his humanity and sense of proportion. He arranged for important and famous people to come and give special "college lectures" once a term. The speakers were all outstanding in their fields and as diverse as Jacquetta Hawkes, the distinguished but bohemian archeologist, Dr Waddington, the controversial geneticist, and the notorious "Red" Dean of Canterbury. Apart from these lectures, there were opportunities to experience the best of art and music. I was later to describe Skilbeck as the main civilising influence on my life. I had also described him in a brief spasm of anger as an insincere hypocrite! How wrong I was. Skilbeck believed passionately in every view he expressed. The result was not always as intended. In his attempt to "preserve society" – by which he was assumed to mean the female students' virginity – he somehow drew attention to forbidden fruits which many of the students then found ingenious ways to taste! If Skilbeck was insincere or hypocritical it was in the politician's mould of accepting falsehood for fact in order to preserve the accepted mores, i.e. nice boys and certainly nice girls did not masturbate! I had chuckled to myself when I heard this view expressed in the common room. Who was kidding who?

I was lucky enough to have Professor Louis Wain FRS as my tutor. Louis Wain was a brilliant teacher and research man. His work with plant protection chemistry had led to a large and productive research unit being established at Wye. This in turn brought older and very gifted postgraduates to enrich college life. I had not done any organic chemistry at Northern Polytechnic. It was possible to pass "Inter" without it and I had missed it out to narrow my overstretched field of study. Now under Louis Wain's tutorship, I went out of my way to master the subject.

Rugby went well and I was soon established as a first team regular. I also found time to play a part in the college review, a spoof on *South Pacific*. Louis Wain flattered: "If you don't make it here, there must be a great career waiting for you on the stage, Lansbury!"

The first term passed quickly and I fell badly in love with a Horticultural student. I had looked round the unsophisticated girl students in their corduroy trousers and baggy jumpers. The older postgraduate ladies were an even less glamorous lot. "What do you expect?" a cynical fellow student commented. "What sort of gals would devote their lives to studying earthworms and messing about in cow muck?"

Although I was still thinking in terms of the girls I was used to mixing with in North London, one girl caught my eye. She had lustrous black hair falling in a fringe of ringlets over her sparkling brown eyes. Her skin was rosy and she had beautifully square shoulders. "Very nice," I said to myself; "she looks a bit like the Queen Mother, Elizabeth Bowes-Lyon, when she was young." I thought of the made-up floozies of Barnet. "Not really my type though." Over the weeks I seemed to see more and more of her. She took coffee at the same time as me at the Wye Hill café, where I loved the fresh hot doughnuts. One day I heard one of her friends ask her if she had had her "daily male". She convulsed with peals of laughter waving her newspaper, the *Daily Mail*. I was delighted that she had a vulgar sense of humour but I did not approve of her taste in Tory tabloids. That evening I walked into the common room *and saw her across the crowded room.* She had changed her hairstyle and looked bold and ravishing. I was in love.

She was a sensible Yorkshire lass and was not impressed by the antics by which I sought her attention. The accomplishment of being able to stand on my head and drink a pint of beer upside down was perhaps not the best way to charm her away from an incensed boyfriend. At the end of term dance, I waltzed with her and as the end of the dance came, I kissed her on the forehead. She giggled demurely. At Christmas I was rewarded. A Christmas card portraying two robins on a bough bore greetings and the words, "Love from Brenda."

I enjoyed five rugger matches with the OMs during the Christmas vac. I did not mention the girl I had fallen for and indeed played the part of my old flirtatious self at the parties at the club and round Mill Hill. Christmas dinner at my sister's house was a very happy occasion. Her twins were now ten years old and seemed to love their wicked uncle. I had been christened "wicked uncle" by Patsy, my niece. I had thrown stones at her window at five in the morning, wanting to be let in after a wild night out, drinking with my mate, Cobbo. Alex was now in a reasonable job, George was in Africa again, this time helping to build a university in the Gold Coast. My dad was in good spirits and there was no pressure of swotting to spoil my recreation. I worked for two weeks as a railway porter to augment my grant and had the embarrassment of meeting some of the posher Old Millhillians waiting for their trains to the city. I tried to rise to the occasion: "Carry your bags, sir!" I cried to one august old boy. The other businessmen who knew me howled with laughter. It still paid to be a clown!

The next term at college, I was very badly in love. Brenda invited me to her twenty-first birthday party. She had gone out with me once to a very unsuccessful dinner dance with another couple. The other boy, a wealthy Cornish landowner's son, had shown off and behaved in a superior and snobbish manner all evening. He had humiliated a well-meaning waitress who had decanted a cheap claret into a decanter to please the young toffs. I could not bear to see simple working girls being pissed about by this spoiled brat and I simmered all evening. Brenda had seemed to be amused by the oaf's antics, and I was sad. I had also found out that Brenda had a boyfriend who was a rugby International. It was with amazement that I learned that it was none other than Dennis Wilkins. Apparently Wilkie had taken her to rugby internationals as his guest and back to his ship at Portsmouth afterwards. I, whose only distinction in life up to then had been my modest success at rugby football, felt completely devalued. I hadn't even made the Middlesex county first team! Furthermore it was obvious from Brenda's comments that Wilkie was a favoured visitor to her father's house in Yorkshire where, apart from being captain of the Royal Navy team, he was also captain of Yorkshire! At Christmas, Wilkie had escorted Brenda to the Royal Tournament at Olympia where he was in charge of the Royal Navy contingent. After the show she had swopped her skirt for his trousers so that she could ride one of the Household Cavalry mounts. Wilkie had tried to wear her skirt, to the assembled servicemen's delight. I was jealous and impressed. It looked like being a tough fight to win her, especially as I was a penniless student with limited prospects and a very unglamorous past.

During the Easter vacation, I went to Twickenham to see England play Ireland. Wilkie the blonde giant I so much admired but now envied was playing. It was a dull match and ended in a draw. My mates and I wandered off into the West End for a drink at Chez Nous, a small drinking club which I had joined after paying a pound membership in order to be able to drink out of hours. The club logo was a picture of the proprietor in his Squadron Leader's uniform framed in a black lavatory seat. I was with a nice Welsh girl from Neath. She had a Master of Science degree and was doing research on rabbit control at Wye. She had a bell-like voice of great charm and loved to sing. I felt stifled in the smoky atmosphere of the poky subterranean club. Leaving the others, I went up to the street above for a breath of fresh air.

Parked outside Oddenino's restaurant was a green 1.5 Riley Coupe, the latest and most de luxe model. It was identical to the one in which Brenda's father had come down to Wye to collect her at the end of term. I was consumed with jealousy. I imagined Brenda and Wilkie celebrating at Grosvenor House after the match and then coming on to Oddenino's. That was the pattern for the filthy rich! I plunged back into the club and drank recklessly. Cobbo and Pam were at first amused and then worried as my behaviour grew worse. I shocked the nice Welsh girl and called her "Rabbity One". She realised something had upset me and tried to cool me down. By now I was ridiculously drunk and unreasonable. I dragged my friends from one seedy club to another. Eventually "Rabbits" persuaded me to let her take me home to Mill Hill. I tried to make love to her in the little cul de sac where my sister lived. Fortunately for the long-suffering girl, even I could not find my way through an old-fashioned panty girdle. She pushed me out of her little two-seater and drove off. My little niece, Patsy, was at the window looking out. She came down and let me in. I was very ill next day.

I could not bring myself to talk to Brenda for the first few days of the following term. I had made up my mind to put her, and all women for that matter, out of my mind. I threw myself into college life with renewed enthusiasm. It could not last. The college community was too small for us not to be thrown together. One afternoon as I left the common room on seeing her in there, I heard her voice. "Don't you think we should have a little talk?" Disarmed and weak-willed, I walked with her down to the River Stour where it flowed through the flat meadows below the college. I found her easy to talk to and confessed the mixture of jealousy and hopelessness which had driven me to behave badly with my friends and to ignore her. She listened patiently as I poured out my misery and self-pity. It was probably the first time I had dropped my guard and been honest, since leaving the protective womb of home to go off to boarding school sixteen long years ago.

Brenda was puzzled. She had never considered her relatively wealthy background to be other than normal. True, she had been to Hawnes, a very ladylike public school, but it had not changed her friendly nature in the least. She was almost unaware of class and position, taking people as she found them. The security of a strong, happy family, up to the time her mother had died, had made her a kind, generous person without a prejudice or resentment of any kind. She was kind and sympathetic to me, a confused, class-conscious young man. It emerged that she had not been in London with Wilkie; I had made a fool of myself for nothing. Brenda found it all a bit of a hoot. Having heard me out and removed the worst chips from my shoulder, she proposed that we should be friends again.

216

From then on, we had a glorious summer. We went down to the beaches at Hythe and Folkestone, taking our books with us as we swotted for the end of year exams. Brenda was a year ahead of me and was swotting for her finals. I had no serious exams to face other than the second year internals which were not important. Nonetheless, I worked very hard indeed, in contrast to most of the other Wye students who affected a casual approach to study. The habits and techniques I had learned at Northern Polytechnic enabled me to plan my revision and reading to maximise the time available. In addition I was reading ahead of Brenda's science subjects in order to be able to hear her and test her on them, as she seemed to find them difficult.

After an early rebuff, I did not try to get my evil way with Brenda as far as sex was concerned. She, for her own reasons, was not going to give in. I was very frustrated, having been out in the free-and-easy, mature world for so long; but I loved her too much to make a real issue of it. We swam and lay on the pebble beaches, revising and laughing in the brilliant sunshine. I, who suffered from appalling acne, even took my shirt off in front of her. I had never done this with another girl. She did not appear to be disgusted by my spottiness and my love for her grew.

I enjoyed the end of year exams. It was really an opportunity to show off. I knew I had done well, thanks to a study timetable between papers which left me unshaven and haggard. Brenda and her fellow finals students thought that I was mad to work so hard for unimportant exams. Soon the exams were all over; there was no more to be done to improve one's chances of success. The students settled down to enjoying the Commemoration Ball and Cricket Week which rounded off the academic year.

I went up to London to meet Brenda after her last exam, a Chemistry practical. She was exhausted and I had arranged to take her to Mill Hill for the night to meet my family. She asked me to stop at a chemist. "It's too bad," she said, "getting the curse in a Chemistry practical!" She laughed at me, brandishing a blue box. I felt proud of this intimacy; someone was treating me as an adult at last.

The previous day, I had jocularly warned my family that I was bringing home a fifteen-stone girl from Leeds. The family were entranced by the well-built but slim girl I presented. Brenda was an instant success and an especial favourite with my dad and the twins. "Will you marry her, Uncle?" asked my niece with shining eyes. "Quiet, Patsy," said her mother; but she too was smiling knowingly. I was unbearably embarrassed but secretly pleased. Brenda seemed to like my bohemian family and had not seemed shocked by the tiny shambolic house into which they all crammed. If she was, she did not show it.

Next morning we travelled back to college in the fearful old banger which I had bought with the last of my savings. It had proved impossible to court a girl at Wye unless one had the means to escape from the ever-present audience of nosey colleagues. My banger was a 1928 Riley Nine open tourer with a fabric body that shed shreds of decaying fabric whenever it got up any speed. It was over thirty years old and had not been treated kindly. Nonetheless it got us about, albeit noisily and followed by a plume of blue smoke. As neither Brenda nor I were too keen on watching college cricket, we drove off most days for the beach.

My dad came down for a day to see the college which I had raved about. While we were sitting having a chat in the Elizabethan Library, Professor Wain came in. I introduced my father. To my surprise and pleasure, the Professor's face lit up and he stepped forward to pump the old man's hand enthusiastically. "We are very proud of your son, Mr Lansbury. I can tell you almost certainly he has done something remarkable." He paused. "But then I can't say any more." The two Lansburys were left in ignorant suspense.

As Dad and I walked out of the college to find a pub meal, a voice hailed us. It was Dunstan Skilbeck: "Congratulations, Terry!" It was the first time he had used my christian name. "Congratulations! I can't think of anyone who has deserved it more!" It transpired that I had won the Paton Figgis Award for the best second year student. In practical terms it carried a cash award of ninety pounds, a fortune to me, and an absolute godsend as I was down to my last fifty or so. Brenda, who had joined us, heard the news without expressing surprise. It was almost as if she expected no less. She smiled at me. I would have loved her to hug and kiss me but it was not her way.

The Commemoration Ball was not an unqualified success. I was depressed by the thought that Brenda was leaving at the end of term. I was morose and drank too much. Brenda tried her best to cheer me up but I was too sad and sorry for myself. I took her back to the female students' Hall at Withersdane. Getting into the back of a conveniently unlocked car parked outside the main entrance, I tried my best to seduce her. It was no use; she was not having it. She said she must go in before the doors were locked. I knew full well that this was an excuse. There were lots of ways into the building which were open to a determined latecomer. I remonstrated in vain.

"Daddy wouldn't like me sneaking in late," she said.

I was outraged. We were bloody adults, were we not?

"Fuck Daddy!" I shouted and lurched off down the road back to the College. "Fuck Daddy," I repeated as I limped sadly along. Curious couples on the way down the road regarded me with amusement. "Fuck Daddy!" I spat at a passing lecturer. "Go to bed, Lansbury, before you get into trouble."

I went to my room and looked sadly at a lamp Brenda had given me. It was made from a Grand Marnier bottle and seemed to symbolise the world she came from and which seemed to be keeping me from really being her man. With a tearful sob, I threw it through the window. There was a crash of glass from across the quadrangle. Next day I reported the damage to the bursar. "Five pounds, please," said the bursar without looking up. "I shall deduct it from your caution money."

I went home to Mill Hill without seeing Brenda. That night I went with my father to see Jose Ferrer in *Cyrano de Bergerac* at the local cinema. The sad, romantic tale of unrequited passion made me feel worse than ever. What a fool I had been.

I had taken a vacation job that summer and went off to work for the Guinness estates as a soil tester. For weeks I used a soil auger, twisting it into the soils of the Weald of Kent, feeling, examining and describing the sample cores before bagging them for chemical analysis. We were relating the soils to the appearance and growth of the hopfields and classifying them for the purposes of hop growing. When this task was complete, I stayed on to run one of the new and experimental hop picking machines.

I was surprised one day to receive a parcel forwarded from Mill Hill. It contained a letter from Brenda and a battered but delicious coffee cake. Also enclosed was a delightful photograph of Brenda inscribed, "To Terry with love". Pinned to the photograph was a small cutting from a magazine. It carried a short poem.

> "It seems but yesterday, dear friend
> That first you took me by the hand
> and looked into my eyes, I knew
> that you would understand."

The letter invited me up to her home for a few days. As soon as I could, I set off for Yorkshire in my ancient Riley car. It was a remarkable vehicle, in spite of its dilapidation, having been one of the first Riley Nines ever built. Its tatty fabric body was equipped with a big black canvas hood. The celluloid side windows were torn or replaced with plywood. Despite its appearance, it was a good runner and I made good time to Yorkshire.

Approaching the village of East Carlton, I did not know what to expect. Brenda obviously came from a fairly well-to-do family; she had been at Hawnes Public School for girls but she had spoken of her father's financial difficulties and had even wondered if she would have to leave Wye if he could not pay the fees. I had done some calculations and found that I had at least enough money to cover one term's fees in my Post Office account. I had assured Brenda that if the worst came to the worst, I would pay for her to stay on, and I meant it.

Coming round the corner into East Carlton, I saw Brenda's home for the first time. My heart sank. It seemed to be an enormous mansion. I nearly slunk away. The Lodge, as it was called, was a fine house looking across open country to the mills of Yeadon. I was made very welcome by a charming lady who I learned was Brenda's brother's mother-in-law, Sybil.

Sybil made me a cup of tea and told me that Brenda had gone to fetch her father's car which he had abandoned at a pub in Bingley. She told me that Brenda's father was unwell. It seemed he had developed an alchohol problem which he was only now overcoming successfully. I was concerned. The awful years my family had endured during my own mother's alcoholism were still fresh in my mind. My heart went out to Brenda. She had never mentioned her father's weakness when I had been pouring out my troubles. She must have been a very strong character.

Despite Brenda's dad's infirmity, I was overawed by his commanding presence. It was obviously not a good time for visitors and although Brenda's brother and his new wife June made me welcome, with many innocent jokes about my eccentricity in owning a dreadful old car like that – in spite of the friendliness, I felt a bit in the way. Brenda suggested that we should drive up to the Lake District. To my surprise her father agreed.

In spite of Brenda's worries, we left the Lodge in high spirits. The weather was good and the old Riley was purring along smoothly. In no time we were coasting down into Skipton, then on past Settle and along the Craven Fault to Clapham. Here we stopped to admire the flat-topped majesty of Ingleborough mountain. I had studied this limestone area for my Geology exams and I was excited to see it in real life rather than in the textbooks.

Pausing at Kirkby Lonsdale, we admired the ancient market cross before tackling the winding road to Kendal. Here, in the ancient grey town, we stopped for a snack, the old Riley earning many cheery comments from bystanders. The faithful old motor started to steam as we climbed the hill out of the town and headed for Windermere. A large bus overtook the struggling car as we were caught up in a traffic queue. The conductor leaned out and waved his cap in the column of steam rising from the brass radiator. "Get that steam engine back on the rails, lad!" he quipped with a smile. Soon we were motoring quietly along the side of Windermere, admiring the smart cruisers at Waterhead but eager to reach the wildness of the Northern Lakes around Keswick. Rydal and Grasmere were as perfect as any artist had ever portrayed them. The water was absolutely still and the golden fells and blue sky were mirrored perfectly in the lakes below. After surmounting Dunmail Raise and cruising along Thirlmere, the old car took the long hill out of Naddle up to Castlerigg without a cough. From then on it was downhill into Keswick.

To our disappointment, the town was crowded with tourists and traffic. Brenda suggested that we should find our way up to the farm where she had spent her childhood holidays. After a long slow drive up the valley, with countless gates to open and close carefully behind us, we arrived at the tiny village high up in the fells. We stayed in separate rooms with the Willie Tysons at Caffle House, Watendlath. After a good crack with the old couple and much reminiscing about Brenda's past family holidays there, we were lulled to sleep by the sound of tinkling streams and the waterfalls below the tarn.

Next day we woke to the new sound of bleating lambs. We went outside and breathed in the pine-scented air. Old Willie admired the old car; he wondered what Brenda's dad had thought of his daughter going off in such a wreck? The next two days were heavenly as we explored the lakes which we both loved so well. Brenda recalled the hills she had climbed when she had stayed at Watendlath as a child; she knew the mountains as well as I did. We walked, climbed and chatted happily. There was to be no sex and I was getting used to the idea of a celibate life. It was a good job that I was worn out at night, I thought ruefully.

Alas, this wonderful break had to come to an end and I went sadly back to Mill Hill. I was not all that despondent though, because I had so much to tell the family about the Yorkshire folk and my glorious trip with Brenda.

Brenda came down to London soon afterwards for a friend's wedding. While she was down the results of her final examination came through. She had passed all the written examinations but had been referred in a Horticultural practical. This was unbelievable as she had been a star pupil in practical matters. I cursed the Horticulture Professor for a fool. Brenda was heartbroken and could not be consoled. She went through the rest of her stay like a sleepwalker. I told her she must come back to college; but her father had booked her into the Constance Spry Flower School in St John's Wood. She said she might return the following summer to resit her final exams.

With the commencement of the Autumn Term, I went back to Wye. Life at college was bleak for me without my friend and beloved. I had, however, been elected Captain of Rugger. This was some compensation. The team was a happy and confident one and we swept all before us. "Best team since the war," said Dunstan Skilbeck one day to my immense pride when, for the first time, the tiny college was able to beat the hitherto unassailable Royal Veterinary College. I was seeing a bit of Brenda at weekends. We went together to theatre and cinemas. Once or twice we went out with Tom Cochrane and the Mill Hill crowd but Brenda did not seem to take to the outrageous gang who I loved dearly. The flip southern humour, which had developed like a secret language between the lads, was lost on her. Apart from that, Brenda and I were very much the odd ones out. All the other couples were either living or at least sexually active together. Brenda's chasteness must have seemed very odd to my old friends. I had got used to it.

I quite enjoyed Christmas with Dad and the family at my sister Daphne's house. I had helped Brenda make flower arrangements in the freezing garage of the house where she was staying. She had gone home for Christmas and I felt very alone. However, I was invited up to Yorkshire for the New Year. Brenda met me at Leeds station. She had had a superb hair cut and was wearing a short black fur coat. She looked beautiful, expensive and sophisticated. She kissed me affectionately and my heart rose.

There was a busy round of parties laid on. Brenda's father had recovered completely and was now the life and soul of the party on

222

straight tonic water. Everyone was commenting on his strength of mind, surrounded by all the heavy drinking. All was well at first but a series of incidents was starting to depress me. Wilkie's name was proudly displayed in the visitor's book. Browsing through the family albums I found pictures of Brenda with her head laid affectionately on Wilkie's huge shoulder. She had never demonstrated affection towards me that way.

All the family friends were arriving in huge, smart new cars. I began to feel out of place again. Brenda's brother did his best to make me feel at home but I was already drifting apart from them. I knew Brenda had had a teenage affair with a local married horseman. I was not, I thought, unduly jealous. Why should I be? I was no saint myself. However a chance reference to the man upset me. I wanted Brenda so very much and loved her; but she was keeping me at arm's length, both emotionally and physically, further than I thought reasonable. Especially as her horsey man had got much further with her than she would allow me. Brenda's dad sensed my sulking silence and was displeased. I went off to bed without saying goodnight. Brenda was warm and friendly next morning but told me off for my bad manners. Only Brenda's stepmother Sybil seemed to sympathise with me; and I wondered how she knew what was passing through my mind. I went home to Mill Hill sadly. I thought it was over.

The rest of the vacation was a blur of wild drinking around Mill Hill and Barnet. I ran into Paula but she was with one of my Barnet friends. I asked how things were at the Red Lion and she flattered me by saying that "Barnet without Lansbury just ain't fun." Rugby with the OMs went well and I was back in the first fifteen in spite of my limited availability. I enjoyed a fabulous victory over Met Police and an equally satisfying draw against London Irish.

Back at college my team continued to sweep all before them, being unlucky to lose narrowly to Imperial College in the semi-final of the University Cup Competition. There was sweet revenge when the tiny college with only just over one hundred male students defeated all the giant colleges to win the university seven-a-sides. I did not pick myself and delegated my friend, Hugh Mattinson, to lead the side and receive the cup. The college Principal, Dunstan Skilbeck, was fulsome in his congratulations. "The best side we have had since the war!" I was asked once more to play for the university but declined. Finals were approaching.

I did not hear from Brenda over Easter. Her letters had become fewer and fewer, a fact not unnoticed by gossiping fellow students. I was very depressed indeed. One day I received a very incoherent eleven page letter from Brenda. It was clearly written by someone in shock. She had been involved in a car accident and was dreadfully upset. I wrote to her and tried to telephone but could not reach her. I phoned her brother but he was embarrassed and could tell me nothing about her feelings towards me. I could not understand why I should be the person she wrote to in shock, unless she wanted me.

Eventually I got a letter telling me that she was coming back to college in a few weeks' time to retake her final exam. I had by this time taken up with my first girl other than Brenda in two years. Christine was a very pretty little thing and I was very fond of her in the way one loves a kitten. Given time, it would probably have developed into something stronger. She was on the brink of true womanhood and I was experienced enough, had I been inclined, to have gently introduced her to the joys of sex, but I did not attempt it. She seemed too vulnerable, indeed breakable. We did a lot of passionate kissing and I was surprised when she said to me one night that lovemaking palled if it went no further than this. It was a tricky time. I had not given up hope that Brenda and I would make up again when she came back to college. On the other hand if she did not want me, then here was a lovely young girl who most students would have given their all for!

I managed somehow to keep my options open. I felt I was behaving very badly to Christine but I was too lonely to give her up. Brenda eventually came back and we went out for a drink straightaway. Someone had already told her about Christine but she did not seem put out, and chattered away happily about the parties she had been to in Yorkshire. She mentioned a John Winterbotham several times and I felt the familiar claw of jealousy. We argued a lot about study programmes. She wanted to knock off for the new Queen's coronation. I, who was no royalist, wanted to work.

I thought she was too thin and told her so. It was not until we went to the beach at Folkestone and she bought me a supper of bacon and eggs, seasoned with HP sauce, that we started to laugh together again.

Christine was very understanding when I told her that I was going back to Brenda. I went up to Christine's parents' family farm, high in the downs above Hastingleigh. The whole family were just coming in from the hillside where they had been putting lucerne hay on tripods to dry. I knew it was Christine's birthday and I gave her a larger box of chocolates than I could afford. She thanked me but her little upthrust chin was quivering. I felt very torn inside. She was so affectionate in a way that Brenda would not or could not show. She was so pretty and so vulnerable but deep down, I knew I could never feel for her the way I ached for Brenda. Her brother Ernest, who I liked very much, smiled. He was looking at me very closely. Meeting my eyes he smiled again. We could have been very good friends; he understood. I refused Christine's mother's offer of a cup of tea and drove back to college confused and with mixed up emotions.

The final examinations came and went in a flurry of journeys to and from the South Kensington examination halls. I greeted Queen Victoria's statue for the fourth and last time. Several of my friends from Northern Polytechnic were there and seemed genuinely pleased and surprised to see that I had made it to finals. I remembered their earlier disbelief in my ability to pass even the Intermediate BSc.

The written finals papers were straightforward and did not seem difficult. When I went for my oral examination, Walter Russell, the external examiner from Oxford, told me that I had done a good written paper in Chemistry. Professor Cooper told the visiting examiner, Professor Ellis, that if I couldn't answer questions on Agriculture to ask me to sing a few rugger songs. They hardly bothered to examine me and I knew I was through. Professor Cooper told me that I had written a very attractive paper. I wondered what that meant.

A day or two later, dressed in academic cap and gown, I carried a beadle's rod in the Commemoration ceremony. I hated the pomp and longed to go off with Brenda. We escaped after lunch and sunbathed on the downs above Brook. I had got to love the place and the Kentish landscape laid out below us.

Feeling thirsty, we went back to college. The ceremonies and speeches were still going on. "Where the hell have you been?" asked a young lecturer. "You have missed your moment of glory. You have won the Harwood Medal and Chemistry prize!"

I remembered the competitive interview some weeks earlier. I had got into a pickle and made heavy weather of a valency problem involving a complex redox reaction. Eventually with a bit of prompting I had extricated myself and drawn the correct equation on the board. I had also been extraordinarily lucky. I had been looking at

Sir John Russell's definition of soil pH in *Soil Conditions and Plant Growth*. Dr Smith asked me to define pH. I rattled it off: "The logarithm to the base ten of the reciprocal of the hydrogen ion concentration in a soil solution." Dr Smith looked at me strangely. "Could you write it on the board, please?" she said. I, who could still see the page in my head, obliged.

Not for the first time in my life, I found that last minute cramming could bring results...

The Commemoration Ball was good fun. Brenda and I capered wildly and happily. This time I did not take her back to Withersdane but off to Camber Beach on Romney Marsh. It was a brilliant moonlit night. We struggled out of our evening dress and swam naked in the sea. When we came out of the warm shallow water, I held Brenda naked in my arms. We kissed but there was no follow-up. That night we tried to sleep chastely in each other's arms. The sand blew over us constantly and was in our eyes and mouths. We were glad to get up, stiff and sleepless, to go back for a warm bath at college.

Next day I waited ages for Brenda in the Wye Hill cafe. She did not come. I looked for her all afternoon but she did not appear. I went to the George Inn and had a few stiff drinks. I was angry. One of the college servants asked me if something was wrong. I swore and said, "Too true." The innocent waiter now told me that he had seen Brenda in Ashford with a young man driving an Aston Martin sports car. Later they had been seen driving about Wye together. Already suffering from frustration, I flew into a jealous rage. I demanded more drink and was uncharacteristically rude to the landlady who flushed tearfully. She was a nice woman and had always seemed fond of me, perhaps because I was usually friendly and not stuck up and arrogant like some of the other students.

By the time I reached the women's residence, Withersdane Hall, for the end-of-year dance, I was very drunk indeed. Someone went and told Brenda I was there. She came hurrying down from her bedroom.

I turned away from her and went out of the front door. I was hideously sick in the ornamental flower bed. I was aware of soft hands on my head and someone kissing me in spite of my foulness. Other hands lifted me into a car and I was aware of being helped up to my room.

Next day I awoke with a thundering headache. I was supposed to go for an interview for a scholarship to Cambridge. Brenda was hammering at my door. "Get going, you idiot!" she called; then less roughly, she said, "Do you feel awful?" I dragged myself up and we just made it to Ashford in time for the London train. We parted at King's Cross and Brenda asked me if I was coming to stay at the Lodge while I took the National Diploma in Agriculture examination at Leeds University. I swallowed a lump in my throat: "It's up to you." Brenda smiled patiently. "Yes, come," she said. The train pulled out taking Brenda away and I walked heavily towards Regents Park . It was a lovely June day but I was not interested in anything much, let alone a scholarship interview.

As time was short, I took a taxi which deposited me outside 48 Cambridge Terrace, one of those Nash facades surrounding Regent's Park. The fine Georgian pillars and curved front were hiding a hideous yellow brick rear elevation. I went in. I was surprised how well the interview went. I did not really want to go to Cambridge and would have preferred to do research at Wye. However, I would have to make the best of it.

Later in the week I travelled up to Leeds where I was met, once more by a radiant Brenda. We walked happily on the Chevin above Otley and we picked bilberries as Brenda's huge and aged yellow Labrador searched fruitlessly for rabbits. We held hands and looked into each other's eyes.

"What's the matter, Terry?" she said.

"I am just so damn jealous. I can't help it. I have waited so long for you and I never seem to get anywhere. I don't want to be just friends."

Brenda spoke; she sounded choked. "You are much more than a friend to me but things have been difficult at home. It has not been easy for me to think clearly."

"What about the guy in the Aston Martin at Wye?"

"Oh, that was awkward. It was Mac, the fellow you pinched me off at the dance when you stood on your head." She laughed at the memory. "He offered me a lift into Ashford and back, that's all. Is that what upset you?" I grunted; perhaps I had been a fool again.

In the post next day there were two long brown envelopes containing the results. Brenda had passed her finals this time and her father was overjoyed. I had also passed. I was a little sad not to be at my sister's house to share my joy with my father and the family.

Without them I would have been nothing.

The next day I went off to the National Diploma in Agriculture examinations, which were being held in Leeds University examination hall. The NDA exams were no problem. One examiner, a Mr Bond from Shuttleworth College, tried to put the wind up me. He clearly did not like Professor Mac Cooper's agricultural philosophy or the Wye candidates and he did his best to take it out on me; but I was in no mood to be bullied. When he criticised one of my suggested cropping programmes, I answered, "That's your opinion; but I disagree." He looked at me for a long time, then closed my papers and indicated that the interview was ended. I did not care. After the exam was over, I met old Mr Hunter Smith from the Hertfordshire Farm Institute, where I had started my college career. He congratulated me on my degree. I was delighted to share my happiness with this fine old gentleman who had encouraged me to try for university.

There seemed no end to my happiness. The news came through that I had passed the NDA and this was followed by the offer of a place at Cambridge. Brenda and I went off to the lakes again in my old car. This time we stayed at the Bridge Hotel at Buttermere. One day near Blea Tarn, Brenda and I sat on a large flat rock looking across the tarn towards Bowfell and the Langdales. A shepherd was bringing his flock down the side of Pike o' Blisco towards Fellfoot Farm.

I turned to Brenda; she was opening a box of Ovaltine biscuits and offered me one. I took it; but before eating it, I looked at her and said as casually as I could, "What would you say if, in a few months' time, I asked you to marry me?"

Brenda tried to swallow a mouthful of biscuit; she laughed a high-pitched nervous laugh. "I don't know; perhaps I might say yes!" I kissed her. She still had a mouthful of biscuit and pushed me away. "Look out, those people are watching!"

I returned, radiantly happy, to London. I had helped Brenda cut and rake up the hay in front of her father's house and in the orchard. One day I had heard the old lady who helped in the house telling Brenda's stepmother Sybil that "Those two are so in love." I noticed that Sybil seemed pleased.

Back at Mill Hill I had been invited together with most of the Lansbury family to the unveiling of a plaque in memory of my granddad, George Lansbury, at the Lido in Hyde Park. The Prime Minister Mr Attlee was to officiate. For once my dad was the star. He was, after all, the old Labour leader's eldest son. Clem Attlee asked

228

him to unveil the plaque with him.   It was a happy occasion. Afterwards, Clem Attlee said to me, "I hear you are doing great things in agriculture; we could do with you in Parliament!"   I who, as a big-headed scientist, considered myself above politics at that time, smiled and shook my head.   All the eminent aunts, uncles and cousins were there. At last I felt an equal to any of them.   My feeling of not belonging had vanished. I was my own man.

It was soon time to go up to Cambridge. I started to read a few relevant books and get myself ready for a return to academic life. Brenda came down to London for a last few days with me and the family. It was now obvious to everyone that we were very close.

Coming home from the cinema, where we had watched Howard Keel and Catherine Grayson in *Kiss me Kate*, a clever updating of *The Taming of the Shrew*, we dallied, neither wanting to go in yet. I was still savouring the romantic theme and took Brenda into the tiny park between the Watford Way and Uphill Road. Sitting her on the little brick bridge over the Silt Stream I got down on my knee in traditional fashion. Taking both her hands, I said, "Will you marry me?" This time Brenda did not laugh. She bent down and kissed me tenderly. "Of course I will marry you!" I stayed on my knee. "Then I will spend the rest of my life making and keeping you happy."

I was a Cambridge man. I had someone of my own.

I was Terry Lansbury and proud of it.

Chapter 13

Blue Skies

The scholarship to Cambridge allowed me the princely sum of £200 to cover my food and recreation. A recent article had appeared in a Sunday paper. It was written by Gilbert Harding, a famous broadcaster and journalist at the time. It was about what a hard time he had had as a penniless pre-war student at Cambridge on £350 a year. Now in 1953, it looked as if I was in for a very bleak time stretching my £200 which was probably the equivalent of £100 in Gilbert's time, to make ends meet.

Fortunately, I had had my golden undergraduate years at Wye College and had little craving for Cambridge University social life. I was engaged to the girl I had yearned for and now I wanted the best qualifications I could get in terms of job eligibility. It was time, in my gypsy friend Bucko's terms, to get "in the cushy". However, it seemed wise to earn what I could during the remainder of the summer vacation and I went back to the Guinness hop farms in East Sussex.

This time, I had been promoted and I was in charge of the No.2 experimental hop stripping machine. This was one of the most advanced machines which had been developed by Brough's of Bristol. The vast heap of machinery filled a large building and consisted of many sets of conveyor belts, chains, flails and fans. I had to operate it with a large gang of very mixed casual workers. They ranged from retired Indian Army majors through college lecturers and students to the roughest of gypsies and roustabouts. Things went well. I drove both the field and machine gangs to new levels of productivity. The roughs respected my strength and stamina, the students feared my command of language and the regular Guinness staff knew me from the past and we got on well. My main problems were with the college lecturers who were used to neither manual work nor taking orders. They too settled down when they realised we were working as a team and were achieving tangible improvements to output as we changed aspects of the operation. I called these changes "experimental factors" for their benefit!

My worst problem was Major Brown. He was a son-in-law of the Guinness family and a director of the Park Royal Brewery. The Mad Major, as he was known to the men, had lost a leg in the war. Someone remarked that the loss of a limb had sharpened his other senses. Certainly he was eagle-eyed and missed nothing. He had a very abrupt military manner and expected to work wonders by looking at our operation, making his on-the-spot decisions and rapping out a few commands for changes. He came close to precipitating a strike at first but once he realised that we knew what was wanted, and were going about it in a systematic way, he became easier to deal with. Major Brown asked us to set things up to test the maximum daily output of hops the machine could produce. At the same time, he wanted a good quality sample. The two aims were antagonistic, but we set to do it. The gang cooperated really well and we achieved record levels of performance, easily beating the larger machine in the next shed where an ex-Wing Commander who had previously flown Sunderland flying boats was in charge. He was a great character with a handlebar moustache and "wizard prang" style of speech, but his gang were mostly Guinness regular staff and were not as flexible as mine.

I had reason to be thankful for the alertness of one of my youngsters. I had impetuously stepped into the path of the hop bine carrier bars. These were about six foot long, slung between two slow-moving chains. I was busy clearing fallen hop bines which threatened to spoil the sample when I felt someone pulling at me. Thinking it was one of the students playing the fool, I resisted but was pulled sharply to one side. I raised a fist to thump the miscreant but realised it was a pleasant young Argentinian who would not have been silly. He pointed behind me and I saw the carrier bar slicing down on the frame I had been leaning over. If he had not warned me so robustly, I would have been severely if not fatally crushed.

It was by no means all work and no play. We were a happy crowd and every night we would carouse in the Bodiam Castle Inn. This was a unique pub in that it was the only licensed premises owned by Guinness. The singing and dancing suited me down to the ground. The seasonal hop pickers, who did the whole job by hand, were cockney families who had come hop-picking for generations. At its height, hop-picking had half-emptied London's East End each August. It was a money-making holiday for the whole family. They stayed in primitive shacks with communal ablutions and were always ready to follow a hard day's work with a hard night's drinking, singing and dancing. One cockney sparrow was a tiny but very deep-chested fellow who wore his cap on the back of his head with a curly mass of hair bursting out over his forehead. He sang wonderful little cockney songs and did little tap dances such as I had seen my own cockney father do. He was delighted when I joined the choruses of "Where did you get that hat?" and "My old man said follow the van". It was at times like this that I felt vague, almost subconscious, yearnings for my cockney roots, so long severed by my family's moves.

I could never resist a bit of flirting despite being so recently spoken for. I danced with the young girls from my team and, more excitingly, with the tough young women from the East End. They somehow managed to emerge spotless, sweet-smelling and "done up to the nines" every evening despite their primitive accommodation where ablutions consisted of a single tap and a steel basin.

I am sorry to say that despite my responsibility as foreman and leader of the gang, I got horribly drunk one night. I had boasted that I could drink ten to twelve pints after a rugby match. One of the locals, knowing his drinks and spotting me for a sap, bet me that I could not drink four pints of Merrydown Cider, turn by turn with four pints of Guinness. This sounded child's play to me and I started in eagerly. By four pints I was struggling; by six, I was in trouble. The world was spinning but I got the last two down to cheers from my team. In the relative privacy of the Gents, the whole lot came back. I washed my face and went back into the hall behind the pub, where we were partying. I tried to dance with a tall redhead who I fancied. After a couple of stumbles, she told me to piss off. Determined not to lose face, I went into my Tarzan routine which had gone down well in the Wye College common room. I started to swing across the steel braces of the roof trusses. This would have been all right if half a dozen young students from Brighton Tech had not tried to follow. The roof structure crackled and shed dust. Terrible screams from the ladies brought in the manager and two policemen.

The two policemen, a sergeant and a constable, pulled me down and gave me a stern lecture. I ought to know better. I was supposed to set the youngsters an example... etc. It was time to go back to our hostel. The gang came out with me, expecting a lift back in my old Riley. I had brought ten of them down, festooned on the running boards, the hood and the space where the rear seats should have been. Now they shouted encouragement as I attempted to swing the starting handle. I was quite unfit to drive but the two policemen stood by and laughed at my efforts.

The lads offered to push-start the car but nothing would make Old Mother Riley so much as cough. I was in any case quite unfit to drive and any less tolerant police would have arrested me. These good fellows had simply immobilised my car by removing the rotor arm to ensure that I did not do myself or anyone else any harm. We walked the three miles back in good voice. Once back, I lay unconscious on a pillow stained and damp from regurgitated Guinness and Merrydown cider. A disgusting pig.

One of my more sober mates gave me the rotor arm next morning and I walked the three miles to collect my car before breakfast which, in any case, I could not have eaten. I was able to start up my hop-stripping machine on time and somehow got through the day. The gang still worked hard for me but with many ribald comments. I worked all day unaware that my ears, neck and hair carried traces of black Guinness. It was some time before I could face the smell or taste of either Guinness or Cider.

I had my second brush with death a week later. I had been carded to play for the OMs 1st XV. I was delighted because with Cambridge colleges playing their games on weekdays, I could get really fit by playing both at Cambridge and in London. The OMs' captain had said they would help with transport for myself and two other players, including Jim Roberts, the England winger-to-be. At last I might get fit enough to break into the Middlesex county side. I had been told that I was in line for a trial. On Friday, I found I had an infected cyst the size of a plum on my earlobe. I could not possibly scrummage and so I cried off.

Later during the weekend, I developed a headache which spread to my back. One of the ex-Indian Army Majors packed me off to the first aid station. An ambulance was called and I was rushed to Hastings Isolation Hospital. I was alarmed by the concern everyone showed. I was not allowed to walk in but was carried in on a stretcher and put, unwashed and dirty, into bed. A large pump and a huge metal cylinder by the bed told me the worst. It was an iron lung. I had poliomyelitis. The pain in my back grew worse but was not acute. The nurses took great precautions against infection as one young girl was brought in followed by another. The 1953 polio epidemic was severe. One of the young girls died the same night but my pains subsided and I had no apparent paralysis. After a week, it was pronounced that I had had an abortive polio and was no longer in danger. Had I not developed the cyst on my ear, I would have played a violent game of rugby while in the early stages of polio. This could have had catastrophic results or been fatal. I settled down to a good rest and read.

Brenda came down to collect me when I was discharged. The ward orderly, a foreign girl, had only seen me as I was brought in, a dirty labourer in filthy overalls. She was bowled over by the sight of Brenda in a stylish red corduroy coat with black accessories and gold jewellery. She looked stunning. "Smart, smart, she smart!" was all the orderly could say. Brenda was obviously considered much too good for me! Brenda had arrived just as I was getting to the last few pages of an excellent novel. I could not insult her by reading in her presence but I could not leave the hospital ignorant of the heroine's fate. I hid in the lavatory! Anxious voices wondered where I was. First Sister, then Matron could be heard exhorting the nurses to find me. Eventually, I turned the last page and came out of the lavatory looking innocent. Unfortunately, the book fell out of my hospital dressing gown where I had hidden it and the game was up. "You rotter!" said Brenda. "I've come all the way from Leeds and you keep me waiting while you bloody well read!" There was no possible excuse. I had survived polio but I was not sure about my engagement!

Brenda, praise the lord, saw the funny side of my iniquity but the Matron and nurses did not. My popularity took a dive and there were stern homilies as I got dressed in the clean clothes which Brenda had brought for me from Mill Hill. However, they all waved goodbye and were smiling as they wished me luck at Cambridge.

We drove up to London in my trusty old Riley. I felt fine apart from an ache and weakness in my lower back where there had been some muscle wastage. After a few days' rest with my family in Mill Hill, we went up to Leeds and I enjoyed a week of luxury living, spiced with nervous anxiety as I plucked up courage to ask Pop Walker for his daughter's hand. I spoke to him in his little bar, which was appropriately called "The Soak". To my surprise he appeared to be delighted and was not too put out when I outlined my very modest prospects. "By, lad! Most prospective sons-in-law spell out their assets! All you've talked about are your liabilities!"

At this he threw back his head and laughed uproariously. Brenda's sister-in-law had been listening and rushed through to the kitchen excitedly to tell the womenfolk. "You close little devil!" she said to Brenda. "You never let on a thing!" When my father-in-law-to-be and I went through to join the ladies, they were equipped with drinks and toasted our engagement. I was in heaven!

It had, of course, to be a long engagement. I had to complete my studies and find a job. I had made some tentative enquiries about careers with the Ministry of Agriculture but the salaries offered to graduate scientific officers were less than Pop Walker paid the labourers at his works. This did not spoil our happiness. I borrowed £50 from my dad to buy Brenda an engagement ring. I asked Pop Walker to look out some rings through his contacts in the trade. He produced a collection of stones and Brenda chose a large pale blue Indian Zircon. There were also eight small diamonds which had belonged to Brenda's mother. He offered to have them made up into an engagement ring if I paid for the work, the gold and two more diamonds so that there could be a cluster of five each side of the big zircon. I was delighted as the stone was big enough for Brenda's strong hands. In due course I put the ring on Brenda's left hand and I went up to Cambridge an officially engaged man. I felt very complete and secure.

Term had started when I arrived at Magdalene College. I met my tutor, a flamboyantly dressed classicist, Mr Scott, a very senior fellow. He was wearing a cape and a broad-brimmed black hat, a blue silk spotted neckerchief and a wonderfully cut grey worsted suit. He told me that as a postgradute with MA status I had considerably more freedom than the undergrads and was not bound by normal Proctor's rules. I need not wear a gown or be subject to the Bulldog's pursuit if out on the town after "curfew". I was to be "in rooms" with a very old lady in McGrath Avenue. "I don't expect a mature man like you will give her much trouble!"

Mature man! This caused great amusement when I told some friends from Wye who were also at Cambridge as Colonial Service trainees. They had by now found their way round the university and were able to bring me up to date very quickly. There were no lectures on Wednesday afternoon so we went to watch the university rugby side. It was hard to be a spectator at the Grange Road rugby ground; I had so much looked forward to rugby at Cambridge and here I was, a mere onlooker.

The academic work proved to be disappointingly elementary. I had been told that the Cambridge Postgraduate Diploma in Agricultural Science was a very tough advanced course and I would have to work very hard indeed to pass the rigorous examinations if I wanted to obtain the coveted honour. I was disappointed to find that the Cambridge School of Agriculture under Professor Engledow and the director, Mr Handley, had become smug and ingrown. The staff were distant and officious. I missed the dynamic enthusiasm of the Wye College research and teaching team. At Wye, we felt we were all involved and at the frontiers of knowledge. At Cambridge, the research was remote and it was as if they were lifting the covers to let us glimpse what was going on as if it were an undeserved privilege. We were not part of the team. Almost the only areas of stimulating interest and value were the lectures on field experimentation and statistics led by Dr Wishart. The Agriculture was unbelievably old hat. I believe that I could have sat the Agricultural examinations straight from the Hertfordshire Farm Institute. We had covered nearly all the postgraduate science course at Cambridge while still undergraduates at Wye College. The Reading University graduates and the Scottish university men felt the same way and several complained to Mr Handley; but he was unheeding and refused to accept their comments. It made us very doubtful about the quality and content of the Cambridge degree course in Agriculture. Perhaps that was why so many sportsmen and aspiring Blues were reading Agriculture. They could afford to miss lectures!

Apart from the low academic level of the lectures, we were treated like school children and expected to sign a register at every lecture! I could not bring myself to do this and abstained. I don't know if the registers were ever checked. There were a lot of Colonial Service trainees on the course. Perhaps the registers were to check that these future civil servants kept up their attendance?

One day I came across a most attractive job in the appointments column of the *Times* newspaper. It was for a Lecturer in Agricultural Chemistry at the new University of the Gold Coast in West Africa. This seemed a wonderful opportunity to use my hard-earned experience and training to benefit the people of emerging Africa. It seemed a good vehicle for my wish, inherited no doubt from my socialist and saintly grandfather, to be altruistic. I ignored Mr Handley's opinion that it was too senior a post for me to apply for and I sent in my application. I suppose I was a bit lucky. Professor Louis Wain was on the selection panel when I was interviewed, together with Professor Phillips who had been my brother George's boss on the groundnut scheme. I returned to Cambridge, pleased with the interview, which had gone well. Some weeks later, I received a letter from Principal David Balme in the Gold Coast, offering me the job at the princely salary of £950 per annum. In those days this was a fortune! It was hard to believe that barely four years ago, I had been an uneducated manual labourer in the fields of Hertfordshire!

Now I was in a position to see Brenda's dad, Pop Walker, about a wedding date.

The job in the Gold Coast was to start in October so we agreed on a late August wedding to be followed by a local honeymoon. We could have broken our flight out to the Gold Coast with a week in Rome but I had not the confidence for a foreign jaunt. I was also too unsure about money to risk such a step into the Eternal City. It was too much of an adventure for me to undertake. Instead, we would go to the Lake District where I knew what was what. This would leave a few days for us to get essential tropical kit and say goodbye to friends and family. Our plan suited Pop Walker very well as he and his new bride, Sybil, his son's mother-in-law, were leaving for India and Pakistan on a long business trip in September.

Brenda visited me in Cambridge whenever she could but her father kept her busy in the gardens of the Lodge and she had little money of her own. I had none to help with her fares from Yorkshire but when she did come, she brought a supply of food to supplement my rations. I had so little money that I had given up eating in the college dining hall. I was living in very cheap rooms on McGrath Avenue. My college, Magdalene, played little part in my life. The undergraduates there were mostly of very aristocratic origins. Many had been to Eton or other top schools. They were incredibly well-supplied with money and clothes. There was little communication between these wealthy undergraduates and the Colonial Service graduates or myself. I was once invited to join a group in their room for coffee but they turned out to be evangelists who were after my soul.

The college, other than for very rare visits to the senior tutor, was just an address where I collected my mail. I had breakfast provided by my geriatric landlady (she went up and downstairs on her hands and knees). She was nearly blind and I occasionally had to discard the bacon when she had failed to see it had blowfly maggots on it. I did not tell her; she would have been mortified. My main meals were soup and bread or tinned stewed steak. There had been a consignment of Jugoslavian tinned stewed steak which the public shunned. I bought a crate for one shilling (5p) a tin. My protein needs were met for weeks by this. Brenda also managed the odd dozen eggs from her father's store. He was a most systematic man and collected his hen's eggs every day and stored them in a huge old fridge for consumption in strict rotation. As the old fridge was barely cool, the eggs did not stay fresh and all the family begged him to let them have some fresh eggs. He would not be shifted from his system. One weekend visit from Brenda resulted in shouts of outrage from my landlady. Brenda had cracked a rotten egg into her frying pan and the foul stench pervaded the house. The old girl may have had impaired eyesight and hearing but there was nothing wrong with her nose or voice! It was a long time before she let Brenda into her kitchen again.

I tried to push the boat out a bit for Brenda's visits by preparing a high tea for her and inviting a few of our old friends from Wye round. I bought what delicacies I could, but it was mainly Brenda's provisions which delighted us. These teas developed into a series of weekly tea parties for me and my friends in various colleges. Eventually Queen's College and particularly the Fisher building became the focus and we settled down to an almost daily meeting for both serious and flippant discussions. This location was a convenient base and close to King's Parade and Downing Street where most of us had lectures. Also important was the supply of free bread from the Queen's College kitchens, which I am afraid we abused terribly, but with great appreciation!

As my future now lay in the colonies, I joined the Colonial Service Club. Here we had a well-balanced community including many men with tropical service who were on refresher courses. Some were Caribbean, some were African and there were a few old colonial hands. It was a well-bonded membership and the contacts and knowledge gained here were amongst the best things of my time at Cambridge. There was a well-stocked drinks cupboard which was run by the secretary, a fellow student. Being a club, there were no "hours" and it was a great place for late drinking when one was in funds. We had a bit of a problem with the old Tanganyika hand who was in charge of all Colonial Service students. There had been a good party when, after singing the ruder version of "Whisky makes you frisky", we were asked to leave the Blue Boar Hotel, so we continued our party at the club. A lantern-jawed rugger blue, hearing the singing, joined us as we walked along King's Parade to Downing Street. Ties were an important means of identifying and classifying individuals within the university. This man's tie either denoted Selwyn College, a largely religious foundation, or the Hawkes Club founded by Lord Hawke for distinguished sportsmen. The lantern-jawed man was very unsteady and fell through the doors of the Inland Revenue office on the floor below our club. We all rolled in after him but did no harm other than to use two of those incredibly tall clerical stools, which Inland Revenue clerks were still using, as rocking horses in mock races across the lino floor. We had a great night. There were one or two mishaps: a chair fell out of a window scaring passersby, and one of my friends fell into the inspection pit at a nearby taxi garage on his way home. He emerged oil-spattered but unharmed in the way that only a drunk can survive an accident without injury. Angry but relieved mechanics abused him as he tottered away.

I too had my problems. On my way home I missed Magdalene Bridge and rode over the punt landing pontoon and into the river Cam. An American serviceman helped me out; and looking down, we could see the lights of my bike still gleaming through the muddy water. I could not do without my only means of transport so I plunged back into the river despite the American's attempts to restrain me. I had stripped to my underpants for the salvage attempt and I think my sodden body made his efforts a bit half-hearted. It certainly made his female companion laugh. The river was only about six feet deep here and I got my bike out safely, helped by the bystanders on dry land. I cycled back to my rooms considerably sobered. My poor landlady, brought down from her warm bed by my knocking, was aghast. A dripping, near-naked man at her door! I, "the mature man", had caused the poor old lady trouble. I well deserved her long drawn out scolding. Her previous student had been a quiet theologian. I was not what she was used to. "Goodness unto me! Whatever next!?"

What came next was far from funny. Her Majesty's Inland Revenue reported a break-in. Her Majesty's Constabulary found a missing stool in the Colonial Service Club. The guardian of Her Majesty's Colonial Service trainees, Mr McKinnon, was not amused. Somehow the finger was pointed at me. "Lansbury," he said, "I am trying to run a club for gentlemen!" I was angered by this inference that I was in some way an outsider. I answered back quietly that as a matriculated member of the university I was, by Royal Charter of King Charles the Second, a Gentleman, so what did he mean? This disconcerted the old boy enough for him to pause. One of my colleagues commented on the lantern-jawed man's presence. "He was either from Selwyn or the Hawkes club." This caused near apoplexy, for the old boy was a Hawkes Club man himself. "No Hawkes Club man would have done this! It must have been a damn trainee parson from Selwyn!"

I was off the hook.

Brenda and I had some lovely walks together. We quartered the backs on sunny afternoons, appreciating the beautiful old buildings and the well-kept gardens. This walk covered a complicated course through college grounds, backwards and forwards across the river Cam. Happy parties lazed in punts or on the green banks of the river watching the antics of punters or, like Brenda and I, were looking into each other's eyes and chatting happily. Punting at Cambridge was made more difficult due to the Cambridge tradition of standing right at the back of the polished stern apron. The more practical if less skilful Oxford punters stood safely in the well of their craft. The Cambridge stance allowed for more precise and elegant progress. I was a total failure at this sport, being too big and clumsy on my feet. My one excursion on the river with Brenda would have been disastrous if we had not taken aboard a young student from St John's who Brenda had known before she met me. He had been in the same squadron as Brenda's brother, flying jet fighters from Norfolk. Larry was an expert and I was very jealous of his skill. It did not matter though; I was unlikely to have much time or money for hiring punts.

Our walks, quartering the backs, took us through magnificent quadrangles, over wondrous bridges and round the lawns of the beautiful buildings. We were amused by the posturing of tubby dons who stood with gowns flapping on the grass lawns, a privilege which was forbidden to ordinary mortals. We peered into dark dining halls admiring the antique oak refectory tables, the minstral galleries and the gilded and brightly coloured crests denoting great associations with historic figures. Best of all, we loved King's College chapel with its lofty vaulted roof and soft music. Sometimes we were lucky and heard the King's Chapel Choir. I suppose the three bridges we remembered best were the Venetian Bridge of Sighs at St John's, the willows weeping over the honey-coloured curve of Clare Bridge with its reflection encircling a lone white swan, and the ugly but fascinating bit of wooden mathematics which bridged the Cam at Queens College.

At last the great day arrived. I had borrowed enough from my dad to hire a dress suit and Pop Walker gave me a length of tweed which I had made up into a smart country suit for going away. The tailor charged me only for the lining silk and his time. He could probably see from my tatty clothes that I could afford no more. The bill was £12!

Brenda wanted a small wedding but her father insisted on a big do with Yorkshire's leading caterer Jack Gilpin in charge and a vast marquee on the lawn. It was a colossal contrast to my own family's situation. They were in a real fix. They had very little money indeed, and lived week by week from financial crisis to crisis. They had no reserves to kit themselves out or for the fares to Yorkshire. For someone like Brenda, living in the security of a prosperous family, it was not easy to realise just how hard up the Mill Hill family were. She knew we were all agnostic and thought the Mill Hill Lansburys were just being awkward about the church wedding fuss. I was, after all, the first of my family to be married in church. My dad eventually found the money to get them all up to Yorkshire and in the event they loved the adventure and the taste of the high life. I was by now down to my last few quid, and quite unable to help them. I had also borrowed a further £50 from my dad to pay for us to go on honeymoon. In spite of my near insolvency, I did still have to host a stag party for my mates who had travelled up from Mill Hill, Cambridge and Kent. I was skating on very thin ice indeed.

The stag party in the Black Horse at Otley got completely out of hand. Starting as a convivial coming together of young men from all the various phases of my life between Prep School and Cambridge, they were like a disparate group of strange dogs, sizing each other up and deciding whether to pal up or fight. Tom Cochrane played the piano and the Mill Hill gang sang ribald songs as usual. The Cambridge men drank heartily and set off to climb every challenge in the room, in the hotel foyer and stairwell and later, up the corniches of the hotel facade. The Yorkshire lads, led by Brenda's brother, persisted in trying their luck with the girlfriends of those of my friends who were staying at the hotel. As ale consumption progressed, behaviour deteriorated. Someone threw a bottle at a wall to admire the burst. This set off much crashing of broken glass and even the imperturbable Tom was forced to abandon the piano in a shower of beer, some of which came in unopened bottles. I gave up when the piano lurched and gave a loud crack and emitted resonant chords under the weight of two climbing drunks. I went to bed, my mind a human cash register wondering about the potential damages bill. I was rudely awoken by two buxom women who burst into my room and, with the help of treacherous friends, carried me naked to the bathroom where they dusted me all over with a mixture of soap powder and Vim. I have no idea who they were or where they came from. One of them laughed at my wilted willy. It certainly amused my mates. Eventually I got some gritty sleep. I was awoken next morning by the tinkle of broken glass. Someone was sweeping up the debris. After breakfast, I was presented with a bill for £36 out of the £50 I had borrowed for the honeymoon!

The wedding service went off very well. I had terrible feelings of guilt before Brenda arrived. Not only about the stag night or my hangover but also because as an agnostic, I felt extremely hypocritical standing there in the lovely old chancel of St Oswald's Church, Guiseley. However as soon as I saw Pop Walker come in with Brenda, looking unbelievably beautiful, my fears vanished. I threw myself into the service, speaking my lines clearly and with feeling. I might have felt less guilty in a registry office but this was what my beloved Brenda and her family wanted. In the event, my awkward family thoroughly enjoyed it. Brenda came down the aisle looking absolutely wonderful. She had been up all night making the bouquets, in order to save me money; but no one would have known.

The reception was super. Uncle Wally, a purple-nosed, genial old soak, made the old friend of the family speech. It was suitably embarrassing, recalling Brenda in nappies, Brenda's first cigarette, her first drink, and his pleasure in satisfying her demands to have her back scratched until decency and her approaching twenty-first birthday made it indecorous. Wally had been a real toper in his time. Rumour had it that he used to follow the Leeds tramlines back to his hotel after a heavy night's drinking. One night he had followed the wrong set and on reaching the Swinegate tram depot he had got out, got undressed and, re-entering the car, fell asleep, leaving his shoes out to be cleaned. The Leeds tram service was resumed once the police had convinced him of his error. The loss of his licence had set his career as a salesman back considerably! On this occasion he ranged widely upon his knowledge of me, the groom, as a washer-up and singer of rugby songs, as a chauffeur and singer of rugby songs, as a gardener and singer of rugby songs! I tried my best to equal his speech, remembering to thank Pop Walker and Sybil, his new wife. Tom Cochrane, my best man, flattered the bridesmaids and then the serious busines of knocking back the bubbly and Yorkshire bitter began.

I did my best to guide Brenda round all the guests but there were many Yorkshire business people and relatives neither of us knew.

Brenda was pretty tired after her night's labours and we were thankful when it was time for us to go. The guests gathered to see us off . Eventually we got away, driven in style in an open Armstrong Siddeley Sapphire. We were chased all over the Wharfedale countryside as we tried to shake off the pursuing cavalcade of cars. We had hidden the car we had borrowed for the honeymoon in an Otley garage. As the last of the revellers decided the beer in the marquee was preferable to racing round Otley, Bramhope and the Chevin, we were at last able to switch cars. No one had found our honeymoon car; or so we thought. I broke the news of the damages bill to my new bride as we drove through Skipton on our way to our first night hotel at Ingleton, in the shadow of Ingleborough Mountain. She was philosophical about it and anyway, the lads had given us some generous cheques; we could still last out until my first salary cheque in the Gold Coast.

We were to skate on thin ice for the next forty glorious years!

As we undid our cases before going to bed, Brenda gave a wail of despair. Confetti blew out all over the room. That little sod, her sister-in-law, had found our hidden luggage! Brenda set to at once, frantically searching for every last piece. She was wetting the tip of her forefinger with a pink tongue to collect the tiny paper discs from a carpet which seemed unwilling to yield them up. She did not want anyone to know that we were on honeymoon. At breakfast, they might look at us and giggle. Brenda couldn't bear to think that they might know what we had been doing! I didn't care. I just wanted to do it!

It had already been a bloody long two-and-a-half year wait!

Next day we went off to the Lake District through the pretty dales, pausing to explore the wonderlands of stalactites and stalagmites in the limestone caves below Ingleborough. I bored Brenda with lectures on the geology, which she appeared to listen to with interest!

The scenery was all related to the underlying geology, with limestone pavements, sink holes, fault escarpments and mesa-like hills capped with millstone grit. As we went on towards Windermere, the countryside softened into valleys containing the humps and bumps of Drumlin domes left behind by the glaciers of the retreating Ice Age.

We stayed at the old White Lion Hotel in Ambleside and the next few days in the South Lakes were quite wonderful as we explored old haunts, walked the summits and rowed on the lakes. Crossing westward over the Hardnott and Wrynose passes, we were in the world of old volcanic rocks and beetling crags beloved of the climbers. We climbed the three highest mountains and swam in the Solway Firth, off Drigg and Ravenglass. There were no radioactive waste outlets at this time, just huge flocks of gulls, terns and oyster catchers which, sadly, have now largely disappeared in the face of the nuclear industry developments.

Later we moved on to the Northern Lakes, staying at the Castle Inn between Keswick and Cockermouth. I had to go back to the scenes of my emergence to manhood and bored Brenda silly with reminiscences. We met Joyce Arrowsmith, my schooldays' crush, and entertained her elderly parents, who had looked after me so well when I was a lost soul. Brenda invited them all to a meal and it seemed strange to have my first and last loves at the same table. Later, Brenda and I scrambled over Striding Edge to the summit of Helvellyn and ran down the grassy side to Wythburn.

Next day my calf muscles had seized up and I could hardly walk. Mountains were out; so we decamped to the Edinburgh Festival. I tried to take Brenda up the Scott Memorial but vertigo hit me on the second stage and Brenda had to abandon her hero and ascend the tower alone! We enjoyed some very amateurish shows and music and a city tour, before returning to the warmth and security of Brenda's Yorkshire home.

Soon it was time to make final purchases and pack for our new life in West Africa. Brenda's father loaned me a further £50 for extra kit and we went down to London to say goodbye to our Mill Hill family and friends.

We were not sure what we were going to. We had seen pictures of round mud huts and very nice bungalows but had little idea of what sort of accommodation we would actually get. I was to lecture on Agricultural Chemistry at the brand new University College of the Gold Coast and hopefully do something to help bring light to the Dark Continent; but that is another story.

In 1954 – just as we left for the exciting sights, sounds and smells of Africa – the last of rationing and austerity ended at home.

The Dark Years were over.

Terry Lansbury J.P.,B.Sc.London, N.D.A.,Dip.Ag.Sci.Cantab
Walklands Keswick 13 December 2013

Lightning Source UK Ltd.
Milton Keynes UK
UKOW03f2330260314

228882UK00001B/110/P